Deconstruction

'An inspiring and dazzling *tour de force* that revolutionised my thinking' Gary Day, *Times Higher Education Supplement*

Academic game? Dangerous weapon? The most important development in twentieth-century literary studies? Setting out to shake not only literary critical assumptions but the very foundations of Western thought, deconstruction remains one of the most controversial yet crucial strands of contemporary critical theory.

Since first appearing in 1982, *Deconstruction: Theory and Practice* has been acclaimed as by far the most readable, concise and authoritative guide to this topic. While in no way oversimplifying its complexity or glossing over the challenges it presents, Christopher Norris's book sets out to make deconstruction more accessible to the open-minded reader. The volume focuses upon the texts of Jacques Derrida which gave rise to this seismic shift in critical thought, as well as the work of Paul de Man, Geoffrey Hartman, J. Hillis Miller and Harold Bloom, the North American critics who have taken Derrida's project in their own directions.

Inherent in the very idea of deconstruction, however, is the need to revisit, rethink, reassess. In this third, revised edition, Norris builds upon his 1991 Afterword to add an entirely new Postcript, discussing the central topics and development in recent critical debate. The Postscript includes an extensive list of recommended reading, complementing what was already one of the most useful bibliographies available. More than ever in this new edition, *Deconstruction* is the book to revolutionize your thinking.

Christopher Norris is Distinguished Research Professor in Philosophy at the University of Cardiff, Wales, having until 1991 taught in the Cardiff English Department. He has also held fellowships and visiting appointments at a number of institutions, including the University of California, Berkeley, the City University of New York and Dartmouth College.

IN THE SAME SERIES

Christopher
Norris

Deconstruction

Theory and Practice

3rd edition

 London and New York

First published in 1982 by Methuen & Co. Ltd
Reprinted in 1986 with a revised bibliography

Revised edition first published in 1991
by Routledge
2 Park Square, Milton Park, Abingdon, Oxon, OX14 4RN

Simultaneously published in the USA and Canada
by Routledge
270 Madison Ave, New York NY 10016

Reprinted 1991, 1993, 1996, 1998, 2000

This edition first published 2002

Transferred to Digital Printing 2006

Routledge is an imprint of the Taylor & Francis Group

© 1982, 1986, 1991, 2002 Christopher Norris

Typeset in Joanna by RefineCatch Limited, Bungay, Suffolk

British Library Cataloguing in Publication Data
A catalogue record for this book is available from the British Library

Library of Congress Cataloging in Publication Data
A catalog record for this book has been requested

ISBN 0–415–28009–5 (Hbk)
ISBN 0–415–28010–9 (Pbk)

CONTENTS

GENERAL EDITOR'S PREFACE

No doubt a third General Editor's Preface to *New Accents* seems hard to justify. What is there left to say? Twenty-five years ago, the series began with a very clear purpose. Its major concern was the newly perplexed world of academic literary studies, where hectic monsters called 'Theory', 'Linguistics' and 'Politics' ranged. In particular, it aimed itself at those undergraduates or beginning postgraduate students who were either learning to come to terms with the new developments or were being sternly warned against them.

New Accents deliberately took sides. Thus the first Preface spoke darkly, in 1977, of 'a time of rapid and radical social change', of the 'erosion of the assumptions and presuppositions' central to the study of literature. 'Modes and categories inherited from the past' it announced, 'no longer seem to fit the reality experienced by a new generation'. The aim of each volume would be to 'encourage rather than resist the process of change' by combining nuts-and-bolts exposition of new ideas with clear and detailed explanation of related conceptual developments. If mystification (or downright demonisation) was the enemy, lucidity (with a nod to the compromises inevitably at stake there) became a friend. If a 'distinctive discourse of the future' beckoned, we wanted at least to be able to understand it.

With the apocalypse duly noted, the second Preface proceeded piously to fret over the nature of whatever rough beast might stagger portentously from the rubble. 'How can we recognise or deal with the new?', it complained, reporting nevertheless the dismaying advance of 'a host of barely respectable activities for which we have no reassuring names' and promising a programme of wary surveillance at 'the boundaries of the precedented and at the limit of the thinkable'. Its conclusion, 'the unthinkable, after all, is that which covertly shapes our thoughts' may rank as a truism. But in so far as it offered some sort of useable purchase on a world of crumbling certainties, it is not to be blushed for.

In the circumstances, any subsequent, and surely final, effort can only modestly look back, marvelling that the series is still here, and not unreasonably congratulating itself on having provided an initial outlet for what turned, over the years, into some of the distinctive voices and topics in literary studies. But the volumes now re-presented have more than a mere historical interest. As their authors indicate, the issues they raised are still potent, the arguments with which they engaged are still disturbing. In short, we weren't wrong. Academic study did change rapidly and radically to match, even to help to generate, wide reaching social changes. A new set of discourses was developed to negotiate those upheavals. Nor has the process ceased. In our deliquescent world, what was unthinkable inside and outside the academy all those years ago now seems regularly to come to pass.

Whether the *New Accents* volumes provided adequate warning of, maps for, guides to, or nudges in the direction of this new terrain is scarcely for me to say. Perhaps our best achievement lay in cultivating the sense that it was there. The only justification for a reluctant third attempt at a Preface is the belief that it still is.

TERENCE HAWKES

ACKNOWLEDGEMENTS

My thanks to all those in Cardiff – especially Carol Bretman, Kathy Kerr, Karen MacDonaugh, Nigel Mapp, and Peter Sedgwick – whose comments and criticisms over the past few years have clarified my thinking and helped to locate the points most in need of further discussion in the Afterword. Also to Terence Hawkes for commissioning this volume, way back in the early 'New Accents' days, and for offering such a wealth of shrewd editorial advice. Any errors that remain are entirely his fault. Jacques Derrida has provided much help and encouragement since the book first went to press, and I hope he will find nothing to regret in this latest printing. My debts nearer home are (yet again) very partially repaid by dedicating this book to my wife Alison and daughters, Clare and Jenny. Finally, greetings to my cultural-materialist comrades in the Red Choir (Côr Cochion Caerdydd) for managing to unite theory and practice in the best possible way.

Cardiff
June 1990

THIRD EDITION (2002)

Ten years on and (again) I have to think of all the people – colleagues, students, friends, correspondents, astute critics of this book in its previous edition – whose ideas, comments or companionship have left their mark in various ways. Since space is limited I shall not even try to name them all but just extend special greetings to Gideon Calder, Clive Cazeaux, Brian Coates, Gary Day, Paul Gorton, Geoff Harpham, Carol Jones, Christa Knellwolf, Dan Latimer, Radmila Nastic, Paul Norcross, Jessica Osborn, Marianna Papastephanou, Daniele Procida, David Roden, Duncan Salkeld, Sean Sayers, Maria Helena Serodio, Rita Stefansson, and Manuel Barbeito Varela. I should also like thank Robin Atffield, Andrew Belsey, Barry Wilkins and everyone in the Philosophy Section at Cardiff for having (just about ten years ago) welcomed a renegade literary theorist to their company. I trust that the various revisions to this book – plus the Postscript – will go some way toward justifying that act of faith.

Cardiff
August 2001

INTRODUCTION

Literature as well as criticism – the difference between them
being delusive – is condemned (or privileged) to be forever
the most rigorous and, consequently, the most unreliable
language in terms of which man names and transforms
himself.

(de Man 1979, p. 19)

This sentence by the critic Paul de Man is a fair sample of the kind of
thinking about literature which is currently termed *deconstruction*. It
bristles with the sorts of paradox which that thinking finds at work not
only in literary texts but in criticism, philosophy and all varieties of
discourse, its own included. What can it mean to reject the distinction
between literature and criticism as merely a delusion? How can a language be at once the most 'rigorous' and the most 'unreliable' source
of knowledge? In what conceivable sense can man 'transform' himself
through a process of naming somehow made possible by this rigorous
unreliability? These are not problems that either resolve themselves on
a more careful reading or require that we accept them (like the paradoxes of Christian theology) as lying beyond the utmost scope of
unaided rational thought. Rather they operate, as more than one dis-
gruntled critic has remarked of de Man, as a positive technique for

making trouble; an affront to every last standard or protocol of disciplined, responsible debate.

Deconstruction is a constant reminder of the etymological link between 'crisis' and 'criticism'. It makes manifest the fact that any radical shift of interpretative thought must always come up against the limits of seeming absurdity. Philosophers have long had to recognize that thinking may lead them inescapably into regions of scepticism such that life could scarcely carry on if people were to act on their conclusions. David Hume (1711–76) called scepticism 'a malady which can never be radically cured, but must return upon us every moment, however we may chase it away . . . Carelessness and inattention alone can afford us any remedy' (quoted in Russell 1954, p. 697). Deconstruction works at the same giddy limit, suspending all that we take for granted about language, experience and the 'normal' possibilities of human communication. Yet this is not to say that it is a freakish or marginal philosophy, the perverse sport of super-subtle minds disenchanted with the workaday business of literary criticism. Hume saw no way out of his sceptical predicament, except by soothing the mind with careless distractions (billiards was apparently the usual solace of his afternoons). Deconstruction is likewise an activity of thought which cannot be consistently acted on – that way madness lies – but which yet possesses an inescapable rigour of its own.

De Man complains that deconstruction has either been 'dismissed as a harmless academic game' or 'denounced as a terrorist weapon'. Both reactions are understandable, though both – as this book will argue – are equally wide of the mark. Deconstruction is the active antithesis of everything that criticism ought to be if one accepts its traditional values and concepts. Beneath all the age-old conflicts of critical method there has always existed a tacit agreement about certain conventions, or rules of debate, without which (supposedly) no serious thinking about literature could be carried on. That literary texts possessed meaning and that literary criticism sought a knowledge of that meaning – a knowledge with its own proper claims to validity – were principles implicit across the widest divergences of thought. However deconstruction challenges the fundamental distinction between 'literature' and 'criticism' implied by those principles. Moreover it challenges the idea that criticism provides a special kind of knowledge precisely in so far as its texts don't aspire to 'literary' status. For the deconstructionist, criticism (like philosophy) is always an activity of writing, and nowhere more rigorous – to paraphrase de Man – than where it knows and reveals this condition of its own possibility.

This is to anticipate whole tracts of argument which will need rehearsing in detail if the reader is to be convinced. Meanwhile I take ambiguous comfort from Derrida's remarks (in *Of Grammatology*) on the strange and deceptive status of 'prefaces' in general. For one thing they are usually – as here! – written last of all and placed up front as a gesture of authorial command. They claim a summarizing function, a power of abstracted systematic statement, which denies the very process and activity of thought involved in the project of writing. Yet they also subvert, in deconstructive fashion, that authority of 'the text' which traditionally attaches to the work itself. As Gayatri Chakravorty Spivak puts it, in her own Translator's Preface to the English version of *Grammatology*:

> the structure preface – text becomes open at both ends. The text has no stable identity, stable origin ... each act of reading 'the text' is a preface to the next. The reading of a self-professed preface is no exception to this rule.
>
> (Derrida 1977a, p. xii)

In this sense what follows is also a 'preface', a deferred involvement with the writings of Derrida, and not to be taken on trust as a handy and 'objective' survey of deconstructionist method. If there is one applied lesson to be taken away, it is the powerlessness of ready-made concepts to explain or delimit the activity of writing.

1

ROOTS: STRUCTURALISM AND NEW CRITICISM

To present 'deconstruction' as if it were a method, a system or a settled body of ideas would be to falsify its nature and lay oneself open to charges of reductive misunderstanding. Critical theory is nowadays a reputable academic business with a strong vested interest in absorbing and coming to terms with whatever new challenges the times may produce. Structuralism, it is now plain to see, was subject from the outset to a process of adaptation by British and American critics who quickly took heart from what they saw as its 'practical' or 'commonsense' uses. What started as a powerful protest against ruling critical assumptions ended up as just one more available method for saying new things about well-worn texts. By now there is probably a structuralist reading, in one guise or another, of just about every classic of English literature. A few minutes' search through the index of any learned journal is enough to show how structuralism has taken hold in the most respectable and cherished quarters of academic study. Old polemics are quietly forgotten because the ground has meanwhile shifted to such an extent that erstwhile opponents find themselves now in a state of peaceful alliance. To trace this history in detail would provide an instructive example of the capacity of Anglo-American academic criticism to absorb and domesticate any new theory that threatens its sovereign claim.

Deconstruction can be seen in part as a vigilant reaction against this tendency in structuralist thought to tame and domesticate its own best insights. Some of Jacques Derrida's most powerful essays are devoted to the task of dismantling a concept of 'structure' that serves to immobilize the play of meaning in a text and reduce it to a manageable compass. This process can be seen at work in the reception of a book like Jonathan Culler's *Structuralist Poetics* (1975), regarded (not without reason) as a sound and authoritative guide to the complexities of structuralist thought. Culler's volume has been widely prescribed as student reading by critics and teachers who otherwise show small sympathy with current theoretical developments. Its appeal, one may fairly conjecture, lies partly in its commonsense dealing with problems of interpretative method, and partly in its principled rejection of other, more extreme kinds of theory which would question any such method. Culler makes no secret of his aim to reconcile structuralist theory with a naturalized or intuitive approach to texts. The proper task of theory, in his view, is to provide a legitimating framework or system for insights which a 'competent' reader should be able to arrive at and check against her sense of relevance and fitness. Culler's main claim for the structuralist approach is that it offers a kind of regulative matrix for perceptions that might otherwise seem merely dependent on the critic's personal flair or virtuosity.

His argument becomes strained when it tries to link this notion of readerly 'competence' with an account of the manifold conventions – or arbitrary codes – that make up a literate response. On the one hand Culler appeals to what seems a loose extension of the linguist Noam Chomsky's argument: that linguistic structures are innately programmed in the human mind and operate both as a constraint upon language and as a means of shared understanding. Thus Culler puts the case that our comprehension of literary texts is conditioned by a similar 'grammar' of response which enables us to pick out the relevant structures of meaning from an otherwise inchoate mass of linguistic detail. On the other hand, he is obliged to recognize that literary texts, unlike the sentences of everyday language, involve certain specialized codes of understanding which have to be acquired and cannot be accounted for in terms of some universal grammar of response. Competence in these terms is a matter of trained intelligence, of justifying one's reading of a text 'by locating it within the conventions of plausibility defined by a generalized knowledge of literature' (Culler 1975, p. 127).

This is structuralism at its most conservative, an outlook that lends support to traditional ideas of the text as a bearer of stable (if complicated) meanings and the critic as a faithful seeker after truth in the text. Culler is non-committal as to whether these interpretative structures are unchangeably vested in the human mind or whether – as seems more likely – they represent the force of established convention, a kind of second nature to the practised reader. Whatever their status, they clearly imply some manner of check or effective restraint upon the freedoms of critical discourse. Hence Culler's doubts (in the final chapter of *Structuralist Poetics*) about the radical claims of those, like Derrida, who seem bent upon dismantling the very bases of interpretative method and meaning.

Deconstruction is avowedly 'post-structuralist' in its refusal to accept the idea of structure as in any sense given or objectively 'there' in a text. Above all, it questions the assumption – so crucial to Culler – that structures of meaning correspond to some deep-laid mental 'set' or pattern of response which determines the limits of intelligibility. Theory, from Culler's point of view, would be a search for invariant structures or formal universals which reflect the very nature of human intelligence. Literary texts (along with myths, music and other cultural artefacts) yield up their meaning to a mode of analysis possessed of a firm rationale because its sights are set on nothing less than a total explanation of human thought and culture. Theory is assured of its methodological bearings by claiming a deep, universal kinship with the systems of meaning that it proposes to analyse.

Deconstruction, on the contrary, starts out by rigorously *suspending* this assumed correspondence between mind, meaning and the concept of method which claims to unite them.

FROM KANT TO SAUSSURE: THE PRISON-HOUSE OF CONCEPTS

'Kantianism without the transcendental subject' is a description often applied to structuralist thought by those who doubt its validity. Culler's line of argument demonstrates the force of this slogan, showing itself very much akin to Kant's transcendental-idealist theory of mind and knowledge. Immanuel Kant (1724–1804) set out to redeem philosophy from the radical scepticism of those, like Hume, who thought it impossible to arrive at any definite, self-validating knowledge of the external world. They had tried and conspicuously failed to discover any necessary link between mind and reality, or 'truths of reason' and 'matters of fact'. Thought seemed condemned to a prison-house of solipsistic doubt, endlessly rehearsing its own suppositions but unable to connect them with the world at large. Sensory evidence was no more reliable than ideas like that of cause-and-effect, the 'logic' of which merely reflected our accustomed or commonsense habits of thought.

Kant saw an escape-route from this condition of deadlocked sceptical reason. It was, he agreed, impossible for consciousness to grasp or 'know' the world in the direct, unmediated form despaired of by Hume and the sceptics. Knowledge was a product of the human mind, the operations of which could only *interpret* the world, and not deliver it up in all its pristine reality. But these very operations, according to Kant, were so deeply vested in human understanding that they offered a new foundation for philosophy. Henceforth philosophy must concern itself not with a delusory quest for 'the real' but with precisely those deep regularities – or *a priori* truths – that constitute human understanding.

It is not hard to see the parallels between Kantian thought and the structuralist outlook presented by a theorist like Culler. Both have their origins in a sceptical divorce between mind and the 'reality' it seeks to understand. In structuralist terms this divorce was most clearly spelled out by the linguist Ferdinand de Saussure. He argued that our knowledge of the world is inextricably shaped and conditioned by the language that serves to represent it. Saussure's insistence on the 'arbitrary' nature of the sign led to his undoing of the natural link that common sense assumes to exist between word and thing. Meanings are bound up, according to Saussure, in a system of relationship and difference that effectively determines our habits of thought and perception. Far from providing a 'window' on reality or (to vary the metaphor) a faithfully reflecting mirror, language brings along with it a whole intricate network of established significations. In his view, our knowledge of things is insensibly structured by the systems of code and convention which alone enable us to classify and organize the chaotic flux of experience. There is simply no access to knowledge except by way of language and other, related orders of representation. Reality is carved up in various ways according to the manifold patterns of sameness and difference which various languages provide. This basic *relativity* of thought and meaning (a theme later taken up by the American linguists Sapir and Whorf) is the starting-point of structuralist theory.

There are, however, various ways of responding to this inaugural insight. Culler exemplifies the Kantian response which strives to keep scepticism at bay by insisting on the normative or somehow self-validating habits of readerly 'competence'. Culler is in search of a generalized theory (or 'poetics') of reading which would fully encompass all the various means we possess for making sense of literary texts. Relativism is thus held in check by an appeal to the reader as a kind of moderating presence, a mind in possession of the requisite intelligence *and* the relevant codes of literate convention. One must, Culler argues, 'have a sense, however undefined, of what one is reading towards' (Culler 1975, p. 163). Interpretation is a quest for order and intelligibility amongst the manifold possible patterns of sense which the text holds out to a fit reader. The role of a structuralist poetics is partly to explain how these powerful conventions come into play, and partly to draw a line between mere ingenuity and the proper, legitimate or 'competent' varieties of readerly response.

What Culler is proposing in the name of structuralism is a more methodical approach to the kind of criticism that has long been accepted as a staple of academic teaching. The virtue of his theory, from this point of view, is the ease with which it incorporates all manner of examples from other 'prestructuralist' critics who happen to illustrate the conventions Culler has in mind. There is room within his generalized notion of literary 'competence' for various insights which had often been arrived at without the benefit of any such systematic theory. This follows logically enough from the analogy he draws with Chomskian linguistics. To demonstrate the complex system of rules and transformations underlying a speaker's grammatical utterance is not, of course, to claim any *conscious* knowledge of that system on the speaker's part. Linguistic 'competence', as Chomsky calls it, is tacit and wholly unconscious except when brought to light by the linguist's peculiar and specialized activity. The 'transcendental subject' (or locus of thought and experience) in Kantian philosophy is likewise capable of exercising its *a priori* powers without being in the least aware of them.

Culler adopts the same attitude to critics whose intuitive approach is undeniably fruitful but lacks any larger, organizing theory of valid response. Typical is his treatment of a passage from William Empson's *Seven Types of Ambiguity*, selected for what Culler sees as its all-but-conscious structuralist implications. The 'poem' in question (see Empson 1961, p. 23) is Arthur Waley's translation of a two-line fragment from the Chinese:

Swiftly the years, beyond recall.
Solemn the stillness of this spring morning.

Culler remarks how Empson's reading brings out the 'binary oppositions' (mainly the extreme contrast of time-scales) which give the lines their effect. This lends support to Culler's argument that, 'in interpreting a poem, one looks for terms that can be placed on a semantic or thematic axis and opposed to one another' (Culler 1975, p. 126). Such strategies arise from the reader's desire to maximize the interest or significance of a text by discovering its manifold patterns of meaning. A 'competent' reading is one that displays both the acumen required to perceive such meanings and the good sense needed to sort them out from other, less relevant patterns. For his notion of 'relevance' Culler appeals once again to a trans-individual community of judgement assumed to underlie the workings of literate response. Structuralism, with its emphasis on distinctive features and significant contrasts, becomes in effect a *natural extension* or legitimating theory of what it is properly to read a text.

Culler has no real quarrel with those among the 'old' New Critics who talked in terms of irony, paradox or (like Empson) types of ambiguity. These and other patterns of response he regards as enabling conventions, produced by the will to make sense of texts in a complex and satisfying way. Culler's relatively modest proposal is that critics continue to read in much the same manner but also reflect on the presuppositions that govern their various reading strategies.

Thus Empson's 'ambiguity' is found to rest on a principle of binary opposition, the presence of which, in structuralist terms, does more to explain its suggestive power. Such structures may not be objectively 'there' in the text but they offer (it is assumed) so basic and powerful a convention of reading as to place their validity beyond serious doubt. Culler's poetics, therefore, involves a double prescription or regulative claim with regard to literary 'competence'. On the one hand it presupposes an activity of reading grounded in certain deeply naturalized codes of understanding. On the other, it assumes that texts must offer at least sufficient hold – in the way of contrastive or structural features – for such an activity to take its own intuitive bearings.

NEW CRITIC INTO STRUCTURALIST?

Culler's implicit equation between 'structure' and 'competence' is precisely the kind of interpretative ploy that deconstruction sets out to challenge. The concept of structure is all too easily allowed to dominate thought and take on a self-sustaining objectivity immune to critical reflection. It is on these terms that structuralism has proved itself a not-too-threatening presence on the academic scene. Least of all does it now seem a menace – as traditionalist critics once argued – through its 'scientific' rigour and taste for abstraction. American New Criticism in its day attracted the same hostility from those who regarded its rhetorical bases – 'irony', 'paradox', 'tension' – as so many bits of monstrous abstract machinery. Yet it soon became clear that, so far from wanting to rationalize poetry or reduce it to logical order, the New Critics were bent upon preserving its uniqueness by fencing it off within the bounds of their chosen rhetoric. The poem as 'verbal icon', in William K. Wimsatt's phrase, became the rallying-point of a criticism devoted to the privileged autonomy of poetic language.

If system and structure were prominent in the New Critics' thinking, the aim was not so much to provide a rationale of poetic meaning – a logic of logical anomalies – but rather to build a criticism capable of warding off such rationalist assaults. New Critical method was rational enough in its mode of argumentation but kept a firm distance between its own methodology and the differently organized workings of poetic language. This distance was emphatically preserved by the rules of interpretative conduct which Wimsatt, philosopher-elect of the movement, raised to a high point of principle (see Wimsatt 1954). Chief among these was their attack on the 'heresy of paraphrase', the idea that poetic meaning could be translated into any kind of rational prose equivalent. The poem, in short, was a sacrosanct object whose autonomy demanded a proper respect for the difference between it and the language that critics used to describe it.

The New Critics' programme soon took hold as an eminently teach-able discipline of literary study. Its erstwhile detractors were easily reconciled to a creed that scarcely challenged the proprieties of critical discourse. The same is true of structuralism in its early, scientistic guise. Culler's arguments demonstrate the ease with which a structuralist gloss can be placed upon strategies of reading basically akin to those of the 'old' New Criticism. Academic discourse has little to fear from a 'scientific' criticism – however sweeping its claims – which holds out the promise of a highly self-disciplined knowledge of the text. Such a specialized activity can be allowed to take its place as one among many alternative methods, relied upon to beat its own disciplinary bounds.

ROLAND BARTHES

Culler's poetics of reading is therefore in accord with one prominent strain of structuralist thought. In the early writing of Barthes, among others, the aim was a full-scale science of the text modelled on the linguistics of Saussure and the structural anthropology of Claude Lévi-Strauss. These ambitions were signalled by the widespread structuralist talk of criticism as a 'metalanguage' set up to articulate the codes and conventions of all (existing or possible) literary texts. Hence the vari-ous efforts to establish a universal 'grammar' of narrative, along with a typology of literary genres based on their predominating figures of

language. This view of structuralism as a kind of master-code or analytic discourse upon language is taken by Barthes in his *Elements of
Semiology* (1967). Natural language, including the dimension of 'connotative' meaning, is subject to a metalinguistic description which
operates in scientific terms and provides a higher-level or 'second-
order' mode of understanding. It is evident, according to Barthes, that
semiology must be such a metalanguage, 'since as a second-order system it takes over a first language (or language-object) which is the
system under scrutiny; and this system-object is *signified* through the
meta-language of semiology' (Barthes 1967, p. 92). This tortuous
explanation really comes down to the belief in structuralist method as a
discourse able to master and explain all the varieties of language and
culture.

At least this is one way of construing Barthes's text, a reading that
brings it into line with accepted ideas of the structuralist activity. There
are, however, signs that Barthes was not himself content with so rigid
and reductive a programme. If semiology sets up as a second-order
discourse unravelling the connotative systems of natural language, why
should it then be immune to further operations at a yet higher level of
analysis? 'Nothing in principle prevents a meta-language from becoming in its turn the language-object of a new meta-language; this would,
for example, be the case with semiology if it were to be "spoken" by
another science' (ibid., p. 93).

Barthes is well aware of the dangers and delusions implicit in a
discourse that claims the last word in explanatory power. The semiolo-
gist may seem to exercise 'the objective function of decipherer' in
relation to a world which 'conceals or naturalizes' the meanings of its
own dominant culture. But this apparent objectivity is made possible
only by a habit of thought which willingly forgets or suppresses its
own provisional status. To halt such a process by invoking some
ultimate claim to truth is a tactic foreign to the deepest implications
of structuralist thought. There is no final analysis, no metalinguistic
method, which could possibly draw a rigorous line between its own
operations and the language they work upon. Semiology has to recognize that the terms and concepts it employs are always bound up
with the signifying process it sets out to analyse. Hence Barthes's
insistence that structuralism is always an *activity*, an open-ended

practice of reading, rather than a 'method' convinced of its own right reason.

Barthes was alive from the outset to the problems and paradoxes involved in refining structuralist theory without introducing such premature claims of method. To enlist him on the side of deconstruction is perhaps misleading in view of his elusiveness from any theoretical standpoint. Barthes was a brilliant stylist and a highly original – at times even wayward – constructor of theories. His writing was self-conscious to the point where style became an intimate probing of its own possibilities, frequently suggesting theoretical insights but just as often foreclosing them through a sense of resistance to any kind of organized theory. His later texts maintain a dialogue not only with structuralism but with Derrida, Jacques Lacan and other post-structuralist thinkers whose influence Barthes both acknowledges and keeps at a certain protective distance. He remains susceptible as ever to the pleasures of system and method, the old fascination with structure as a totalizing order of thought. But he now seems to view such ideas as 'fantasmatic' images projected by desire upon the polymorphous surface of text, language and culture. The dream of total intelligibility, like 'structure' in its metalinguistic sense, belongs (he implies) to a stage of thinking that is self-blinded by its own conceptual metaphors. The element of rhetorical *play* is present everywhere. Its effects in critical discourse may be ignored, but they are not effaced by the structuralist 'science' of semiotics.

This ambivalent attitude to language and structure is one of the themes Barthes takes up in his fragmentary 'autobiography', translated into English in 1977. It might seem an act of supreme 'bad faith' to produce such a work while proclaiming, like Barthes, the 'death of the author' as a wished-for escape from the tyranny of subjectivity. But the reader is soon made aware that Barthes is not to be caught – by anyone except himself – with his textual defences down. He is, as always, shrewdly beforehand with the *hypocrite lecteur* who thinks to ensnare him with simplified versions of his own way of thinking. There is a consummately neat example in Barthes's recollection of an American student ('or positivist, or disputacious: I cannot disentangle') who took it for granted that 'subjectivity' and 'narcissism' were the same thing: 'a matter of speaking well about oneself'. The student was a victim, Barthes reflects,

> of the couple, the old paradigm: *subjectivity/objectivity*. Yet today the subject apprehends himself elsewhere, and subjectivity can return at another place on the spiral: deconstructed, taken apart, shifted, without anchorage: why should I not speak of 'myself' since this 'my' is no longer 'the self'?
>
> (Barthes 1977, p. 168)

What Barthes thus offers, in the guise of autobiography, is a sequence of deftly turned reflections on the experience of writing, the duplicities of language and the irreducibly *textual* nature of whatever they communicate. As one such playful alibi (or 'shifter' as Barthes would call it, borrowing the term from Roman Jakobson), he writes always in the narrative third person, addressing the various topics of his own obsessive interest with a kind of quizzical detachment. As the book's epigraph helpfully suggests, 'it should all be considered as if spoken by a character in a novel'.

Barthes undermines not only the natural conventions of language but also those methods (his own included) that claim to have mastered their working. The early, 'structuralist' Barthes is called to account by this later *alter ego* for his pursuit of system and method, a deluded quest but still a source of considerable pleasure. The dialogue-of-one becomes a kind of mocking catechism:

> You keep the notion of 'meta-language', but in the category of image-reservoir. This is a constant procedure in your work: you use a pseudo-linguistics, a metaphorical linguistics ... these concepts come to constitute allegories, a second language, whose abstraction is diverted to fictive ends.... And meaning itself – when you watch it functioning, you do so with the almost puerile amusement of a buyer who never tires of pulling the switch of some gadget.
>
> (ibid., p. 124)

This perfectly catches the movement of thought by which Barthes manages to 'discompose' his own ideas and restore them to a textual dimension evoking all the suppleness and vagaries of pure linguistic play.

This aspect of Barthes marks the point at which deconstruction begins to shake and unsettle the structuralist project. It has been quietly passed over by critics anxious to domesticate structuralism by presenting it as a 'method' sometimes provocative in its claims but basically amenable to commonsense uses. The apparent eccentricities of Barthes's later writing are mostly regarded as harmless whimsical diversions on the part of a critic who required some form of 'creative' escape from the exigencies of high-powered theory. This attitude, typical of Anglo-American criticism, draws a firm line between the discipline of thinking about texts and the activity of writing which that discipline is supposed to renounce or ignore in its own performance. Criticism as 'answerable style' (in Geoffrey Hartman's phrase) is an idea that cuts right across the deep-grained assumptions of academic discourse. It is, as I shall argue, one of the most unsettling and radical departures of deconstructionist thought. A properly attentive reading of Barthes brings out the extent to which critical concepts are ceaselessly transformed or undone by the activity of self-conscious writing.

This vertiginous textual movement is resisted by readers who see no connection between the 'structuralist' Barthes and the wayward, dandified discourse of his later writings. Such a reader is Philip Thody, whose book on Barthes (subtitled *A Conservative Estimate*) presents him as a gifted but erratic thinker, full of good ideas but sometimes apt to go off at an odd theoretical tangent (Thody 1977). Thody is convinced that beneath all the fireworks there is a structure of assumptions not so very different from those of the old New Criticism. Barthes is on the one hand a dazzling performer, a master of verbal subterfuge, and, on the other, a decently methodical thinker dressed up in the current Parisian style. His subversive tactics come down to an inordinate fondness for paradox disguising a commitment to order and method.

Thody's recuperative reading is plainly intended to make sense of Barthes for conservative-minded British consumers. His bluff commonsensical tone combines with the attitude that neatly drives a wedge between the acceptable face of structuralist method and its other, more radical implications. Hence his slight impatience with Barthes's paradoxical strain, a tendency Thody regards as peripheral and probably betraying some strong but repressed 'creative' drive. That paradox might be at the root of Barthes's thinking, rather than merely an ornament of 'style', is a notion scarcely to be entertained. Yet this is precisely the import of numerous passages in his writing which show Barthes consciously confronting reason and method with twists of argument beyond their power of absorption. One of the fragments from his pseudo-autobiography makes this 'reactive formation' the source and motive of all Barthes's writing.

> A *doxa* (a popular opinion) is formulated, intolerable; to free myself of it, I postulate a paradox; then this paradox turns bad, becomes a new concretion, itself becomes a new *doxa*, and I must seek further for a new paradox.
>
> (Barthes 1977, p. 71)

Thody's attitude reflects a belief that paradox and suchlike figures of thought belong to the province of 'literary' language and can play only a marginal or self-indulgent role in criticism. It is the same demarcation that the New Critics set between the figural devices of poetry and the rational language of prose explication.

This boundary was always subject to periodic raids and incursions by the more adventurous New Critics, especially those poets and novelists among them who felt uneasy with a discipline that drove a doctrinal wedge between the two kinds of writing. The issue was more than a matter of critical technique. What the orthodox New Critics sought in the language of poetry was a structure somehow transcending human reason and ultimately pointing to a religious sense of values. Walter Ong makes the point most effectively in his essay 'Wit and Mystery'. There is a direct relation, he argues, between the New Critics' emphasis on poetic 'wit' (with its correlative figures of irony, paradox, etc.) and their general allegiance to Christian belief. 'At the point to which the trail of wit leads, the very texture of poetry itself . . . is seen to come into fundamental contact with the heart of Christian doctrine' (Ong 1962, p. 90). R. P. Blackmur reaches a similar conclusion in discussing the role of poetic 'analogy', the way in which poems can suggest without stating the conflicts and tensions of existence: 'Only in analogy are the opposites identical . . . and it was a similar perception which led Saint Augustine to say that in every poem there is some of the substance of God' (Blackmur 1967, pp. 42–3). It thus becomes a matter of deep doctrinal commitment that criticism should respect the peculiar sanctions of poetic language and restrict its own operations to the separate realm of rational prose statement. To confuse the two is to break down the disciplined awareness which strives to preserve the authentic 'mystery' of poetic truth.

Thus the autonomy of poetry became not merely an issue in aesthetics but a testing-point of faith in relation to human reason. Behind the New Critical rhetoric of irony and paradox is a whole metaphysics of language, where poetic and religious claims to truth are bound up together. At the same time there were those who assented in principle to this discipline of thought but found it in practice hard, if not impossible, to live with. Allen Tate, for instance, adhered to the basic New Critical belief that poetic 'tension' and 'paradox' were the hallmarks of a knowledge superior to reason and linked to the ineffable certitudes of faith. Yet he also wrote of the 'intolerable' strain imposed upon the critical mind by the very nature of its 'middle position between imagination and philosophy' (Tate 1953, p. 111). Tate, like Blackmur in his speculative moments, seems to be struggling with the protocols of New Critical doctrine and venturing – albeit very warily – on to different ground. Take the following passage from Blackmur's *A Primer of Ignorance*:

> Just as the imagination is never able to get all of itself into the arbitrary forms of art and has to depend on aids from the intellect, from conventions ... so the intellect in dealing with imagination is itself imperfect and has to depend upon conventions of its own, some quite formalistic.
>
> (Blackmur 1967, pp. 77–8)

Blackmur and Tate are both uneasily aware that the languages of literature and criticism by no means obey the rigid territorial imperative laid down by orthodox fiat.

BEYOND NEW CRITICISM

The challenge became stronger when critics like Geoffrey Hartman announced their intention of breaking altogether with New Critical method and moving 'beyond formalism'. That the stakes were more than aesthetically loaded is clear from the response of rearguard New Critics, including W. K. Wimsatt, whose essay 'Battering the Object' (1970) sought to recall American criticism to its proper methods and ends. Wimsatt was defensively reacting to a new school of thought which questioned the privileged autonomy of poetic form and claimed a much greater degree of speculative freedom for the literary critic. The sources of this thought were in continental theory, and its American representatives – among them Paul de Man and J. Hillis Miller – were later to become the protagonists of deconstruction.

It is possible, then, to make out a parallel shift of awareness affecting both the structuralist activity and the deep-laid foundations of American New Criticism. It would, of course, be wrong to push this parallel too far. Structuralist theory never took on the kind of quasi-religious orthodoxy invoked by New Critical method. But it was, as I have tried to show, subject to various domesticating pressures which effectively sealed off its more disturbing implications. Culler's appeal to the moderating judgement of the 'competent' reader is one such response, attempting to ground critical theory in an all-but-transcendental philosophy of mind. Thody's treatment of Barthes is a cruder but no less determined effort to isolate what is useful and methodical and consign the rest to a harmless realm of stylistic indulgence. New Criticism and structuralism each had its orthodox side, an aspect that lent itself to wholly conformable uses. At the same time they both tended to generate, in livelier minds, a sense of unease or frustration which called their very methods into question.

For American critics the waning of New Critical hegemony coincided with a sudden new interest in French theoretical ideas. This came at a time when structuralism was already being subjected (in the texts of Derrida especially) to a searching critique of its own suppositions and methodical claims. The effect of this convergence is manifest in the writings of Geoffrey Hartman, J. Hillis Miller and others whose passage 'beyond formalism' led them, through various stages, to an avowedly deconstructionist position. In 1970 Hartman was still finding it difficult to imagine where this speculative quest might lead. 'To go beyond formalism', he wrote (1970, p. 113), 'is as yet too hard for us and may even be, unless we are Hegelians believing in absolute spirit, against the nature of understanding.' His state of perplexity recalls the problems faced by Blackmur and Tate in their speculative musings. The difference lies partly in Hartman's rejection of any absolute doctrinal adherence, and partly in the much wider range of ideas created by structuralist debate.

These new-found freedoms are very much at work in Hartman's essay on Milton, which exuberantly breaks with New Critical assumptions about language, style and the place of critical theory (see 'Adam on the Grass with Balsamum', in Hartman 1970). That Milton should be chosen as fighting ground is further indication of the challenge being offered to New Critical opinion. The New Critics mostly followed Eliot in using the 'problem' of Milton's style as a cover for their deep dislike of his radicalism in politics and religion. Hartman sets out to overturn this powerful consensus. He defends not only Milton's style but the critic's freedom to adopt a charged and 'answerable' style of his own in order to counter the weight of received opinion. Hartman wants to initiate 'a more adventurous hermeneutic tradition, even at the risk of deepening, provisionally, the difference between criticism and interpretation'. By 'criticism' Hartman means that disciplined and self-denying ordinance of method which keeps a safe distance between the literary text and the discourse that seeks to comprehend it. The 'hermeneutic' tradition, on the other hand, takes account of the interpreter's puzzles and perplexities by including them within the terms of a full and generous response. Such a style is 'answerable' in its sense of those constant provisional adjustments the critic has to make between the text's claim upon us and our claim upon the text. It thus works to forestall any cramping or excessively rigid method.

Hartman, like Barthes, asserts the critic's freedom to exploit a style that actively transforms and questions the nature of interpretative thought. In itself this marks a decisive break with the scrupulous decorum of critical language maintained in Eliot's wake. Eliot famously defined the 'perfect critic' as one who showed 'intelligence itself swiftly operating the analysis of sensation to the point of principle and definition'. This is to argue that theory, in so far as it is valid at all, is strictly a matter of placing some orderly construction upon the 'immediate' data of perception. Barthes and Hartman totally reject this careful policing of the bounds between literature and theory. Where Eliot proposes a disciplined or educating movement of thought from perception to principle, they discover an endlessly fascinating conflict, the 'scene' of which is the text itself in its alternating aspects of knowledge and pleasurable fantasy.

This is deconstruction in one of its modes: a deliberate attempt to turn the resources of interpretative style against any too rigid protocols of method or language. It emerged, as we have seen, through the impingement of post-structuralist thought on an American New Critical tradition already showing symptoms of internal strain and self-doubt. But deconstruction has another, more toughly argumentative aspect which starts out from similar questioning motives but pursues them to a different end. Its readings, though suspicious of method and system, are themselves rigorously argued and as remote from Hartman's virtuoso language as Hartman is from the academic style he seeks to explode. Jacques Derrida is the philosophic source of this powerful critique, and Paul de Man at present its foremost American exponent.

In the hands of less subtle and resourceful readers deconstruction can become – it is all too clear – a theoretical vogue as uniform and cramping as the worst New Critical dogma. At best it has provided the impetus for a total revaluation of interpretative theory and practice, the effects of which have yet to be fully absorbed.

2

JACQUES DERRIDA: LANGUAGE AGAINST ITSELF

The texts of Jacques Derrida defy classification according to any of the clear-cut boundaries that define modern academic discourse. They belong to 'philosophy' in so far as they raise certain familiar questions about thought, language, identity and other longstanding themes of philosophical debate. Moreover, they raise those questions through a form of critical dialogue with previous texts, many of which (from Plato to Husserl and Heidegger) are normally assigned to the history of philosophic thought. Derrida's professional training was as a student of philosophy (at the École Normale Supérieure in Paris, where he taught until recently), and his writings demand of the reader a considerable knowledge of the subject. Yet Derrida's texts are like nothing else in modern philosophy, and indeed represent a challenge to the whole tradition and self-understanding of that discipline.

One way of describing this challenge is to say that Derrida refuses to grant philosophy the kind of privileged status it has always claimed as the sovereign dispenser of reason. Derrida confronts this preemptive claim on its own chosen ground. He argues that philosophers have been able to impose their various systems of thought only by ignoring, or suppressing, the disruptive effects of language. His aim is always to draw out these effects by a critical reading which fastens on, and skil-fully unpicks, the elements of metaphor and other figural devices at work in the texts of philosophy. Deconstruction in this, its most rigor-ous form acts as a constant reminder of the ways in which language deflects or complicates the philosopher's project. Above all, decon-struction works to undo the idea – according to Derrida, the ruling illusion of Western metaphysics – that reason can somehow dispense with language and achieve a knowledge ideally unaffected by such mere linguistic foibles. Though philosophy strives to efface its textual character, the signs of that struggle are there to be read in its blind-spots of metaphor and other rhetorical strategies.

In this sense Derrida's writings seem more akin to literary criticism than philosophy. They rest on the assumption that modes of rhetorical analysis, hitherto applied mainly to literary texts, are in fact indispens-able for reading *any* kind of discourse, philosophy included. Literature is no longer seen as a kind of poor relation to philosophy, contenting itself with mere fictive or illusory appearances and forgoing any claim to philosophic dignity and truth. This attitude has, of course, a long prehistory in Western tradition. It was Plato who expelled the poets from his ideal republic, who set up reason as a guard against the false beguilements of rhetoric, and who called forth a series of critical 'defences' and 'apologies' which runs right through from Sir Philip Sidney to I. A. Richards and the American New Critics. The lines of defence have been variously drawn up, according to whether the critic sees himself as *contesting* philosophy on its own argumentative ground, or as operating outside its reach on a different – though equally privileged – ground.

In the latter camp it is F. R. Leavis who has most forcefully asserted the critic's right to dissociate his habits of thought from the logical checks and procedures demanded of philosophic discourse. Criticism on Leavis's terms is a matter of communicating deep-laid intuitive responses, which analysis can point to and persuasively *enact*, but which it can by no means *explain* or *theorize* about. Philosophy is kept at arm's length by treating literary language as a medium of 'lived' or 'felt' experience, a region where the critic's 'mature' responses are his only reliable guide and where there is no support to be had from abstract methodology. Hence Leavis's insistence on the virtues of 'practical' criticism (or close reading), allied to such moral imperatives as 'relevance', 'maturity' and an 'open reverence before life'. The effect of this programme is to draw a firm line of demarcation between literary language and the problems of philosophy. Leavis rejects the idea that criticism need concern itself with epistemological problems, or rhetorical modes of working, implicit in literary texts. His ideal critic works within a discipline defined by qualities of responsiveness and intuitive tact, rather than subtlety of philosophic grasp.

Such was the tenor of Leavis's famous 'reply' to René Wellek, who had asked (in an otherwise appreciative essay) why Leavis should not provide a more coherent or worked-out rationale for his critical judgements (see Leavis 1937). To do so would amount to a betrayal, it seemed, of the different but equally disciplined activity required of the literary critic. That activity was justified in so far as it preserved the life-giving wholeness of critical response from the deadening weight of abstract theory.

Leavis represents the most rooted and uncompromising form of resistance to philosophy on the part of literary criticism. The American New Critics, with their penchant for rhetorical system and method, tended to strike a somewhat more ambivalent stance. I have already quoted Allen Tate, in speculative mood, writing despairingly of criticism as a middle-ground activity torn between the warring poles of imagination and philosophic reason. Typically, the New Critics managed to contain these tensions by devising a rhetoric of figure and paradox which closed the poem off within its own formal limits. Poetry (and fiction, so far as they dealt with it) took on a kind of self-authenticating status, confirmed by the various dogmas of critical method. Conceptual problems – like that of relating poetic 'form' to communicable 'meaning' – were neatly side-stepped by being treated as if they were somehow constitutive of poetry's uniquely complex mode of existence. Paradox and irony, which Tate saw as bearing (to some extent at least) on the critic's own predicament, were generally regarded by the New Criticism as objectively 'there' in the poem's structure of meaning.

Hence the circularity and self-sufficient character of New Critical rhetoric. It kept philosophy at bay, not, like Leavis, by flatly denying its relevance, but by translating its questions into a language of irreducibly *aesthetic* paradox and tension. As critics came to interrogate this rhetoric of closure, so it became more evident that the problems had merely been repressed or displaced, and that criticism had yet to discover its relation to the modes and exigencies of 'philosophic' discourse. It was at this point in the history of American criticism and its discontents that Derrida's influence came as such a liberating force. His work provided a whole new set of powerful strategies which placed the literary critic, not simply on a footing with the philosopher, but in a complex relationship (or rivalry) with him, whereby philosophic claims were open to rhetorical questioning or *deconstruction*. Paul de Man has described this process of thought in which 'literature turns out to be the main topic of philosophy and the model of the kind of truth to which it aspires' (de Man 1979, p. 113). Once alerted to the *rhetorical* nature of philosophic arguments, the critic is in a strong position to reverse the age-old prejudice against literature as a debased or merely deceptive form of language. It now becomes possible to argue – indeed, impossible to deny – that literary texts are less deluded than the discourse of philosophy, precisely because they implicitly acknowledge and exploit their own rhetorical status. Philosophy comes to seem, in de Man's work, 'an endless reflection on its own destruction at the hands of literature'.

Derrida's attentions are therefore divided between 'literary' and 'philosophical' texts, a distinction which in practice he constantly breaks down and shows to be based on a deep but untenable prejudice. His readings of Mallarmé, Valéry, Genet and Sollers are every bit as rigorous as his essays on philosophers like Hegel and Husserl. Literary texts are not fenced off inside some specialized realm of figurative licence where rational commentary fears to tread. Unlike the New Critics, Derrida has no desire to establish a rigid demarcation of zones between literary language and critical discourse. On the contrary, he sets out to show that certain kinds of paradox are produced across all the varieties of discourse by a motivating impulse which runs so deep in Western thought that it respects none of the conventional boundaries. Criticism, philosophy, linguistics, anthropology, the whole modern gamut of 'human sciences' – all are at some point subjected to Derrida's relentless critique. This is the most important point to grasp about deconstruction. There is no language so vigilant or self-aware that it can effectively escape the conditions placed upon thought by its own prehistory and ruling metaphysic.

BLINDNESS AND INSIGHT: DECONSTRUCTING THE NEW CRITICISM

The passage 'beyond formalism' was broached in various ways. Some critics (like Geoffrey Hartman) have adopted a wayward and teasingly indirect style, while others – notably Paul de Man – have attempted to think through the paradoxes of New Critical method. De Man's essays in *Blindness and Insight* (1971) are devoted to a deconstructive reading of critical texts from various schools, movements or traditions of thought. To approach the New Critics with an eye to their founding metaphors is to discover, in de Man's terminology, a 'blindness' inseparable from their moments of greatest 'insight'. Their formalist notion of the poem as 'verbal icon' – a timeless, self-possessed structure of meaning – is shown to deconstruct its own claim through unrecognized twists of implication. Their obsession with 'organic' form was undermined by those very 'ambiguities' and 'tensions' which they sought out in order to praise, and so contain, them. 'This unitarian criticism', as de Man puts it, 'finally becomes a criticism of ambiguity, an ironic reflection on the absence of the unity it had postulated' (de Man 1971, p. 28). 'Form' itself turns out to be more an operative fiction, a product of the interpreter's rage for order, than anything vested in the literary work itself. The organicist metaphors of New Critical parlance result from what de Man calls the 'dialectical interplay' set up between text and interpreter. 'Because such patient and delicate attention was paid to the reading of forms, the critic pragmatically entered into the hermeneutic circle of interpretation, mistaking it for the organic circularity of natural processes' (ibid., p. 29).

Deconstruction draws no line between the kind of close reading appropriate to a 'literary' text and the strategies required to draw out the subtler implications of critical language. Since *all* forms of writing run up against perplexities of meaning and intent, there is no longer any question of a privileged status for literature and a secondary, self-effacing role for the language of criticism. De Man fully accepts the Derridean principle that 'writing', with its own dialectic of blindness and insight, precedes all the categories that conventional wisdom has tried to impose on it.

This amounts to a downright refusal of the system of priorities which has traditionally governed the relation between 'critical' and 'creative' language. That distinction rested on the idea that literary texts embodied an authentic or self-possessed plenitude of meaning which criticism could only hint at by its roundabout strategies of reading. For Derrida, this is yet another sign of the rooted logocentric prejudice which tries to reduce writing – or the 'free play' of language – to a stable meaning equated with the character of *speech*. In spoken language (so the implication runs), meaning is 'present' to the speaker through an act of inward self-communing which ensures a perfect, intuitive 'fit' between intention and utterance. Literary works have often been regarded as uniquely exempt and privileged in this respect, a notion resulting (in Derrida's view) from the deep mistrust of textuality which pervades Western attitudes to language. This mystique of origins and presence can best be challenged by annulling the imaginary boundaries of discourse, the various territorial imperatives which mark off 'literature' from 'criticism', or 'philosophy' from everything that stands outside its traditional domain.

This redistribution of discourse implies some very drastic shifts in our habits of reading. For one thing, it means that critical texts must be read in a radically different way, not so much for their interpretative 'insights' as for the symptoms of 'blindness' which mark their conceptual limits. De Man puts the case most succinctly:

> Since they are not scientific, critical texts have to be read with the same awareness of ambivalence that is brought to the study of non-critical literary texts, and since the rhetoric of their discourse depends on categorical statements, the discrepancy between meaning and assertion is a constitutive part of their logic.
>
> (ibid., p. 110)

This argument cuts both ways when it comes to defining the critic's position *vis-à-vis* the literary text. Clearly it denies him the kind of methodical or disciplined approach which has been the recurrent dream of a certain critical tradition. On the other hand it offers a way beyond the rigid separation of roles which would cast him as a mere attendant upon the sovereign word of the text. What it loses in methodical self-assurance, criticism stands to regain in rhetorical interest on its own account. A similar reversal of priorities occurs in the deconstructive reading of 'literary' texts. There is no longer the sense of a primal authority attaching to the literary work and requiring that criticism keep its respectful distance. The autonomy of the text is actively invaded by a new and insubordinate style of commentary which puts in question all the traditional attributes of literary meaning. But at the same time this questioning raises literature to a point of rhetorical complexity and interest where its moments of 'blindness' are often more acutely revealing than anything in the discourse of philosophy.

Such has been the effect of Derrida's writing on a deeply entrenched conservative tradition – that of American New Criticism – which had already started to question its own ideology. What might have carried on as a series of skirmishing tactics (or virtuoso exercises in Hartman's manner) was galvanized by Derrida into something far more radical and deeply unsettling. We can now look more closely at the major texts in which Derrida sets forth the terms and implications of deconstructive reading. Rather than take his books one by one, I shall fasten upon certain crucial themes and argumentative strategies, acting as far as possible on Derrida's reiterated warning that his texts are not a store of ready-made 'concepts' but an *activity* resistant to any such reductive ploy.

LANGUAGE, WRITING, *DIFFERANCE*

If there is a single theme which draws together the otherwise disparate field of 'structuralist' thought, it is the principle – first enounced by Saussure – that language is a *differential* network of meaning. There is no self-evident or one-to-one link between 'signifier' and 'signified', the word as (spoken or written) vehicle and the concept it serves to evoke. Both are caught up in a play of distinctive features where differences of sound and sense are the only markers of meaning. Thus, at the simplest phonetic level, *bat* and *cat* are distinguished (and meaning is generated) by the switching of initial consonants. The same is true of *bag* and *big*, with their inter-substitution of vowels. Language is in this sense *diacritical*, or dependent on a structured economy of differences which allows a relatively small range of linguistic elements to signify a vast repertoire of negotiable meanings.

Saussure went on from this cardinal insight to construct what has become a dominant working programme for modern linguistics. His proposals broke with traditional thinking in two main respects. He argued, first, that linguistics could be placed on a scientific basis only by adopting a 'synchronic' approach, one that treated language as a network of structural relations existing at a given point in time. Such a discipline would have to renounce – or provisionally suspend – the 'diachronic' methods of historical research and speculation which had dominated nineteenth-century linguistics. Second, Saussure found it necessary to make a firm distinction between the isolated speech-act or utterance (*parole*) and the general system of articulate relationships from which it derived (*la langue*). This system, he reasoned, had to underlie and pre-exist any possible sequence of speech, since meaning could be produced only in accordance with the organizing ground-rules of language.

Structuralism, in all its manifold forms and applications, developed in the wake of Saussure's founding programme for modern linguistics. This is not the place for a detailed account of that development, which the reader will find expounded in Terence Hawkes's *Structuralism and Semiotics* (1977). Briefly, structuralism took over from Saussure the idea that *all* cultural systems – not only language – could be studied from a 'synchronic' viewpoint which would bring out their various related levels of signifying activity.

The precise status of linguistics in regard to this new-found enterprise was a topic of considerable debate. Saussure had argued that language was but one of many codes, and that linguistics should therefore not expect to retain its methodological pre-eminence. With the advent of a fully fledged *semiotics*, or science of signs, language would assume its proper, participant place in the social life of signs in general. Paradoxically, it was Roland Barthes – the most versatile of structuralist thinkers – who originally wanted to reverse this perspective and reinstate linguistics as the master-science of semiology. Barthes was quick to exploit the possibilities of structuralist method across a diverse field of cultural codes, from literary texts to cookery, fashion and photography. Yet in his *Elements of Semiology* (1967) Barthes is to be found expressing the conviction that 'the moment we go on to systems where the sociological significance is more than superficial, we are once more confronted with language'. And this, he explains, because 'we are, much more than in former times . . . a civilization of the written word' (Barthes 1967, p. 10).

Of course, this text belongs to an early stage of Barthes's development, a phase he was later to criticize precisely for its overdependence on concepts of metalinguistic or 'scientific' knowledge. I showed in Chapter I how far he eventually travelled toward deconstructing such concepts through a textual activity aware of its own shifting and provisional status. But the kind of linguistic analogy that Barthes once deployed is representative of structuralism at a certain definite point in its development. It was at this point that Derrida intervened, with the object of wrenching structuralism away from what he saw as its residual attachment to a Western metaphysics of meaning and presence. In particular, he questioned the role of linguistics in dictating the methodological priorities of structuralist thought. Derrida's critique of Saussure, in his essay 'Linguistics and Grammatology' (in Derrida 1977a, pp. 27–73), is therefore a crucial point of encounter for the deconstructive enterprise.

The argument turns on Saussure's attitude to the relative priority of *spoken* as opposed to *written* language, a dualism Derrida locates at the heart of Western philosophic tradition. He cites a number of passages from Saussure in which writing is treated as a merely derivative or secondary form of linguistic notation, always dependent on the primary reality of speech and the sense of a speaker's 'presence' behind his words. Derrida finds a dislocating tension here, a problem that other structuralists (Barthes included) had been content to regard as a puzzling but unavoidable paradox. What are we to make of this privileged status for speech (*parole*) in a theory which is otherwise so heavily committed to the prior significance of language-as-system (*langue*)? Barthes presents the question most succinctly:

A language does not exist properly except in 'the speaking mass'; one cannot handle speech except by drawing on the language. But conversely, a language is possible only starting from speech; historically, speech phenomena always precede language phenomena (it is speech which makes language evolve), and genetically, a language is constituted in the individual through his learning from the environmental speech.

(Barthes 1967, p. 16)

The relation of language and speech is thus 'dialectical'; it sets in train a process of thought which shuttles productively from one standpoint to the other.

Where Derrida differs with Barthes is in his refusal simply to accept this paradox as part of a larger, encompassing project (that of semiology) which would overcome such apparent contradictions. For Derrida, there is a fundamental *blindness* involved in the Saussurian text, a failure to think through the problems engendered by its own mode of discourse. What is repressed there, along with 'writing' in its common or restricted sense, is the idea of language as a signifying system which exceeds all the bounds of individual 'presence' and speech. Looking back over the passage from Barthes quoted above, one can see how 'speech' terminology prevails, even where the argument is ostensibly stating the rival claims of language-as-system. Thus Barthes (drawing on Saussure) refers metaphorically to 'the speaking mass' in a context which purportedly invokes the totality of language, but which appeals even so to actual speakers and their speech as the source of that totality. Barthes may state, as a matter of principle, that language is at once the 'product and the instrument' of speech, that their relationship is always 'dialectical' and not to be reduced to any clear-cut priority. In practice, however, his theorizing leans upon metaphors which implicitly privilege individual speech above the system of meaning that sustains it.

Derrida's line of attack is to pick out such loaded metaphors and show how they work to support a whole powerful structure of presuppositions. If Saussure was impelled, like others before him, to relegate writing to a suspect or secondary status, then the mechanisms of that repression are there in his text and open to a deconstructive reading. Thus Derrida sets out to demonstrate

1   that writing is systematically degraded in Saussurian linguistics;

2   that this strategy runs up against suppressed but visible
    contradictions;
3   that by following these contradictions through one is led
    beyond linguistics to a 'grammatology', or science of writing and
    textuality in general.

Derrida sees a whole metaphysics at work behind the privilege granted
to speech in Saussure's methodology. *Voice* becomes a metaphor of
truth and authenticity, a source of self-present 'living' speech as
opposed to the secondary lifeless emanations of writing. In speaking
one is able to experience (supposedly) an intimate link between sound
and sense, an inward and immediate realization of meaning which
yields itself up without reserve to perfect, transparent understanding.
Writing, on the contrary, destroys this ideal of pure self-presence. It
obtrudes an alien; depersonalized medium, a deceiving shadow which
falls between intent and meaning, between utterance and understanding. It occupies a promiscuous public realm where authority is sacrificed to the vagaries and whims of textual 'dissemination'. Writing, in
short, is a threat to the deeply traditional view that associates truth with
self-presence and the 'natural' language wherein it finds expression.

    Against this tradition Derrida argues what at first must seem an
extraordinary case: that writing is in fact the *precondition* of language and
must be conceived as prior to speech. This involves showing, to begin
with, that the concept of writing cannot be reduced to its normal (i.e.
graphic or inscriptional) sense. As Derrida deploys it, the term is
closely related to that element of signifying *difference* which Saussure
thought essential to the workings of language. Writing, for Derrida, is
the 'free play' or element of undecidability within every system of
communication. Its operations are precisely those which escape the
self-consciousness of speech and its deluded sense of the mastery of
concept over language. Writing is the endless displacement of meaning
which both governs language and places it for ever beyond the reach of
a stable, self-authenticating knowledge. In this sense, oral language
already belongs to a 'generalized writing', the effects of which are
everywhere disguised by the illusory 'metaphysics of presence'. Language is always inscribed in a network of relays and differential 'traces'
which can never be grasped by the individual speaker. What Saussure

calls the 'natural bond' between sound and sense – the guaranteed self-knowledge of speech – is in fact a delusion engendered by the age-old repression of a 'feared and subversive' writing. To question that bond is to venture into regions as yet uncharted, and requires a rigorous effort of conceptual desublimation or 'waking up'. Writing is that which exceeds – and has the power to dismantle – the whole traditional edifice of Western attitudes to thought and language.

The repression of writing lies deep in Saussure's proposed methodology. It shows in his refusal to consider any form of linguistic notation outside the phonetic-alphabetical script of Western culture. As opposed, that is, to the non-phonetic varieties which Derrida often discusses: hieroglyphs, algebraic notions, formalized languages of different kinds. This 'phonocentric' bias is closely allied, in Derrida's view, to the underlying structure of assumptions which links Saussure's project to Western metaphysics. So long as writing is treated as a more or less faithful transcription of the elements of speech, its effects can be safely contained within that massive tradition. As Derrida puts it:

> The system of language associated with phonetic-alphabetic writing is that within which logocentric metaphysics, determining the sense of being as presence, has been produced. This logocentrism, this *epoch* of the full speech, has always placed in parenthesis, *suspended*, and suppressed for essential reasons, all free reflection on the origin and status of writing.
>
> (Derrida 1977a, p. 43)

There is a deep connection between the craving for self-presence, as it affects the philosophy of language, and the 'phonocentrism' which prevents linguistic method from effectively broaching the question of writing. Both are components of a powerful metaphysic which works to confirm the 'natural' priority of speech.

Derrida shows that these assumptions, though consistent and mutually reinforcing at a certain level, lie open to disruption as soon as one substitutes 'writing' for 'speech' in the conceptual order that governs them. The effect is unsettling not only for linguistics but for every field of enquiry based on the idea of an immediate, intuitive access to meaning. Derrida traces the exclusion or degradation of writing as a gesture perpetually re-enacted in the texts of Western philosophy. It occurs wherever reason looks for a ground or authenticating method immune to the snares of textuality. If meaning could only attain to a state of self-sufficient intelligibility, language would no longer present any problem but serve as an obedient vehicle of thought. To pose the question of writing in its radical, Derridean form is thus to transgress – or 'violently' oppose – the conventional priority of thought over language.

Such is the deconstructive violence to which Derrida subjects the texts of Saussure and his structuralist successors. It is not a question, he repeats, of rejecting the entire Saussurian project or denying its historical significance. Rather it is a matter of driving that project to its ultimate conclusions and seeing where those conclusions work to challenge the project's conventional premises. In Derrida's words,

> It is when he is not expressly dealing with writing, when he feels he has closed the parentheses on that subject, that Saussure opens the field of a general grammatology . . . then one realizes that what was chased off limits, the wandering outcast of linguistics, has indeed never ceased to haunt language as its primary and most intimate possibility. Then something which was never spoken and which is nothing other than writing itself as the origin of language writes itself in Saussure's discourse.
>
> (ibid., pp. 43–4)

Saussure is thus not merely held up as one more exemplar of a blind and self-deceiving tradition. Derrida makes it clear that structuralism, whatever its conceptual limits, was a necessary stage on the way to deconstruction. Saussure set the terms for a development which passed beyond the grasp of his explicit programme but which could hardly have been formulated otherwise. By repressing the problem which his own theory of language all but brought into view, Saussure transcended the express limitations of that theory. The very concept of 'writing' was enlarged through this encounter into something primordial and far removed from its place in traditional usage.

The point will bear repeating: deconstruction is not simply a strategic reversal of categories which otherwise remain distinct and unaffected. It seeks to undo both a given order of priorities *and* the very system of conceptual opposition that makes that order possible. Thus Derrida is emphatically not trying to prove that 'writing' in its normal, restricted sense is somehow more basic than speech. On the contrary, he agrees with Saussure that linguistics had better not yield uncritically to the 'prestige' that written texts have traditionally enjoyed in Western culture. If the opposition speech/writing is not subjected to a thorough-going critique, it remains 'a blind prejudice', one which (in Derrida's phrase) 'is no doubt common to the accused and the prosecutor'. Deconstruction is better provided with texts, like Saussure's, which foreground the problematic status of writing precisely by adopting a traditional perspective. A repressed writing then reasserts itself most forcibly through the detours and twists of implication discovered in Saussure. It is the 'tension between gesture and statement' in such critical texts which 'liberates the future of a general grammatology'.

Deconstruction is therefore an activity of reading which remains closely tied to the texts it interrogates, and which can never set up independently as a method or system of operative concepts. Derrida maintains an extreme and exemplary scepticism when it comes to defining his own methodology. The deconstructive leverage supplied by a term like *writing* depends on its resistance to any kind of settled or definitive meaning. To call it a 'concept' is to fall straight away into the trap of imagining some worked-out scheme of hierarchical ideas in which 'writing' would occupy its own, privileged place. We have seen (in Chapter I) how structuralism proved itself amenable to such uses. The *concept* of structure is easily kidnapped by a tame methodology which treats it as a handy organizing theme and ignores its unsettling implications. Derrida perceives the same process at work in the structured economy of differential features which Saussure described as the precondition of language. Once the term is fixed within a given explanatory system, it becomes (like 'structure') usable in ways that deny or suppress its radical insights.

Hence Derrida's tactical recourse to a shifting battery of terms which cannot be reduced to any single, self-identical meaning. *Différance* is perhaps the most effective of these, since it sets up a disturbance at the level of the signifier (created by the anomalous spelling) which graphically resists such reduction. Its sense remains suspended between the two French verbs 'to differ' and 'to defer', both of which contribute to its textual force but neither of which can fully capture its meaning. Language depends on 'difference' since, as Saussure showed once and for all, it consists in the structure of distinctive oppositions which make up its basic economy. Where Derrida breaks new ground, and where the science of grammatology takes its cue, is in the extent to which 'differ' shades into 'defer'. This involves the idea that meaning is always *deferred*, perhaps to the point of an endless supplementarity, by the play of signification. *Différance* not only designates this theme but offers in its own unstable meaning a graphic example of the process at work.

Derrida deploys a whole range of similar terms as a means of preventing the conceptual closure – or reduction to an ultimate meaning – which might otherwise threaten his texts. Among them is the notion of 'supplement', itself bound up in a supplementary play of meaning which defies semantic reduction. To see how it is put to work we can turn to Derrida's essays on Rousseau and Lévi-Strauss, where the theme is that of writing in the context of anthropology and the cultural 'sciences of man'.

CULTURE, NATURE, WRITING: ROUSSEAU AND LÉVI-STRAUSS

For Derrida, writing (in its extended sense) is at once the source of all cultural activity and the dangerous knowledge of its own constitution which culture must always repress. Writing takes on the subversive character of a 'debased, lateralized, displaced theme', yet one that exercises 'a permanent and obsessive pressure . . . a feared writing must be cancelled because it erases the presence of the self-same (*propre*) within speech' (Derrida 1977a, p. 139). This passage occurs in the course of a chapter on Rousseau, whose *Essay on the Origin of Languages* is the starting-point for one of Derrida's most remarkable meditations.

Rousseau thought of speech as the originary form and the healthiest, most 'natural' condition of language. Writing he regarded with curious distrust as a merely derivative and somehow debilitating mode of expression. This attitude of course falls square with Rousseau's philosophy of human nature, his conviction that mankind had degenerated from a state of natural grace into the bondage of politics and civilized existence. Language becomes an index of the degree to which nature is corrupted and divided against itself by the false sophistications of culture. What Derrida does, in a remarkable tour of argument, is to show that Rousseau contradicts himself at various points in his text, so that far from proving speech to be the origin of language, and writing a merely parasitic growth, his essay confirms the priority of writing and the illusory character of all such myths of origin.

Rousseau, for instance, treats of writing as the 'supplement' of spoken language, existing in a secondary relation to speech just as speech itself – by the same token – is at one remove from whatever it names or describes. Such arguments have a long prehistory in Western thought. Like Plato's doctrine of transcendental forms, the effect is to devalue the activities of art and writing by constant appeal to a realm of self-present, self-authenticating truth, their distance from which condemns them to an endless play of deceitful imitation. For Derrida, the 'supplementarity' of writing is indeed the root of the matter, but not in the derogatory sense that Rousseau intended. Writing is the example *par excellence* of a supplement which enters into the heart of all intelligible discourse and comes to define its very nature and condition. Derrida shows that Rousseau's essay submits to this reversal even in the process of condemning the subversive influence he attributes to writing and its 'supplementary' character. A whole strange thematics of the supplement runs through the detail of Rousseau's argument like a guilty obsession and twists his implications against their avowed intent. That Rousseau cannot possibly *mean what he says* (or say what he means) at certain crucial junctures is the outcome of Derrida's perverse but utterly literal reading. Rousseau's text, like Saussure's, is subject to a violent wrenching from within, which prevents it from carrying through the logic of its own professed intention.

Music was one of the manifold interests which went toward the Rousseauist philosophy of culture, and Derrida has some fascinating pages relating Rousseau's ideas on the subject to the general theme of speech *versus* writing. The argument turns on Rousseau's preference for the vocal or melodic style, which he identified with the Italian music of his time, as against the harmonic or contrapuntal, which typified the supposed weakness and decadence of French tradition. As a matter of musical history this view is open to all kinds of scholarly question.

Derrida, however, is not concerned so much with musicological fact as with the *textual* symptoms of doubt and duplicity which mark Rousseau's argument. The primacy of melody in music is held to follow from its closeness to song, which in turn represents the nearest approach to the passionate origins of speech itself. Harmony enters music by the same 'degenerate' process of supplementarity which marks off writing from speech. As music developed, melody (as Rousseau explains it) 'imperceptibly lost its former energy, and the calculus of intervals was substituted for nicety of inflection' (quoted in Derrida 1977a, p. 199).

Derrida fastens upon this and similar passages in Rousseau's text, and shows that what Rousseau is really describing is the condition, not of music in a phase of historical decline, but of *any* music which aspires beyond the stage of a primitive, inarticulate cry. Forgetfulness of origin may be the ruse by which harmony and writing manage to efface the primordial 'warmth' of a pure communion with nature. Yet Rousseau is forced obliquely to acknowledge (through the blind-spots and contradictions of his text) that music is strictly *unthinkable* without the supplement of harmony, or swerve from origin, which marks it from the outset. Rousseau's 'embarrassment' is plainest when he attempts to define the originary nature of melody and song. If song is already, as Rousseau suggests in his *Dictionary of Music*, 'a kind of modification of the human voice', then how can he assign to it (Derrida asks) 'an absolutely characteristic (*propre*) modality' (ibid., p. 196)? The text unconsciously confesses what Rousseau is at such pains to deny: that thought is incapable of positing a pure, unadulterated origin for speech or song. Rousseau's argument, as Derrida describes it,

> twists about in a sort of oblique effort to act as *if* degeneration were not prescribed in the genesis and as if evil *supervened upon* a good origin. As if song and speech, which have the same act and the same birthpangs, had not always already begun to separate themselves.
>
> (ibid., p. 199)

Rousseau's text cannot mean what it says, or *literally* say what it means. His intentions are skewed and distorted by the 'dangerous supplement' of writing as it approaches the theme of origin.

Derrida perceives such discrepancies at every turn of Rousseau's argument. Wherever the authenticity of 'nature' (or speech) is opposed to the debasements of 'culture' (or writing), there comes into play an aberrant logic which inverts the order of priority between those terms. Thus Rousseau's quest for the 'origin' of language turns out to presuppose an already articulate movement of production which must be cut off at source from any such originating presence. The supplement has to be inserted, Derrida writes, 'at the point where language begins to be articulated, is born, that is, from falling short of itself, when its accent or intonation, marking origin and passion within it, is effaced under that other mark of origin which is articulation' (ibid., p. 270).

'Accent', 'intonation' and 'passion' are bound up together as positive terms in Rousseau's philosophy of language and nature. They all belong to that ruling ideology of voice-as-presence which equates the primacy of speech with the virtues of an innocent, uncorrupted self-knowledge. Rousseau constructs an elaborate mythology based on the contrast between 'natural' languages which remain close to their sources in passionate utterance, and 'artificial' languages where passion is overlaid by the rules and devices of convention. The former he associates with 'the South', with a culture largely indifferent to progress and reflecting in its language the gracefulness and innocence of origins. The latter is identified with those 'Northern' characteristics which, for Rousseau, signalize the decadence of progress in culture. Passion is overcome by reason, community life invaded by the forces of large-scale economic order. In language the polarity (according to Rousseau) is equally marked. In the passionate, mellifluous, vowel-based language of the South one encounters speech near the well-spring of its origin. The tongues of the North, by contrast, are marked by a harsh and heavily consonantal structure which makes them more efficient as communicative instruments but widens the rift between feeling and signification, between instinct and expression.

For Derrida, this Rousseauist mythology is a classic instance of the reasoning that always comes up against its limits in trying to locate any origin (or 'natural' condition) for language. He shows how Rousseau associates the threat of writing with that process of 'articulation' by which language extends its communicative grasp and power. 'Progress' involves a displacement from origin and a virtual supersession of all those elements in speech – accent, melody, the marks of passion – which bound language to the speaking individual and community at large. To deconstruct this mythology of presence, Derrida has only to pursue that 'strange graphic of supplementarity' which weaves its way through Rousseau's text. What emerges is the fact that language, once it passes beyond the stage of a primitive cry, is 'always already' inhabited by writing, or by all those signs of an 'articulate' structure which Rousseau considered decadent. As with Saussure's linguistic methodology, so with Rousseau's historical speculation: speech in its imaginary plenitude of meaning is disrupted at source by the supplement of writing.

This is why Rousseau occupies such a central place in *Of Grammatology* and Derrida's writing generally. He represents a whole constellation of themes which, in one form or another, have dominated subsequent discourse on language and the 'sciences of man'. His texts exhibit a constant, obsessive repetition of gestures which miss their rhetorical mark and display the insufficiency of language when it strives for an origin beyond all reach. The deadlocked prolixity of Rousseau's text is also a lesson to the modern philosopher or linguist:

> Our language, even if we are pleased to speak it, has already substituted too many articulations for too many accents, it has lost life and warmth, it is already eaten by writing. Its accentuated features have been gnawed through by the consonants.
>
> (ibid., p. 226)

Speech itself is always shot through with the differences and traces of non-present meaning which constitute articulate language. To attempt to 'think the origin' in Rousseau's fashion is therefore to arrive at a paradox which cannot be resolved or surpassed: 'The question is of an originary supplement, if this absurd expression may be risked, totally unacceptable as it is within classical logic.' The supplement is that which both signifies the lack of a 'presence', or state of plenitude for ever beyond recall, and *compensates* for that lack by setting in motion its own economy of difference. It is nowhere present in language but everywhere presupposed by the existence of language as a pre-articulated system. Philosophies that take no account of its activity are thereby condemned (Derrida argues) to a ceaseless repetition of the paradoxes brought to light in his reading of Rousseau.

This critique is extended to the structuralist anthropology of Claude Lévi-Strauss, where Derrida finds the same issues raised in terms of nature versus culture. Lévi-Strauss was among the first to perceive that the insights of structural linguistics could be applied to other 'languages' or signifying systems in the attempt to elucidate their underlying codes. This gave rise to what is perhaps the most impressive single achievement of structuralism in its broad-based interpretative mode. Lévi-Strauss rests his analyses of myth and ritual on the conviction that, behind all the surface varieties thrown up by the world's different cultures, there exist certain deep regularities and patterns which reveal themselves to structural investigation. It is a matter of looking beyond their manifest content to the structures of symbolic contrast and resemblance that organize these various narratives. At a certain level of abstraction, he argues, it is possible to make out patterns of development and formal relations which cut right across all distinctions of culture and nationality. Myths can then be seen as a problem-solving exercise, adapted to context in various ways but always leading back to the great abiding issues of human existence – mainly the structures of law and taboo surrounding such institutions as marriage, the family, tribal identity, and so forth. The end-point of such analysis may well be to discover, as Lévi-Strauss frequently does, a formula of algebraic power and simplicity to express the logic underlying a dispersed corpus of myths.

Derrida reads Lévi-Strauss as an heir to both Saussure's 'phonocentric' bias and Rousseau's nostalgic craving for origins and presence. The two lines of thought converge in what Derrida shows to be a subtle but weighted dialectic between 'nature' and 'culture'. The phonocentric basis of Lévi-Strauss's method derives, quite explicitly, from the structural linguistics of Saussure and Roman Jakobson. But along with this methodological commitment there is also, according to Derrida, a 'linguistic and metaphysical phonologism which raises speech above writing'. In effect, Lévi-Strauss is seen as performing for modern (structuralist) anthropology the same ambiguous service that Rousseau performed for the speculative science of his day. The nature/culture opposition can be shown to deconstruct itself even as Lévi-Strauss yields to the Rousseauistic dream of an innocent language and a tribal community untouched by the evils of civilization.

Derrida's arguments are largely based on a single brief excerpt – 'The Writing Lesson' – from Lévi-Strauss's book *Tristes Tropiques* (1961). Here the anthropologist sets out to analyse the emergence of writing and its consequences among a tribe (the Nambikwara) whose transition to 'civilization' he describes with undisguised feelings of sadness and guilt. He records how the motives of political power ('hierarchization, the economic function . . . participation in a quasi-religious secret') manifested themselves in the earliest responses to written language. Lévi-Strauss gives expression, like Rousseau, to an eloquent longing for the lost primordial unity of speech-before-writing. He takes upon himself the burden of guilt produced by this encounter between civilization and the 'innocent' culture it ceaselessly exploits. For Lévi-Strauss, the themes of exploitation and writing go naturally together, as do those of writing and violence.

Derrida's answer is not to deny the inherent 'violence' of writing, nor yet to argue that it marks a stage of irreversible advance beyond the 'primitive' mentality. On the one hand he points out that the Nambikwara, on Lévi-Strauss's own evidence, were already subject to a tribal order marked 'with a spectacular violence'. Their social intrigues and rituals of power are in manifest contrast to the retrospective feelings of the anthropologist, who elsewhere presents an idealized picture of their tranquil and harmonious society. Moreover, as Derrida argues, this suggests that writing is always already a part of social existence, and cannot be dated from the moment when the anthropologist, that guilty spectator, introduced its merely graphic conventions. In truth, there is no such pure 'authenticity' as Lévi-Strauss (like Rousseau) imagines to have been destroyed by the advent of writing in this narrow sense. 'Self-presence, transparent proximity in the face-to-face of countenances . . . this determination of authenticity is therefore classic . . . Rousseauistic but already the inheritor of Platonism' (Derrida 1977a, p. 138). From this point it is possible for Derrida to argue that the violence of writing is there at the outset of all social discourse; that in fact it marks 'the origin of morality as of immorality', the 'non-ethical opening of ethics'.

Thus Derrida's critique of Lévi-Strauss follows much the same path as his deconstructive readings of Rousseau and Saussure. Once again it is a matter of taking a repressed or subjugated theme (that of writing), pursuing its various textual ramifications and showing how these subvert the very order that strives to hold them in check. Writing, for Lévi-Strauss, is an instrument of oppression, a means of *colonizing* the primitive mind by allowing it to exercise (within due limits) the powers of the oppressor. In Derrida's reading this theme of lost innocence is seen as a romantic illusion and a last, belated showing of the Rousseauist mystique of origins. 'Writing' in Lévi-Strauss's sense is a merely derivative activity which always supervenes upon a culture already 'written' through the forms of social existence. These include the codes of naming, rank, kinship and other such systematized constraints. Thus the violence described by Lévi-Strauss presupposes, 'as the space of its possibility, the violence of the arche-writing, the violence of difference, of classification, and of the system of appellations' (ibid., p. 110).

This latter has to do with the function of *names* in Nambikwara society, their significance and mode of designation. Lévi-Strauss offers a casual anecdote about some children who took out their private animosities by each revealing the other's name in a round of mutual revenge. Since the Nambikwara, according to Lévi-Strauss, place strict prohibitions on the use of proper names, this episode becomes symbolic of the violence that intrudes upon preliterate cultures when their language gives way to promiscuous exchange (or writing). Derrida counters with evidence – again from Lévi-Strauss's own text – that these were *not*, in fact, 'proper names' in the sense the anecdote requires, but were already part of a 'system of appellation' – a social arrangement – which precludes the idea of personal possession. The term 'proper name' is itself improper, so the argument runs, because it carries an appeal to authentic, individuated selfhood. What is really involved is a system of classification, a *designated* name which belongs to the economy of socialized 'difference' and not to the private individual. In this instance, what is prohibited by the Nambikwara is not the breach of any personal rights but rather the utterance of 'what *functions* as the proper name':

> The lifting of the interdict, the great game of the denunciation . . . does

not consist in revealing proper names, but in tearing the veil hiding a classification . . . the inscription within a system of linguistico-social differences.

(ibid., p. 111)

Derrida's strategies are most clearly on view in these pages devoted to Lévi-Strauss. The 'nature' which Rousseau identifies with a pure, unmediated speech, and Lévi-Strauss with the dawn of tribal awareness, betrays a nostalgic mystique of presence which ignores the self-alienating character of *all* social existence. Writing again becomes the pivotal term in an argument that extends its implications to the whole prehistory and founding institutions of society.

Moreover, the evidence pointing to this conclusion is there in the texts of Lévi-Strauss, as it was in the writings of Rousseau and Saussure. It is not some novel and ultra-sophisticated 'method' of reading devised to keep criticism one jump ahead. Nor does it impinge from outside and above, like certain forms of Marxist criticism which treat 'the text' as a handy support for their own superior knowledge of its meaning or mode of production. (I shall return to this topic at a later point.) Indeed, one of the chief logocentric assumptions that Derrida seeks to expose is the notion that writing is somehow *external* to language, a threat from outside which must always be countered by the stabilizing presence of speech. Carried down through a long tradition, from Plato to Saussure, this idea is most visibly (and paradoxically) inscribed in the Rousseauistic leanings of Lévi-Strauss. Writing becomes an exteriorized agency of violence and corruption, constantly menacing the communal values so closely identified with speech. Derrida's aim to is to show that, on the contrary, writing emerges both within the very *theme* of speech and within the *text* which strives to realize and authenticate that theme. Deconstruction is in this sense the active accomplice of a repressed but already articulate writing. In Derrida's much-quoted phrase, 'Il n'y a pas de hors-texte' ('There is no "outside" [or nothing "external"] to the text').

3

FROM VOICE TO TEXT: DERRIDA'S CRITIQUE OF PHILOSOPHY

It should be clear by now why Derrida attaches such importance to the task of freeing structuralism from Saussure's phonocentric approach. The human voice is the ultimate sanction of all philosophies – like that of Rousseau – which base themselves more or less explicitly on a metaphysics of origins and presence. Among Derrida's first published works was a book on Husserl (*Speech and Phenomena* 1973) in which he examined the claim that philosophy could provide indubitable grounds for knowledge through a rigorous, self-critical reflection on the *a priori* modes of thought and judgement. Edmund Husserl (d. 1938) was the founder of modern phenomenology, a movement of thought to which Derrida is much indebted, although his debt takes the form (as usual) of a thorough critique and re-writing of its premisses. I shall later have various detailed points to make about this crucial encounter, in which Derrida prepares the ground for his deconstructive project. At this point, however, it may be more useful to state the central issue in terms of my discussion so far.

Phenomenology sets out to isolate those structures of experience and judgement which cannot be doubted or called into question by even the most sceptical mind. Husserl believed that the only valid foundation for knowledge was an attitude that accepted nothing on trust, rigorously suspending or 'bracketing' all ideas and assumptions that might be products of delusion. This 'bracketing' of experience would then provide the basis for a philosophy secure in its grasp of the world and immune from the ravages of scepticism. Husserl thought this project all the more vital in view of the self-doubting mood which had overtaken many branches of philosophy towards the end of the last century. A gap had opened up between the 'hard' sciences (those based on experiment and factual observation) and other fields of thought where *interpretative* method played a greater role. This rift was further widened by the naïve or unreflective positivism which had begun to get a hold on philosophy itself. New systems of logic were being devised which, for all their explanatory power, lacked any grounding in the self-conscious process of thought. Unless the mind could arrive at such conclusions by reflecting on the process that produced them – by establishing, that is, an account of its own logical working – philosophy would still be a prey to sceptical doubt. For Husserl, this divorce between knowledge and reflection was approaching a crisis-point which threatened not only the human sciences but the entire project of Western thought (see Husserl 1970). Hence his attempt to provide philosophy with a new rationale which would avoid the twin perils of an unreflecting objectivity and a mere retreat into irrationalism.

The technicalities of Husserl's undertaking need not concern us here. What has to be grasped is the fact that his philosophy denies any resort to mere subjectivism, even while appealing to the 'transcendental ego' (or reflective self-awareness) as an ultimate guarantee. Husserl wanted to demonstrate once and for all that such a ground of appeal was possible without abandoning philosophy to the whims of subjective introspection. This called for a firm distinction between those acts of consciousness which defined the very nature of thought and perception, and that other realm of private-individual psychology which offered no such hold for understanding. What Husserl called the process of 'phenomenological reduction' was precisely this endeavour to separate the basic, constitutive structures of perception from the mass of indeterminate or 'merely' subjective experience. In short,

Husserl revived for modern philosophy the project of thought which Descartes had initiated three centuries earlier: that of re-establishing the certitudes of reason by systematically doubting everything that could be doubted. Descartes discovered his own indubitable truth in the thinking subject whose existence in the act of thought was (to his mind) beyond all question. Even *that* residual certainty has since been attacked (by the structuralists, among others) for its confusions of linguistic and logical statement. Husserl's main object was to break this charmed circle of consciousness by showing how the mind took possession of experience, relating thought to the object-of-thought through an act of structured perception. Thinking no longer takes place in a solipsistic realm of reflection cut off from the reality it vainly strives to grasp. Philosophy is reconstructed on the pared-down but firm foundations of a knowledge in and of the world.

What Derrida fastens on to in Husserl's various texts is the element of subjectivism which he sees still at work once the 'transcendental reduction' has been carried through. Husserl himself was far from consistent in explaining just how far the process needed to be taken if the charge of psychologism was to be rebutted, and philosophy placed on a new and firm footing. His early work admitted certain phenomena of consciousness which could well be regarded as belonging more to individual psychology than to any universal structure of mind. In later texts Husserl strove to purge these elements by insisting more rigorously on the 'transcendental' nature of phenomenological reflection. The mind whose operations are experienced and analysed is *not*, he reiterates, the 'empirical' or pre-reflective ego of everyday awareness. It is a form of conscious self-surveillance critically trained upon its own logical workings and thus redeemed from the errors and uncertainties of common mental experience. For Derrida, however, the question remains whether Husserl was *able* to break so completely with presuppositions which – in one form or another – have dominated the whole of Western intellectual tradition.

His argument turns (as one might expect) on Husserl's treatment of the relation between language and thought. Phenomenology is seen to derive its sense of purpose from the intimate relation assumed to exist between consciousness (or self-presence) and linguistic expression. Husserl draws a cardinal distinction between two kinds of sign, the 'indicative' and the 'expressive'. The latter alone is endowed with meaning (*Bedeutung*) in Husserl's sense of the word, since it represents the communicative purpose or intentional force which 'animates' language. Indicative signs, by contrast, are devoid of expressive intent and function merely as 'lifeless' tokens in a system of arbitrary sense. We have already seen how Derrida set about dismantling a similar opposition in the texts of Rousseau and Lévi-Strauss. In their case the argument was cast in terms of speech versus writing, the former endowed with all the metaphorical attributes of life and healthy vitality, the latter with dark connotations of violence and death. Derrida finds the same powerful metaphors at work in Husserl's meditations on language and thought. 'Indicative' signs are banished to a region of exterior darkness, as remote as possible from the life-giving sources of language. Like Rousseau's feared and disruptive 'writing', they seem to threaten the self-presence of speech by wrenching it away from origin into an endless play of unmotivated, random significations.

Derrida contests this priority by showing once again how the privileged term is held in place by the force of a dominant *metaphor*, and not (as it might seem) by any conclusive logic.

> Although spoken language is a highly complex structure, always containing *in fact* an indicative stratum, which, as we shall see, is difficult to confine within its limits, Husserl has nonetheless reserved for it the power of expression exclusively – and thereby pure logicality.
>
> (Derrida 1973, p. 18)

This latter connection – the link between 'expression' and 'pure logicality' – is crucial to Husserl's undertaking. He seeks to provide a new grounding for logic, not as a self-contained system of axiomatic truths, but as a structure built up from acts of consciousness which grasp the necessity of their own production. Thus logic itself belongs to the expressive (or 'meaningful') activity of thought, as opposed to any purely formal dimension. For Husserl this implies a further distinction between reasoning that is genuinely possessed of its own productive nature and other modes of thought which merely take over an existing methodology.

Behind this opposition, once again, is the idea that consciousness can be fully *authentic* only when its workings express the present activity of a human subject. And from this point, as Derrida shows, it is no great distance to the metaphors of voice and self-presence which govern traditional philosophy. Expression as the 'breath' or 'soul' of meaning, and language as the mere physical 'body' which it comes to animate – such are the covert figurative ploys of Husserlian phenomenology. But, as Derrida argues,

> although there is no expression or meaning without speech, on the other hand not everything in speech is 'expressive'. Although discourse would not be possible without an expressive core, one could almost say that the totality of speech is caught up in an indicative web.
>
> (ibid., p.31)

This disturbing possibility – that 'expression' may be tainted at root by the encroachments of 'indicative' meaning – is enough to shake the whole edifice of Husserl's thought.

The term *différance* plays a major dislocating role in the deconstruction of Husserlian themes. It is first introduced by way of describing those elements of non-intended signification which point to a domain of 'indicative' sense beyond the grasp of immediate conscious awareness. Derrida's logic is simple but devastating. Language can fulfil the condition of self-present meaning only if it offers a *total and immediate* access to the thoughts that occasioned its utterance. But this is an impossible requirement. We simply cannot have what Derrida calls 'a primordial intuition of the other's lived experience'. In which case, following Husserl's own distinction, it has to be admitted that language must always fail to achieve expressive self-presence, and must always partake of the indicative character which marks, for Husserl, the suspension of meaning. This may be, according to traditional prejudice, 'the process of death at work in signs'. But that tradition has nothing to fall back upon once its underlying motives and metaphors have thus been questioned. 'Whenever the immediate and full presence of the signified is concealed, the signifier will be of an indicative nature' (ibid., p. 40). And this, as Derrida goes on to argue, is not just a local aberration but a defining characteristic of all uses of language, written or spoken.

Différance thus comes into play (as it did in the essay on Saussure) at the point where meaning eludes the grasp of a pure, self-present awareness. The idea of a temporal *deferring* is also made explicit in relation to Husserl's phenomenology. His quest for a grounding philosophy of conscious experience required that Husserl gave some account of time and its various modalities. This was the topic of his book *The Phenomenology of Internal Time-Consciousness* (first published in 1929), in which Husserl set out to analyse the different relations and levels of intelligible order which 'made sense' of time for the experiencing mind (see Husserl 1964). From the phenomenological standpoint, this involved showing how the 'living present' of awareness is the privileged point from which memories, both long- and short-term, are organized and accorded their due temporal significance. Among Husserl's most important distinctions is that between *retention* and *representation*, the former having to do with immediate (sensory) traces, the latter with experiences recalled over a greater distance of time. It is here that Derrida inserts the deconstructive lever of *difference*. He points out that Husserl is constantly obliged, by the logic of his own argument, to treat the present as a moment compounded of manifold retentions and anticipations, never existing in the isolated instant of awareness. Time is an endless deferring of presence which drives yet another paradoxical wedge into the project of phenomenology.

This brings about the virtual collapse of all those distinctions Husserl set up in order to preserve the 'living present' in its privileged position. 'Representation' can no longer be distinguished from 'retention', since both are involved in the same ceaseless movement of temporal distancing. What separates them is not the 'radical difference' which Husserl wanted between 'perception and non-perception'; it is, rather, 'a difference between two modifications of non-perception'. In other words, there is no privileged locus of consciousness from which thought could ever organize or control the flux of temporal experience. Husserl's main object was to separate perception from representation in such a way that the latter – the realm of 'mediated' signs and impressions – should not interfere with the primary self-evidence of knowledge. What his text in fact reveals, against its own intention, is the 'movement of difference' which always inhabits 'the pure actuality of the now'. This movement undermines Husserl's phenomenology in the same way that writing questions and subverts the privilege of speech. Perception is always already representation, just as speech presupposes (and wills itself to forget) the *différance* of writing.

PHENOMENOLOGY AND/OR STRUCTURALISM?

Derrida is as far from 'rejecting' Husserl as he is from simply dismissing the linguistics of Saussure or the structural anthropology of Lévi-Strauss. In the texts of all three he discovers a set of paradoxical themes, at odds with their manifest argument, which opens them up to a deconstructive reading. On the other hand, these texts are selected precisely for the rigour and tenacity with which they raise the questions that Derrida wishes to press. That the pressure is brought to bear in ways Derrida can twist, so to speak, against their own intentions is not to be taken as wholly undermining their project. This issue came up in the course of an interview with Julia Kristeva (reprinted in the volume *Positions*, translated 1981). What exactly was the status of deconstructive 'method'? Did it hold out any notion of a 'truth' denied to the texts it called into question? How – more pointedly – could Derrida square his vigilant mistrust of metaphysical language with the fact that he had to work, of necessity, within that language, even while claiming to dismantle its whole conceptual structure?

Derrida replied characteristically by turning the question round to reveal its oversimplified terms of argument. If there is no possibility of breaking altogether with Western metaphysics, it is equally the case that every text belonging, however rootedly, to that tradition bears within itself the disruptive potential of a deconstructive reading. As Derrida puts it, 'in every proposition or in every system of semiotic research . . . metaphysical presuppositions coexist with critical motifs' (Derrida 1981, p. 36). Deconstruction is therefore an activity performed by texts which in the end have to acknowledge their own partial complicity with what they denounce. The most rigorous reading, it follows, is one that holds itself provisionally open to further deconstruction of its own operative concepts.

This is why Derrida returns so often to writers like Husserl whose texts are problematic in ways that defy any settled or definitive reading. They make it possible to define more exactly the point at which thought encounters an *aporia* – or self-engendered paradox – beyond which it cannot press. This term is used frequently by Derrida and those of his more rigorous disciples, such as Paul de Man, who pursue deconstruction to its furthest bounds of possibility. The *Oxford English Dictionary* rather sidesteps the problem of a worked-out definition but does offer two early instances – both from rhetorical handbooks – which convey something of the suspicion and unease evoked by the word. Puttenham, in his *English Poesie* (1589), refers to 'Aporia, or the Doubtfull. So called . . . because oftentimes we will seem to cast perills, and make doubt of things when by a plaine manner of speech wee might affirme or deny him.' Less moralistic but equally perplexed is an entry from 1657: 'Aporia is a figure whereby the speaker sheweth that he doubteth, either where to begin for the multitude of matters, or what to do or say in some strange ambiguous thing.' Clearly the concept of *aporia* occupied a suspect, even sinister, place in the system of traditional rhetoric. These entries give more than a hint of the unsettling uses to which it will be put in the rhetoric of deconstruction.

Aporia derives from the Greek word meaning 'unpassable path', a sense that fully lives up to its later paradoxical development. In Derrida's hands it represents the nearest one can get to a label or conceptual cover-term for the effects of *différance* and the 'logic' of deviant figuration. What deconstruction persistently reveals is an ultimate impasse of thought engendered by a rhetoric that always insinuates its own textual workings into the truth claims of philosophy. To pursue these workings is to glimpse the possibility of reversing philosophy's age-old repression of writing. This would give rise, in Derrida's words, to a 'writing within which philosophy is inscribed as a place within a system which it does not command'. But this prospect can be grasped only momentarily, in the process of engaging with texts that remain – like the deconstructive project itself – inseparably tied to Western philosophy. Within Derrida's writing there runs a theme of utopian longing for the textual 'free play' which would finally break with the instituted wisdom of language. It is a theme that emerges to anarchic effect in some of his later texts (to which I shall return in subsequent pages). For the most part, however, Derrida argues that deconstruction must 'bore from within', or work to dismantle the texts of philosophy with concepts borrowed from philosophy itself.

This reciprocal dependence is nowhere more evident than in Derrida's relationship to Husserl. In his essay 'Genesis and Structure' (in Derrida 1978), he attempts to locate the moment of suspense or hesitation where Husserl is faced with an *impossible* choice between two equally 'valid' but mutually exclusive schemes of explanation. These schemes are, broadly speaking, phenomenological and structuralist. The one seeks to account for knowledge and experience by offering a 'genetic' explanation of how the mind (the 'transcendental ego' of Husserlian parlance) constitutes its own reality. The other eschews such a method – suspecting it, perhaps, of some complicity with subjectivism – and turns instead to the concept of 'structure' as a locus of objective truth. These two dimensions of thought are the poles between which Husserl has to steer if his project is not to be captured by uncritical motives and themes.

And this, Derrida argues, is a problem not only for Husserlian phenomenology but for all philosophical thinking which penetrates beyond a certain level of awareness. Subjectivism is not the only trap philosophy has to avoid. Structuralism has its own special dangers, the nature of which Husserl was quicker to grasp than most of its present-day practitioners. The concept of structure (as we have already seen) can easily be immobilized by assuming it to possess some kind of 'objective' or self-validating status. In this sense it is possible to argue, like Derrida, that 'a certain structuralism has always been philosophy's most spontaneous gesture'. The explanatory props of 'structure' are always available when thought tries to ignore the question of how its own regulative concepts are brought into play. What Husserl's writings demonstrate is the gap (or *aporia*) between structuralism in its objectivist guise and everything that cannot be accounted for in structuralist terms. His entire undertaking is an effort to reconcile two different orders of thought which can never be reduced to each other's terms but which none the less cannot be assumed to exist in self-sufficient isolation. The 'structuralist' quest, as Derrida reads it, is always for 'a form or function organized according to an internal legality in which elements have meaning only in the soldarity of their correlation or their opposition' (ibid., p. 157). The 'genetic' demand, on the other hand, is 'the search for the origin and the foundation of the structure'. In *Speech and Phenomena* the object had been mainly to deconstruct such ideas of 'origin' and 'foundation' by showing them to be always already inscribed in a differential structure of meaning. In 'Genesis and Structure' the argument is angled, not from the opposite side, but from a larger perspective which admits the necessity of both (irreducible) systems of thought.

Derrida's critique of structuralism is continued in the essay 'Force and Signification', which likewise questions the internal self-sufficiency of a theory given over to system and concept. Structuralism always asserts itself where thinking yields to the attractions of order and stability. Its achievements, however impressive, are intrinsically limited to 'a reflection of the accomplished, the constituted, the *constructed*' (Derrida 1978, p. 5). What is suppressed by this static conceptualization is the 'force' or animating pressure of intent which exceeds all the bounds of structure.

Derrida here seems remarkably close to Husserl's insistence on the life-giving content of 'expression', which redeems signs from the fixity of dead convention. He goes so far as to compare the results of structuralist analysis with a city laid waste by some mysterious 'catastrophe' of natural or human creating. But the point of these metaphors is not to reinstate a thematics of presence or expression, as opposed to the *différance* of structural inscription. Rather, it is to demonstrate that structuralism itself arises from the break with an attitude (the phenomenological) it cannot reject but must perpetually put in question. The concept of structure is wrenched from within by denying it its conceptual status and showing how it functions as a *metaphor* to contain the unruly energies of meaning. Structuralism and phenomenology are locked in a reciprocal *aporia* from which neither can emerge with its principles intact, but on which both depend for their moments of maximum insight.

Conventional accounts of modern French criticism tend to reduce this relationship between phenomenology and structuralism to a matter of successive 'schools' or waves of interest. Structuralism, it is assumed, grew out of phenomenology and then, in the other sense of the phrase, 'grew out' of it – rejected its assumptions and developed an alternative theoretical approach. This idea is plausible up to a point. Phenomenology certainly helped to lay the ground for structuralism by focusing attention more keenly on the ways in which consciousness perceives and makes sense of the world. It offered a philosophy of language where the idea of structure was already implicit, since meaning was seen as a productive interplay between the text and the reader's quest for intelligibility. Where it differed from structuralism was in the assumption (following Husserl) that meaning was always a kind of creative *excess*, surpassing any possible account of its origin based on the notion of structure.

Maurice Merleau-Ponty, Husserl's most distinguished successor, states the issue with perfect clarity. Language – and speech in particular – represents

> that paradoxical operation through which, by using words of a given sense, and already available meanings, we try to follow up an *intention* which necessarily outstrips, modifies and in the last analysis stabilizes the meanings of the words which translate it.
>
> (Merleau-Ponty 1962, p. 389)

According to this view, language in its 'creative' uses outruns what might be accounted for in terms of purely 'structured' or pre-existent meaning. Contrary to structuralist thinking, it reveals an 'excess of the signified over the signifying' which places it beyond all reach of reductive explanations.

This theme of the creative or intentional 'surplus' in meaning goes a long way to explain the rift between structuralism and phenomenology. The activating principle of structuralist thought, at least in its earlier manifestations, was precisely the *refusal* to acknowledge any meaning outside or beyond the constraints of a pre-existent language. Yet it is not hard to see how a dialogue might now be reopened between phenomenology and the post-structuralist themes of text, writing and deconstruction. Merleau-Ponty himself seems to move in this direction – as is apparent if one looks more closely at some of his later essays, especially those collected in the volume *Signs* (1964). Merleau-Ponty's reflections persistently dwell on the sheer *impossibility* of distinguishing 'structure' from 'meaning', or expression from that which precedes it and makes it possible. Language, he suggests at one point, can only be conceived of as 'a surpassing of the signifying by the signified which it is the very virtue of the signifying to make possible'

(Merleau-Ponty 1964, p. 90). In its sense of an irreducibly two-way dependence, this description marks a definite shift from Merleau-Ponty's earlier position. It acknowledges the claims of structure while still holding on to the necessity of thinking beyond their more rigid application.

The point is made most tellingly in an essay on Matisse, occasioned by a documentary film of the artist at work. It would be wrong, Merleau-Ponty suggests, to 'believe' in what the film portrays as an inspired but at the same time *premeditated* build-up to the finishing stroke. By a simple gesture Matisse is made to resolve 'the problem which in retrospect seemed to imply an infinite number of data'. The process of creation is unthinkable in terms which insist on the simplified either/or of expressive versus structural description. Rather, as Merleau-Ponty carefully phrases it,

> the chosen line was chosen in such a way as to observe, scattered out over the painting, twenty conditions which were unformulated and even informulable for anyone but Matisse, since they were only defined and imposed by the intention of executing *this painting which did not yet exist.*
>
> (ibid., p. 46)

This manages to state, more clearly than any abstract account, the paradox Merleau-Ponty discovers at the heart of language and all signifying systems. The 'surpassing' of structure by meaning cannot be described simply in terms of subjective 'intention'. Merleau-Ponty is at one with the structuralists in seeing that meaning is always necessarily inscribed in a pre-existent economy of sense which it can never fully control. On the other hand, he shows that this very condition, by creating such a complex background of constraints, makes it possible for meaning to emerge in new and unforeseeable ways. Merleau-Ponty's later philosophy is a constant search for that 'fecund moment' when meaning discovers the structure which will 'make it manageable for the artist and at the same time accessible to others'.

It is this same ultimate paradox that structuralism approaches, so to speak, from the opposite side. Where Merleau-Ponty finds meaning perpetually on the brink of investing itself with structure, Barthes would see structures endlessly producing new possibilities of sense. Derrida is pointing to a similar moment of convergence in his essays on structuralism and phenomenology. By deconstructing the play of concept and metaphor behind these two philosophies, Derrida arrives at his own formulation of the problems encountered by Merleau-Ponty. Structuralism lives on what he calls 'the difference between its promise and its practice'. The practice has mostly given way to those enticing metaphors, derived from structural linguistics, which elevate 'form' at the expense of 'force', or structure to the detriment of what goes on within and *beyond* structure. The 'promise' survives in that other, self-critical strain of structuralist thought which implicitly questions its own methodical grounding. There is always, according to Derrida, an 'opening' which baffles and frustrates the structuralist project. 'What I can never understand, in a structure, is that by means of which it is not closed' (Derrida 1978, p. 160). Hence the importance of Husserlian phenomenology as an intimate running critique of structuralist thought. What Husserl powerfully demonstrates, often against his immediate intention, is 'the principled, essential, and structural impossibility of closing a structural phenomenology' (ibid.).

Derrida's sights are thus firmly set against the idea that structuralism has brought about a total and irreversible break with its own prehistory. This heady delusion – still current in some quarters of the structuralist Left – ignores the dangers of pre-emptive closure and conceptual rigidity which Derrida brings to light. It would also be wrong, and for much the same reason, to regard deconstruction as 'post-structuralist' in the sense of displacing or invalidating the structuralist project. Without that specific tension between 'practice' and 'promise' exemplified in structuralist thought, Derrida could hardly have broached the questions that animate his own writing. Deconstruction is a constant and vigilant reminder of what structuralism *must be* if it is to avoid the traps laid down by its seductive concepts of method.

By virtue of its innermost intention, and like all questions about language, structuralism escapes the classical history of ideas which already presupposes structuralism's possibility, for the latter naïvely belongs to the province of language and propounds itself within it.

(ibid., p.4)

This 'innermost intention' is the aspect of structuralist thinking which eludes methodical reduction and which Derrida strives to maintain. Otherwise – as he shows most clearly in the case of Saussure – structuralism is destined simply to rejoin the tradition it promised to transform.

4

NIETZSCHE: PHILOSOPHY AND DECONSTRUCTION

Friedrich Nietzsche (1844–1900) remains for most modern philosophers what he was for his contemporaries: a scandal wrapped in layers of enigma. One reaction in recent times has been to brand him as a dire precursor of the Nazi phenomenon, a thinker whose supposedly 'irrationalist' outlook and megalomaniac pretensions paved the way for Hitler and his ideologues. These charges cannot be altogether rejected. They rest on a partial reading of Nietzsche which was actively encouraged by certain of his followers and no doubt exercised some baleful influence, if not on the scale imagined by his latter-day detractors. Suffice it to say that Nietzsche's doctrinaire mythology, his ideas of the 'superman' and 'eternal recurrence', have suffered considerable guilt by association.

But alongside these writings Nietzsche also conducted a critique of Western philosophy and its presuppositions which has lost nothing of its power to provoke and disturb. It is this aspect of Nietzsche's thought which has left its mark on the theory and practice of deconstruction. To speak of 'influence' here would be somewhat misleading, since the word implies a handing-down of concepts and themes as if within a centralized tradition of authority. What Derrida brings out, after all, is the way in which writing exceeds all the various proprietory claims laid down by the conventional 'history of ideas'. If texts are unbounded by authorial intent and open to radical deconstruction, then clearly there is no question of Derrida's having simply absorbed Nietzsche's influence and put his ideas to work in a modern, post-structuralist context. What Nietzsche provides, on the contrary, is a *style* of philosophic writing which remains intensely sceptical of all claims to truth – its own included – and which thus opens up the possibility of liberating thought from its age-old conceptual limits.

Nietzsche is not to be taken at his own self-estimate, as having once and for all put a close to the deluded quest of Western metaphysics. Like Saussure or Husserl, he remains to some extent a prisoner of the themes and rooted conventions of thought which his writing begins to question. These themes, as Derrida so often reminds us, run deep in the logic and communicative structure of language, so deep indeed that to break with them entirely would be to risk madness or total non-communication. (Nietzsche himself was declared insane and produced nothing more than random, unintelligible jottings during the last sixteen years of his life.) More than any philosopher in the Western tradition, Nietzsche pressed up against those limits of language and thought which Derrida attempts to define. He anticipates the style and strategy of Derrida's writing to a point where the two seem often engaged in a kind of uncanny reciprocal exchange.

The reasons for this are not far to seek. Nietzsche often seems to spell out in advance the programme and systematic ruses of deconstruction, adopting the same attitude of sceptical rigour and denying himself any secure resting-place in method or concept. Philosophers, he argued, were the self-condemned dupes of a 'truth' which preserved itself simply by effacing the *metaphors*, or figurative discourse, which brought it into being. If language is radically metaphorical, its meanings (as Saussure was later to show) caught up in an endless chain of relationship and difference, then thought is deluded in its search for a truth beyond the mazy detours of language. Only by suppressing its origins in metaphor had philosophy, from Plato to the present, maintained the sway of a tyrannizing reason which in effect denied any dealing with figural language. Reason had crushed out the imaginative life of philosophy, just as – in Nietzsche's view – it had destroyed the joyous or

'Dionysian' element in classical Greek tragedy. Socrates stands – with Christ in Nietzsche's inverted pantheon – as the pale destroyer of all that gives life, variety and zest to the enterprise of human culture. To restore that buried tradition is to show how 'reason' usurped its place by systematically coopting or repressing the rhetorical gambits of language.

An arresting image from Nietzsche conveys the extent of his scepticism about knowledge and truth. What remains of such notions, Nietzsche asks, once we have seen through the twists and displacements by which language simultaneously hides and perpetuates its own devious workings? Truth, he concludes,

> is a mobile marching army of metaphors, metonymies and anthropomorphisms ... truths are illusions of which one has forgotten that they *are* illusions ... coins which have their obverse effaced and which are no longer of value as coins but only as metal ...
>
> (quoted by Spivak, in Derrida 1977a, p. xxii)

For Nietzsche this insight led to the conclusion that *all* philosophies, whatever their claim to logic or reason, rested on a shifting texture of figural language, the signs of which were systematically repressed under the sovereign order of Truth. This bottomless relativity of meaning, and the ways in which philosophers have disguised or occluded their ruling metaphors, are the point of departure for Derrida's writing like Nietzsche's before him.

Of course there are plenty of precedents for the idea that language is radically metaphorical in character. The doctrine took shape among the German Romantics, and passed down through Coleridge to modern critics like I. A. Richards, whose *Philosophy of Rhetoric* (1936) expounded what might seem an uncompromising line on the central importance of metaphor. 'Thought is metaphoric,' Richards declared, 'and the metaphors of language derive therefrom.' In contesting the traditional view of metaphor (that it is merely a grace or incidental supplement of language), and in thus reversing an entrenched priority, Richards goes some way towards a deconstructionist approach. The difference appears when he proposes that 'to improve the theory of metaphor' we must 'take more notice of the skill in thought which we possess' and 'translate more of our skill into discussable science' (Richards 1936, p. 116). There is still the implication, despite Richards's high claims for metaphor, that a 'science' or logical metalanguage exists which can step outside the figural domain and survey its peculiar contours.

This assumption runs deep in Richards's thinking, as it does across virtually the entire domain of modern Anglo-American philosophy and criticism. In his early writings Richards put forward an 'emotive' theory of poetic language, according to which poetry could be valued for its powers of evocative and life-enhancing metaphor, while escaping the rigid truth-conditions of logical-positivist philosophy. His distinction was seized upon by the American New Critics, and became (as we have seen) the basis of their various rhetorical modes of explication. A gulf was thus fixed between poetry and rational knowledge, a no-man's-land which permitted no crossing except by a strict observance of the saving and peculiar 'logic' of figural language. Structuralism in its early, scientistic guise was subject to the same general ordinance. Criticism aspired to the condition of a metalanguage or encompassing theory of the text which derived its explanatory power from precisely this sense of disciplined objectivity.

Derrida follows the Nietzschean lead in his break with this self-accrediting notion of method and validity. 'Science', in Derrida's usage, is a discourse linked to the repressive ideology of reason, which in turn (as Nietzsche argued) took rise from the Greek equation between truth and logic. What is in question, for Nietzsche and Derrida, is not some 'alternative' logic of figural language but an open plurality of discourse where all such priorities dissolve into the disconcerting 'free play' of signs. Derrida writes (in his essay 'Structure, Sign and Play') of the two 'interpretations of interpretation' which between them stake out the region traversed by modern debates on language and method. Both are 'structuralist' in the extended sense of the term which, as we have seen, Derrida applies to a long and diverse tradition of Western thought. They are both concerned, that is to say, with interpreting the means by which thought makes sense of an otherwise inchoate experience. Where they differ is in the degree of order and stability imposed by their respective quests for meaning. On the one hand is the attitude – exemplified here by Lévi-Strauss – which clings to the concept of structure as a refuge from the giddying motions of pure difference. On the other is posed the more radical choice, that which involves, as Derrida describes it, 'the Nietzschian affirmation . . . of the play of the world and of the innocence of becoming . . . of a world of signs without fault, without truth, and without origin which is offered to an active interpretation' (Derrida 1978, p. 292). It is this dimension of Nietzsche's thought which has not merely 'influenced' but in many ways uncannily pre-empted the work of deconstruction.

NIETZSCHE, PLATO AND THE SOPHISTS

Nietzsche's critique of philosophy was as far-reaching in its historical scope as in the zest with which it set out to attack all current ideas of knowledge and truth. It involved a full-scale 'genealogy' of Western thought, a diagnostic survey which worked right back to the ancient Greek origins of philosophy itself. For Nietzsche it seemed that this tradition had been firmly set on course by the style of dialectical argument invented by Socrates and passed on through the texts of his student Plato. The dialectical method of eliciting 'truth' from a carefully contrived encounter of wisdom and ignorance was – according to Nietzsche – no more than a rhetorical ploy. Its persuasiveness, however, was such as to monopolize for itself all claims to reason, dignity and truth. As a result, philosophy renounced any dealing with rhetoric and looked upon the arts of language (especially writing) as sources of error and delusion. Among the contemporary targets of Socratic disdain was the school of rhetorician-philosophers known as the sophists, a name that still connotes – as it did for Plato – verbal ingenuity mixed with persuasive guile. Socrates is shown running circles of argument round one of their number in Plato's dialogue The Gorgias. Here dialectic wins out, as always, by placing its questions with strategic skill and forcing the opponent into a position of weakness on Socrates' terms. The upshot, crudely summarized, is to demonstrate that rhetoric possesses neither reason nor moral self-knowledge; that its powers of persuasion are ethically indifferent and open to all manner of abuse.

Nietzsche's response is not to deny the potential aberrations of rhetoric but to argue, on the contrary, that Socrates himself is a wily rhetorician who scores his points by sheer tactical cunning. Behind all the big guns of reason and morality is a fundamental will to persuade which craftily disguises its workings by imputing them always to the adversary camp. Truth is simply the honorific title assumed by an argument which has got the upper hand – and kept it – in this war of competing persuasions. If anything, the sophist comes closer to wisdom by implicitly acknowledging what Socrates has to deny: that thinking is always and inseparably bound to the rhetorical devices that support it.

DECONSTRUCTION ON TWO WHEELS

Nietzsche's transvaluation of philosophy therefore demanded a return to source and an effort to deconstruct the ruling metaphors of reason itself. There is an odd but revealing parallel to this in Robert Pirsig's novel *Zen and the Art of Motorcycle Maintenance* (1974), where the narrative interest has more to do with Greek philosophy than with Zen Buddhism, as many readers have no doubt been puzzled to find. The central figure is a man on the verge of breakdown and despair who sets out on a coast-to-coast motorcycle trip across America in search of self-understanding. What emerges gradually in the course of this quest is a whole buried prehistory of psychic and intellectual conflict which – we come to realize – led up to the events of the novel. Through a sequence of dimly remembered episodes the narrator reconstructs a portrait of his own previous life, the last few months of which were spent as a student of philosophy at the University of Chicago. Under the pseudonym 'Phaedrus' – adopted for reasons which soon become clear – this doomed *alter ego* is shown in the process of challenging all the basic assumptions handed down by his teachers on pain of academic excommunication.

When Phaedrus begins to read back into the sources, especially the texts of Plato and Aristotle, he finds their arguments not only unconvincing but deviously angled in such a way as everywhere to misrepresent their forgotten opponents. The sophists, in particular, are held up to philosophic ridicule by a method of argument which twists their case into a parody of its own just-visible outline. From Socrates down through Plato and Aristotle, the evidence points to a massive suppression and misinterpretation of everything that threatened the sovereign power of dialectical reason.

Phaedrus himself is cast as a latter-day victim of this same 'conspiracy', suffering the taunts of professors and students unwilling to question received wisdom. The 'Church of Reason' is too firmly established in Chicago, with its neo-Aristotelian stress on the virtues of clear-cut logical analysis and firmly categorical thinking. The trouble comes to a head for Phaedrus when his class is taken over – ominously – by the Chairman for the Committee on Analysis of Ideas and Study of Method. What ensues – at least in Phaedrus's inflamed imagination – is an ultimate duel of wits between 'dialectic' and 'rhetoric', with rhetoric decisively winning the day. The turning-point comes with his realization that ' "dialectic" had some special meaning that made it a fulcrum word – one that can shift the balance of an argument, depending on how it's placed'. By challenging the Chairman to explain the provenance of dialectic – its 'genealogy', in Nietzschean terms – Phaedrus shows it to rest on a willed and systematic forgetting of its own rhetorical origins. Reason, or the supposed self-evidence of reason, is thrown into doubt by its manifest failure to justify its methods on other than purely tautological grounds. Hence Phaedrus's triumphant conclusion:

> The halo round the heads of Plato and Socrates is now gone. He sees that they are consistently doing that which they accuse the Sophists of doing – using emotionally persuasive language for the ulterior purpose of making the weaker argument, the case for dialectic, appear the stronger. We always condemn most in others, he thought, that which we most fear in ourselves.
>
> (Pirsig 1974, p. 378)

But that way madness lies. Phaedrus cannot communicate his discovery within the norms of institutionalized knowledge and 'dialogue' so zealously preserved by the Chicago Aristotelians. He leaves the university and suffers (like Nietzsche) a protracted – though in his case not terminal – nervous collapse.

The 'original' Phaedrus, in Plato's dialogue of that title, is yet another foil for Socrates, a young and vaunting rhetorician whose headlong gambits are neatly anticipated at every turn (see Plato 1973). As far as the latter-day Phaedrus is concerned, this exchange simply follows the standard pattern of an argument ignoring its own complicity with the tricks and devices of which it sternly disapproves. The *Phaedrus* is also, as it happens, a crucial text for Derrida's reading of Greek philosophy. It contains Plato's most vigorous attack upon writing, couched in the same familiar terms – 'presence' versus 'absence', living speech versus the dead letter – as made up the argument of Rousseau's essay. Writing is the dangerous 'supplement' which lures language away from its authentic origins in speech and self-presence. To commit one's thoughts to writing is to yield them up to the public domain, thus exposing them to all the promiscuous wiles of interpretation. Writing is the 'death' that lies in wait for living thought, the subtle agent of corruption whose workings infect the very sources of truth. Plato's case against rhetoric is therefore of a piece with his attitude to writing. Both are seen as the rebellious servant to a master (truth or dialectic) whose authority they flout by setting themselves up as alternative paths to wisdom.

As Pirsig's Phaedrus accounts for it, rhetoric was denatured and deprived of its force through being treated as merely a collection of classified devices, reducible to system and order. Aristotle brought this process to a high point of rational perfection: 'Rhetoric has become an object, and as an object has parts. And the parts have relationships to one another and these relations are immutable' (Pirsig 1974, p. 368). Whence, incidentally, the motorcycle connection: a machine for Phaedrus is more than the sum of its parts as laid out in a service manual.

Curiously enough, the novel never mentions Nietzsche, though its manner of engaging philosophic issues is everywhere prompted by a Nietzschean spirit of critique. The crucial question Phaedrus poses – whence the authority of Socratic reason? – is posed and answered by Nietzsche in strikingly similar terms. It is rhetoric, not dialectic, which takes us back furthest toward the origin of thought in man's encounter with experience: 'Dialectic, which is the parent of logic, came itself from rhetoric. Rhetoric is in turn the child of the myths and poetry of ancient Greece' (ibid., p. 391). Phaedrus is thus led back to the pre-Socratic philosophers, those shadowy figures whom Nietzsche admired for having the courage of their own metaphors. These thinkers had identified reality with various elemental forces in the natural world. For Thales the 'immortal principle' was that of water, while

Anaximenes varied the metaphor to air, and Heraclitus – the philosopher of change and flux – saw fire as the element of all things. Their 'explanations' were of course a species of poetic analogy, and yield small sense to the rational (or post-Socratic) mind. But, as Phaedrus declares, 'everything is analogy', including the presumptive generalizations involved in dialectical argument. The difference is that the dialectician, unlike his 'irrational' precursor, fails to recognize this operative movement in the process of thought itself.

WRITING AND PHILOSOPHY

Deconstruction begins with the same gesture of turning reason against itself to bring out its tacit dependence on another, repressed or unrecognized, level of meaning. Phaedrus's glimpse of how the concept *dialectic* could be used as a 'fulcrum' to achieve this reversal is very much in keeping with Derrida's textual strategies. In his texts on Greek philosophy Derrida traces some of the ruses and devices by which writing is systematically opposed to the values of truth, self-presence and origin. But why this animus towards writing? The likeliest historical explanation, adopted by many scholars, is that writing was a relatively new development at this stage in Greek cultural life, and that Plato tended to mistrust what he saw as its dangerous diffusion of knowledge and power. This argument clearly has much in common with the Nietzschean-Derridean view of Socratic reason as a tyrannizing force of repression. On the other hand it ignores the textual strategies and the deep-grained metaphysics of presence which a deconstructive reading uncovers. For Derrida the suppression of writing is no mere accident of chronology or quirk of a culture in transition. It operates, in Plato and his numerous descendants, through a mode of self-perpetuating rhetoric unglimpsed by the conventional historian of ideas.

That this attitude to writing has remained deeply entrenched can be seen from a text like F. M. Cornford's *Before and After Socrates* (1932), a widely read introduction to Greek philosophy and its background. Cornford shows a kind of condescending patience with the sophists, treating them as adolescent rebels on the way to Socratic wisdom and dignity. When he comes to the relationship between Socrates and Plato, his comments perfectly illustrate the marked devaluation of writing by a powerful mystique of origins. Socrates, according to Cornford, was one of those choice spirits who by 'living the truth' bequeathed an example more potent than any mere text.

> They have divined in our nature unsuspected powers which only they have as yet, in their own persons, brought to fulfilment. . . . Conviction is slowly carried to posterity by the example of their lives, not by any record they bequeath in writing. For, with few exceptions, they have not written books. They were wise, and knew that the letter is destined to kill much (though not all) of the life that the spirit has given.
>
> (Cornford 1932, p. 62)

Nothing could show more clearly the Socratic equation between truth, presence and the primal authority of speech. Without fully endorsing Plato's idea of writing as a childish invention, an affront to mature wisdom, Cornford yet manages to imply that Socrates preserved his truths intact by not having to submit them to the infantile lures of textuality.

Derrida pursues these sanctions against writing deep into the labyrinth of Plato's thought. He discovers a further opposition between 'good' and 'bad' writing, the one envisaged as 'natural' and inscribed upon the soul by the laws of reason, the other a debased and 'literal' script which obtrudes its shadow between truth and understanding. As Derrida shrewdly notes, this distinction is made possible by a *metaphoric* switch wherein the figurative ('good') writing becomes more real and immediate than its literal counterpart. In Christian as in Platonic tradition, the material script is devalued in favour of a spiritual writing imprinted directly on the soul without the aid of material instruments. This 'simulated immediacy' then becomes the source of all authentic wisdom and truth. What cannot be acknowledged within this Platonic scheme is the fact that it depends on a root *metaphor* of writing, one that it strives to repress even while perpetually playing variations on its terms. Deconstruction insists – paradoxically enough – on the literal status of this seemingly strange and recondite metaphor. It is not, as Derrida says, 'a matter of inverting the literal meaning and the figurative meaning but of determining the "literal" meaning of writing as metaphoricity itself' (Derrida 1977a, p. 15). It is here that deconstruction finds its rock-bottom sense of the irreducibility of metaphor, the *différance* at play within the very constitution of 'literal' meaning. It finds, in short, that there is no literal meaning.

Greek philosophy is not the only source for this double valuation of 'good' and 'bad' writing. Derrida cites a multiplicity of texts, including those many biblical passages which distinguished the ineffable 'writing' of God – vouchsafed to the soul through divine illumination – from the fallen, material inscriptions of worldly language (see ibid., pp. 16 ff.). By thus creating a twofold order of writing in its 'sensible' and 'intelligible' aspects, theology seconded the Platonist belief in a 'writing of the soul' which had to be protected from the mere physicality of signs. The *logos* of revealed truth, whether Platonist or Christian, harks back to a state of linguistic grace before the 'fall' of language into a mode of debased and corporeal written substance. In medieval theology the two traditions came together: 'the intelligible face of the sign remains turned toward the word and the face of God'.

It is the same distinction between 'sensible' and 'intelligible' orders of meaning which Derrida sets out to deconstruct in the texts of Husserl. Indeed, its effects can be seen, he argues, in every philosophy committed to the notion of a meaning somehow anterior to the signs that serve to convey it. This applies even to Saussure's cardinal distinction between 'signifier' and 'signified', the terms of which – for all their radical potential – remain caught up in a version of Platonic dualism. This bifurcated image of the sign belongs, as Derrida argues,

> to the totality of the great epoch covered by the history of metaphysics, and in a more explicit and a more systematically articulated way to the narrower epoch of Christian creationism and infinitism when these appropriate the resources of Greek conceptuality.
>
> (ibid., p. 13)

Structuralism and semiotics remain a part of this tradition so long as they preserve the Saussurian bar between signifier and signified, 'sensible' token and 'intelligible' concept.

BEYOND INTERPRETATION?

Yet thought cannot altogether break with this distinction, no matter how rigorously it strives to suspend — or place within brackets — the conceptual terms it has to work with. We arrive once again at that Nietzschean-Derridean limit where the only possible way forward is a vigilant textual practice aware of its own metaphysicalliabilities. Nietzsche is fully as rigorous as Derrida when it comes to deconstructing his own rhetorical motives and denying himself any claim to consistency of method.

This would seem to raise problems, as I hinted earlier, with those passages where Derrida cites the Nietzschean text in a clearly positive or approving manner. Such a response can only be at odds with Nietzsche's *tout court* rejection of truth values and his refusal to engage in the kind of argument that would specify terms for its own correct interpretation. Nietzsche, on the contrary, permits his reader no such comforting assurance that the 'truth' of his writing is there to be discovered by a careful passage from signifier to signified. To interpret him thus is to fall once again into the great Platonic illusion of a realm of purely intelligible meaning obscured by the material artifice of language. Nietzsche, like Barthes and Derrida, deploys every means of resisting this drift toward interpretation in its various traditional forms. His plurality of styles and cultivation of paradox are strategies intended to arrest understanding, as far as possible, at the level of the text where signification has not yet congealed into meaning or concept. His image of writing as a 'dance of the pen' is one to which Derrida often reverts in order to suggest this free play of sense.

But, again, this seems to take the word for the will in a manner paradoxically opposed to Nietzsche's (and, indeed, Derrida's) way of thinking. How does one begin to interpret a text that denies the very logic of interpretative thought, and hence undercuts the reader's every move to assimilate its meanings into some kind of ordered intelligibility? And — more tellingly from Derrida's standpoint — where can deconstruction find a hold for interpreting texts that so shrewdly rehearse and anticipate its own Nietzschean call for an end to interpretation?

NIETZSCHE AND HEIDEGGER

These questions are driven to the brink of deliberate absurdity in Derrida's latest encounter with Nietzsche (*Spurs*, 1979). This text offers little in the way of 'serious' argumentation, at least of the kind that most philosophers would accept or know how to reckon with. It mostly settles for a style of fantastical juggling with images and wild – even faked – etymologies. The object of these shuttling tactics is not so much Nietzsche as Heidegger's influential reading of Nietzsche, an interpretation Derrida regards as both exemplary of its kind and – for precisely that reason – open to deconstruction. Martin Heidegger (1889–1976) was a German philosopher who exercised a powerful influence on modern existentialist and hermeneutic thought. 'Hermeneutics', as Heidegger conceived it, was the founding philosophy of all interpretation, an attempt to provide the human sciences with a self-understanding adequate to their task. For Heidegger this meant a questing back to the pre-Socratic sources of Western thought and a gradual unveiling of truths obscured by the subsequent accretions of abstract, 'metaphysical', or logico-conceptual reason. Heidegger's 'influence' on Derrida is a topic of great complexity which the reader can find most usefully outlined in Gayatri Chakravorty Spivak's Preface to the English *Grammatology* (Derrida 1977a). For the moment we can focus more specifically on Heidegger's critique of Nietzsche and the way in which Derrida intervenes to disrupt and reverse its effect.

Heidegger mounts a project of 'hermeneutic' recovery which aims to interpret the meaning and significance of Nietzsche's text through a full understanding of the motives and tradition that produced it. Nietzsche is seen as the last and desperate spokesman for a Western metaphysics run aground on its rationalist assumptions, and vainly trying to surmount the various problems of its own engendering. Nietzsche is a vital figure in the history of thought because, according to Heidegger, he represents reason up against its limits and incipiently harking back to a Being, or point of origin, that preceded all the obfuscating wiles of rationality. That Nietzsche ultimately failed in this attempt is a sign that he remained partly captive to a system of thought he could only *reject* or *invert*, without seeing back beyond its limiting suppositions. What this would entail, for Heidegger, is a bracketing of

all those logical assumptions that inhabit the very grammar and predicative structure of Western thought. Language itself perpetuates the
rationalist parcelling-out of experience into categories like 'subject'
and 'object', distinctions that obey the analytic drive towards the mastery of nature by reason. To think one's way beyond such categories is
to ask, with Heidegger, not *how* or *what* things exist but *why* they should
exist in the first place. Hence his crucial distinction between 'Being'
and 'beings', the former identified with the call of an 'authentic'
thinking prior to all merely conceptual knowledge, the latter as the
realm of existent entities that are always already subject to conceptual
categorization.

This gross simplification of Heidegger's thought will perhaps at least
serve to bring out its challenging significance for Derrida. Up to a
point there is clearly much in common between deconstruction and
the Heideggerian project of undoing the conceptual knots and ties
implicit in Western philosophy. In each case it is a matter of making do
with the language bequeathed by that tradition, while maintaining a
rigorous scepticism about its ultimate validity or truth. Indeed, one
of Derrida's most typical strategies for achieving this suspension of
concepts comes directly from Heidegger's textual practice. This is the
device of placing words *sous rature* or 'under erasure', signified by crossing them through in the text and thus warning the reader not to accept
them at philosophic face value. Thus, in *Of Grammatology*: 'the sign ~~is~~ that
ill-named ~~thing~~, the only one, that escapes the instituting question of
philosophy' (Derrida 1977a, p. 19). The marks of erasure acknowledge
both the *inadequacy* of the terms employed – their highly provisional
status – and the fact that thinking simply cannot manage without them
in the work of deconstruction. By this graphic means, much akin to the
anomalous spelling of *différance*, concepts are perpetually shaken and
dislodged.

Thus far, then, Derrida and Heidegger seem to pursue very similar
deconstructive ends. Their difference opens up at the point where
Heidegger locates the source and ground of authentic thought: that is,
in the moment of Being or plenitude which precedes articulate discourse. For Derrida this can only represent another classic case of the
familiar metaphysical hankering after truth and origins. Heidegger's
hermeneutic project is founded on a notion of truth as self-presence

which ultimately seeks to efface, or claims to precede, the play of signification. Where Nietzsche looked back beyond Socrates to a diverse and vivid 'prehistory' of philosophic thought, Heidegger looks to a source of authentic truth in the unitary ground of Being. His 'destruction' of metaphysics is intended not, like Derrida's, to release a multiplicity of meaning but to call thinking back to its original, long-forgotten vocation. Heidegger thus stands as Derrida's nearest tactical ally and yet — by this crucial divergence — as his major modern antagonist.

The struggle is enacted most visibly in their respective readings of Nietzsche. Heidegger's treatment is itself confined, as Derrida sees it, to 'a hermeneutic space of the question of truth (of Being)'. It partakes of the same logocentric myth – the craving for origins, truth and presence – which Derrida is everywhere at pains to deconstruct. Here it is a question, he argues, of noting the uncanny disruptions and obliquities of *style* which wrench Heidegger's project away from its professed aim. His reading irresistibly yields 'to a violent yet almost internal necessity and, although not actually undone, . . . is forced to open onto still another reading which for its part refuses to be contained there' (Derrida 1979, p. 115). The unsettling power of Nietzsche's text is such as to place it beyond reach of a philosophy aimed, like Heidegger's, towards truth and the ultimate presence of meaning. Hence the style of outlandish virtuosity — the ruses of metaphor and image — which Derrida by contrast brings to his reading of Nietzsche. Interpretation is no longer turned back in a deluded quest for origins and truth. Rather, it assumes the vertiginous freedom of writing itself: a writing launched by the encounter with a text which itself acknowledges no limit to the free play of meaning.

NIETZSCHE'S UMBRELLA

This ludic or playful dimension is very much a part of Derrida's refusal to subjugate 'writing' to 'philosophy', or style to the kind of repressive regime that treats figurative language as a blemish on the surface of logical thought. Pushed to an extreme, this means suspending all question as to Nietzsche's likely or intended import, and accepting that his texts exist in a realm of open potential, beyond any hope of assured 'hermeneutic' recovery. Derrida treads the giddy brink of absurdity in the pages he devotes to a marginal jotting in Nietzsche's notebooks: 'I have forgotten my umbrella.' He makes ingenious play with the possible 'meanings' of this fragment, only to conclude – again with Heidegger and the 'hermeneuts' chiefly in view – that its context is irretrievable and its meaning therefore a total enigma. Suggestions of a Freudian reading are briefly entertained, then dismissed as betraying that same inveterate itch to make sense – to discover some hidden but 'true' significance – which besets the hermeneutic enterprise. The sentence, Derrida concludes, is neither more nor less 'significant' than any other passage of Nietzsche's writing. Because this text, like any other, is 'structurally liberated' from intentions or living speech, it might always be the case 'that it means nothing, or that it has no decidable meaning . . . the hermeneut cannot but be provoked and disconcerted by its play' (ibid., pp. 131–2).

Derrida thus turns the tables most effectively on Heidegger's reading of Nietzsche as the 'last of the metaphysicians'. In Derrida's account it is Heidegger who uses the traditional sanctions of truth and authenticity to recapture the Nietzschean text for his own hermeneutic purposes. Against this philosophy Derrida deploys every possible means of liberating Nietzsche's stylistic energies, allowing his text to 'disseminate' sense beyond all the bounds of conceptual closure. This strategy is often wildly at odds with Nietzsche's manifest meaning. Thus Derrida draws some strange metaphorical connections between Nietzsche's image of *Woman* ('her seductive distance, her captivating inaccessibility, the ever-veiled promise of her provocative transcendence') and writing as the non-truth of philosophy, the dissolver of concepts and categorical distinctions (ibid., p. 89). Remembering Nietzsche's notorious misogynist streak ('You are visiting a woman? Don't forget to take your whip'), feminists will doubtless find this as baffling as will most philosophers, faced with Derrida's style of argumentation.

But this is to misunderstand the 'question of the woman' as Derrida half-playfully expounds it from the hints and obliquities of Nietzsche's text. He goes on to admonish Heidegger for having silently subsumed 'the sexual question' under the 'more general question of truth'. Hermeneutics is supposedly riven, or wrenched from its quest for truth, by a language of erotic suggestion and teasing *différance* which breaks down its claims to interpretative mastery. Heidegger's reading merely 'idles offshore' in so far as it ignores the disruptive influence of woman in Nietzsche's proliferating chains of metaphor. Derrida can quote very much to the point from a text like *Ecce Homo*, which indeed seems to equate the multiplicity of styles in Nietzsche's writing with his intimate knowledge of women ('perhaps I am the first psychologist of the eternally feminine'). His point, however, is not to document the character of Nietzsche's erotic sensibility but to trace those *textual* feints and suggestions that elude any normative logic of sense. Of course there is nothing self-evident about Derrida's curious equation between woman, sexuality and the swerve from logic into figural language. What he is out to convey is the effect of a reading which 'perversely' cuts across the normal conventions of relevance and hermeneutic tact.

In Barthes's later writing (notably *A Lover's Discourse*, trans. 1979) there is a similar desire to eroticize language, to yield as it were to the seductive repertoire of images and figures where reason loses its mastery. This is very much in line with Barthes's growing scepticism about the use and attractiveness of structuralist thought when applied with too much methodological rigour. His eroticized 'theory' of the text is a constant nimble evasion of any paternal law which might threaten the pleasures – albeit the highly intellectualized pleasures – of reading. Barthes achieves this effect by a glancing impressionistic way with ideas which nowhere allows them to settle into method or concept. It is therefore no coincidence that Nietzsche provides so many of the starting-points and texts for meditation in *A Lover's Discourse*. Nietzsche's dissolution of philosophic concepts and categories is for Barthes the very image of erotic desire and self-abandon.

Derrida likewise deploys an eroticized reading of Nietzsche to unfix and disconcert the hermeneutic project. The 'question of the woman' in Nietzsche 'suspends the decidable opposition of true and non-true . . . whereupon the question of style is immediately unloosed as a question of writing' (Derrida 1979, p. 57). Where Barthes rests content with a wayward and glancing approach to the text, Derrida is impelled to engage its metaphors in a far more strenuous way, responding to the Nietzschean challenge with a strange but rigorously *argued* reading. The philosophic 'problem' of Nietzsche's style is shown to open up into the larger question of how philosophy has for so long managed to repress or forget its own status as writing. Nietzsche is not 'the last metaphysician' but – as Derrida reads him – the first knowingly to unwrite or deconstruct the history of metaphysics. Along with his compatriot and near-contemporary Karl Marx, he stands among the great demythologizing figures of modern thought. Between them Marx and Nietzsche stake out the main possibilities and rival claims of poststructuralist criticism.

5

BETWEEN MARX AND NIETZSCHE: THE POLITICS OF DECONSTRUCTION

An interview with Derrida, published in the volume *Positions* (1981), raises the question of political commitment and the link – if any – between Marxism and deconstruction. The interviewers, Jean-Louis Houdebine and Guy Scarpetta, were both speaking for the brand of *Marxisant* textual semiotics associated with the Parisian journal *Tel Quel*. Their questioning took an aggressive line, attempting to pin Derrida down on the issue of whether his 'methods' were allied – or implicitly opposed – to the Marxist analysis of language and ideology. Derrida's response was to argue, in effect, that the texts of Marx and Lenin have yet to be *read* in a rigorous fashion which could draw out their modes of rhetorical and figurative working. They cannot simply be interpreted, he argues, according to a preconceived method which would 'seek out a finished signified beneath a textual surface'. Deconstruction would have to emphasize what Derrida calls the 'heterogeneity' of the Marxist text, the ways in which it breaks with idealist tradition (notably Hegel) while yet showing signs of being governed, at a deeper level, by various metaphysical themes.

Houdebine and Scarpetta tried to nudge the dialogue towards some sort of tactical alliance, perhaps between 'contradiction' (as the mainspring of Marxist dialectic) and Derrida's thematics of *différance*. His replies go to show how radically incompatible are the claims of a self-styled materialist 'science of the text' and those of a deconstruction which sees no prospect of any such total break with ideology. For Derrida, the language of dialectical materialism is shot through with *metaphors* disguised as *concepts*, themes that carry along with them a whole unrecognized baggage of presuppositions. It must henceforth be a question, Derrida says, of taking that language and investigating 'all the sediments deposited [in it] by the history of metaphysics' (see Derrida 1981, pp. 39–91).

This encounter, though brief and inconclusive, points to a major topic of contention in and around the development of Derrida's ideas. Is deconstruction merely – as some of its opponents claim – a new-fangled form of textual mystification, helping to keep history and politics at bay? Is it 'undialectical' in its concern with themes of presence and *différance* which persist down the ages and bear no mark of socio-economic change? What is the relation, in short, between Derridean deconstruction and those varieties of Marxist literary theory which have emerged in the wake of structuralism? An approach to these questions can best be made by tracing the two great rival influences on post-structuralist thinking, those of Marx himself and his compatriot Friedrich Nietzsche.

Deconstruction in the Nietzschean mode has produced a discourse of extreme sceptical rigour and rhetorical self-consciousness. The Marxist critique has been equally powerful, on the one hand adopting certain structuralist ideas in developing its own theoretical basis, while on the other rejecting what are seen as elements recalcitrant to Marxist thought. Between these two main trends of post-structuralist theory there has emerged a complex antagonism which brings out the radical *différance* of deconstruction.

DERRIDA ON HEGEL

Derrida's long period of silence in regard to Marx can only be construed as a strategic postponement, a refusal as yet to engage Marxist thought on its own textual ground. Indeed, Derrida devotes a whole

chapter to Hegel (in *Writing and Difference*) without so much as mentioning the Marxist critique and materialist inversion of Hegelian thought.
His reading seeks to isolate the point in Hegel's philosophy where
history and consciousness, so far from uniting in a plenitude of intelligible meaning, find themselves subject to a dislocating movement
beyond the utmost grasp of dialectical reasons. Hegelian logic suffers a
rhetorical swerve from purpose which betrays it into self-contradiction
through a surplus of unmanageable meaning. The 'restricted economy'
of Hegel's system is displaced and invaded by a 'general economy'
which Derrida equates with the effects of writing or textuality. Concepts are unfixed from their 'lawful' philosophic place, subjected to a
violent 'mutation of meaning' and turned back against the sovereignty
of reason. 'Since no logic governs, henceforth, the meaning of interpretation, because logic is an interpretation, Hegel's own interpretation can be reinterpreted – against him' (Derrida 1978, p. 260). In
typical Derridean fashion, the essay approaches Hegel not directly but
via another reading – that of Georges Bataille – whose perceptions and
blind-spots are a further pretext for deconstructive treatment. Hegel's
argument is cunningly enmeshed in a web of intertextual significations
which place it beyond any single controlling logic.

Elsewhere in *Writing and Difference* Derrida broaches the relation
between text and politics, suggesting briefly that deconstruction offers
'the premises for a non-Marxist reading of philosophy as ideology'.
Certainly his reading of Hegel brings out the conflict between deconstruction and anything like a Marxist understanding of textual
ideology. Hegelian dialectic becomes just one chapter in the Western
tradition of logocentric discourse pushed up against its limits by the
'general economy' of writing. There is little sense of its historical root-
edness, or indeed of its role as an antagonist-precursor to Marxist
thought. History is reduced to the play of *representations* by which the
mind, on Hegel's account, attempts to take hold of its own understanding and the stages of historical thought which led up to it. At the
limit-point of conscious reflection, history dissolves into the figures of
rhetoric where all claims to knowledge are deconstructed. Hegel's dialectic of power and knowledge can be turned on its head by a reading
which fastens on those points where metaphor disrupts the very logic
of his argument. Hegelian history can be read 'from left to right or

from right to left, as a reactionary movement or as a revolutionary movement, or both at once' (ibid., p. 276). The figural play or 'supplementarity' of writing makes it impossible to subordinate meaning to a preconceived system or explanatory scheme. The conceptual 'totality' is always undone by the ruses of signification, those 'slidings and differences of discourse' that deconstruction is at pains to reveal.

As we have seen, it was Nietzsche who first brought such a sceptical critique to bear on the systematic edifice of Hegelian philosophy. For Nietzsche, as for Derrida, the project of absolute knowledge was deluded at source by its forgetfulness of how *language* creates and capriciously misleads the processes of thought. Nietzsche saw nothing but blindness and multiplied error in the various attempts to arrive at truth through logic or conceptual analysis. Philosophy had based itself unwittingly on a series of buried metaphors none the less potent and beguiling for their common and commonsense usage. Nietzsche carries out what amounts to a full-scale programme of deconstruction, attacking every last vestige of philosophic truth and certainty. The fundamental 'laws' of Aristotelian logic are held to be expressions of our present *inability* to think beyond them, rather than possessing an absolute validity. Logic is the product of a will to understand which selectively arranges the habits of thought so as to make some sense of immediate experience. Concepts are formed on the groundless supposition that our *knowledge* of objects in the world comes directly from our *experience* of what it is to perceive them. The link between empirical self-evidence and conceptual truth is, according to Nietzsche, a product of metaphorical displacement, raising the contingent into the necessary by a constant (though unrecognized) leverage of tropes.

Nietzsche therefore stands as a precursor to that line of post-structuralist thought which questions the very concepts of method and 'structure' in the name of a demystifying rhetoric. As Derrida makes clear in his essay on Hegel, this questioning extends to the field of historical knowledge, in so far as such knowledge lays claim to a viewpoint above and beyond its own temporal condition. The 'meaning of history' and the 'history of meaning' are bound up together in that quest for self-authenticating truth that is endemic to Western thought. Hegel's belief in the 'ontological unity of method and historicity' is the point at which Derrida locates the repeated hankering for origins and self-presence. Hegel treats history and consciousness as converging towards a stage of maximum lucidity and consummate understanding. Derrida – like Nietzsche before him – sets out to deconstruct this idealized knowledge and the concepts of method which belong to it.

In so doing, he throws down an outright challenge to the powers of historical explanation. This might seem merely another, more sophisticated version of the quarrel between 'synchronic' and 'diachronic' modes of thought which marked the early stages of structuralist debate. Lévi-Strauss presented the issues most clearly in his essay 'History and Dialectic' (in Lévi-Strauss 1966). This took the form of a reply to those (including Sartre) who had condemned structuralism as an abstract methodology and a flight from the realities of history and lived experience. Such objections were merely, in Lévi-Strauss's view, a product of the outworn illusion that attached historical significance to meanings secreted by the individual mind in the process of self-projection. History was rather to be seen as a series of shifting configurative patterns, the 'meaning' of which becomes increasingly opaque with the passage of time. 'Events which are significant for one code are no longer so for another'; what meaning they possess is entirely dependent on how they strike a contemporary. Historical understanding is only possible in so far as it adopts a synchronic standpoint, 'classes of dates each furnishing an autonomous system of reference'. Sartre's idea of 'totalization' – of history unfolding its significance through a sweep of interpretative hindsight – is dismissed by Lévi-Strauss as a wishful belief in the wholeness and continuity of human experience. This belief attaches a 'spurious intelligibility' to events that have only a shifting and provisional significance. To 'socialize the Cogito' in Sartre's fashion is to fall into the twin Hegelian traps of 'individualism and empiricism'.

MARXISM, STRUCTURALISM AND DECONSTRUCTION

This quarrel was taken up by critics like Frederic Jameson, Marxists of a broadly structuralist persuasion who felt that the claims of synchronic thought must somehow be reconciled with those of historical understanding. Jameson agrees with Lévi-Strauss in so far as he treats interpretation as a process of perpetual 'transcoding', a rhetorical activity conscious of its own operations and never coming to rest in a single, determinate 'truth'. Such a method would result, Jameson argues, in a new-found openness of critical discourse and a way of transcending the antimony of, 'form' and 'content'. Where his argument distinctly lacks force is in the claim that this open plurality of codes would effectively involve both critic and literary work in a process of deeper *historical* engagement. After so much tight-knit argumentation, Jameson's phraseology here is revealingly loose and metaphorical. By showing the variety of codes at work on both sides of every interpretative act, structuralism promises 'to reopen text and analytic process alike to all the winds of history' (Jameson 1971, p. 216).

Jameson's confident *rapprochement* between rhetoric and Marxist dialectic can only seem premature in the light of subsequent developments. Others, like Terry Eagleton, have recognized more clearly that an open-ended free play of rhetorical transcoding – with the ideal of an infinitely 'plural' text – is resistant to the purposes of Marxist criticism. Jameson pins his theory to a faith that *method* can retain some absolute validity even when history and meaning have been reduced to a constantly shifting interplay of tropes. He sides, in other words, with that element in Lévi-Strauss's thinking which seeks to preserve 'structure' as a mode of intelligibility immune to the assaults of sceptical doubt.

It is precisely this 'version' of structuralism that Derrida so deftly dismantles in the texts of Saussure and Lévi-Strauss. His object is not to deny or invalidate the structuralist project but to show how its deepest implications lead on to a questioning of method more extreme and unsettling than these thinkers wish to admit. The very notion of 'structure' is shown to be a metaphor dependent, at the limit, on a willed forgetting of its own rhetorical status. Two of Derrida's most powerful essays – 'Force and Signification' and 'Structure, Sign and Play' – are devoted to precisely this end of bringing out the radical metaphoricity of 'structure' as a term and an operative concept. Otherwise, he argues, one remains for ever trapped in the circular logic of a discourse which ceaselessly confirms its own truth. 'Structure' is ultimately a reflex image of the visual or spatial metaphors to which Western thought has so often resorted in its quest for understanding.

To think without the aid of such figurative props may well be beyond the powers of mind. To accept them, on the other hand, without deconstructing their effects is to risk 'being interested in the figure itself to the detriment of the play going on within it metaphorically' (Derrida 1978, p. 16). Derrida is following Nietzsche's critique of the delusions engendered by moving metaphorically from image to concept without subjecting that movement to a close rhetorical scrutiny. The great virtue of structuralism, on Derrida's account, is that it poses this necessity in the most urgent terms: 'Does the fact that language can determine things only by spatializing them suffice to explain that, in return, language must spatialize itself as soon as it designates and reflects upon itself?' (ibid.). Constantly to raise such questions about its own methods and validity is for Derrida the only means by which structuralism can avoid the reified concept of 'structure'.

As I have argued, it is difficult to square deconstruction in this radical, Nietzschean guise with any workable Marxist account of text and ideology. Such attempted fusions in the name of a Marxian post-structuralist theory are fated, for reasons I shall now pursue, to an endlessly proliferating discourse of abstraction. To deconstruct a text in Nietzschean-Derridean terms is to arrive at a limit-point or deadlocked *aporia* of meaning which offers no hold for Marxist-historical understanding. The textual 'ideology' uncovered by Derrida's readings is a kind of aboriginal swerve into metaphor and figurative detour which language embraces through an error of thought unaccountable in Marxist terms.

Eagleton's one brief reference to Nietzsche in *Criticism and Ideology* (1976) manifests the unease a Marxist must feel in the face of such thoroughgoing scepticism. His immediate target is the Parisian journal *Tel Quel*'s brand of 'libertarian' textual theory, which equates radical politics with the free play of an infinitely pluralized meaning. This attitude typically inverts itself (on Eagleton's reading) 'into a mirror-image of bourgeois social relations'. To invest all meaning in the freedom from a single, authoritative meaning – invoking it only to deny – is an impotent gesture of defiance. But Eagleton's real quarry here is Nietzsche and the Nietzschean challenge to a Marxist interpretative theory. There are, he remarks, other kinds of radical break with tradition

which are not fixated in the moment of release which follows on the

> dethronement of the ultimate donor of meaning – which accept that if
> God is dead there is no need to resurrect Nietzsche, since their
> reference-point is the 'taken-for-granted' post-atheism of Marx rather
> than the 'always-to-be-validated' post-atheism of his compatriot.
>
> (Eagleton 1976, p. 43)

Nietzschean scepticism becomes here a kind of infantile disorder, shown up for what it is by the certified maturity of Marxist-historical thought. Deconstruction might be seen in the same negative terms: a discourse fixated upon the 'transcendental signified' of logocentric thought, self-locked (like Nietzsche) in the toils of endless demystification.

But on what ground precisely does Eagleton rest this higher dialectical knowledge? On the precondition, as he states it (following Althusser), that criticism must 'break with its ideological prehistory, situating itself outside the space of the text on the alternative terrain of scientific knowledge' (ibid., p. 43). The metaphors here are manifestly visual and spatial. They cry out to be deconstructed, not merely in a spirit of perverse oneupmanship, but in order to follow through their implications for Marxist epistemology. Eagleton's imagery of textual 'space' and scientific 'terrain' derives from a refined but omnipresent version of the base/superstructure metaphor. Theory (or a putative 'science of the text') is seen as placing itself outside and above the domain of lived ideology. The literary text stands midway between them, a rich but confused source of knowledge, more 'immediate' than theory in its access to experience but so representing and working that experience as to make it accessible (visible) to theory. Such is the basis for Eagleton's 'science of the text': 'In yielding up to criticism the ideologically determined conventionality of its modes of constructing sense, the text at the same time obliquely illuminates the relation of that ideology to real history' (ibid., p. 101). The argument here is entirely in the charge of its sustaining metaphors, the process envisaged as a vertical ascent to a plane of science and lucidity from the 'vivid but loose contingencies' of lived experience. The 'oblique illumination' offered by the literary text is oblique in so far as it occupies that relatively dense middle region; 'illuminating' in so far that it lends itself to a rigorous scientific knowledge. The metaphors of light and darkness co-operate with those of hierarchical structure to produce a perfect *image* – or visual analogy – for the textual science that Eagleton has in mind.

Derrida's essay 'White Mythology' (1974b) has much to say about the figural implications of light and darkness as they permeate the texts of Western philosophy. Reason, the natural light of intelligence, is typically opposed to the opaque materiality not only of inanimate nature but of writing as an alien and obtrusive medium. This is, of course, the root strategy of logocentric discourse which Derrida turns back against itself by forcing its logic to the point of implicit reversal. That consciousness can be present to itself in the pure light of reason, delivered from the snares of opaque textuality, is a recurrent dream of Western thought. It is deeply embedded in the Marxist theory of text, ideology and representation, even where that theory is meticulously purged of crude deterministic thinking. The 'science' proposed by Eagleton, Pierre Macherey and other Althusserian Marxists cannot in the end break loose from the visual and spatial metaphors that determine its logic. Texts are treated as a more or less 'dense', 'opaque' or 'obliquely' translucent writing placed between the raw stuff of lived experience and the penetrating light of knowledge. The etymological link between 'theory' and 'seeing' (Greek *thea* = spectacle) becomes a forgotten or sublimated metaphor underlying the certitudes of science.

The figurative texture of Eagleton's language is most in evidence where his theory comes up against the problems of defining 'representation' in a materialist but non-reductive sense. The text 'represents' ideology by revealing 'in peculiarly intense, compacted and coherent form the categories from which those representations are produced' (Eagleton 1976, p. 101). The argument here is borne up by a circular exchange of metaphorical values attaching to the spatial and visual connotations of the language employed. A sense of rigour and explanatory power is conveyed by the abstract term 'categories', which yet remains contextually ill defined. Its want of specificity is made up for rhetorically by the hints of a concrete, vivid directness in words like 'intense' and 'compacted'. The visual-projective metaphors of 'form' and 'representation' complete the work of *conceptualizing* this tight-knit cluster of images. What the literary text reveals is the condition of its own intelligibility as *viewed* from precisely this metaphoric standpoint.

Eagleton does indeed qualify his position, but in equally symptomatic language:

> 'Reveals' is perhaps a misleading term here, for not every text displays its ideological categories on its surface: the visibility of those categories depends on the text's precise modes of working them, as well as on the nature of the categories themselves.
>
> (ibid., p. 85)

The metaphors here are even more insistent. Ideology is 'displayed' by the text, at whatever depth from its specular surface, through a mode of more or less 'visible' working produced by those same abstract 'categories'. Eagleton's elaborate argumentation cannot conceal its dependence on these basic and proliferating figures of thought. It is ironic that he should elsewhere criticize Althusser and Macherey for their retreat into a 'nebulously figurative' discourse which gives their arguments a 'merely rhetorical quality'. For all his alertness to this slippage into metaphor, Eagleton exhibits the same liability, most often indeed when he is expounding a new Marxist 'science' which will mark the break with such ideological discourse. The Marxist model of representation, however refined in theory, is caught up in a rhetoric of tropes and images that entirely controls its logic.

NIETZSCHE *CONTRA* MARX?

This puts a very different slant on Eagleton's summary contrast between Marx and Nietzsche. The 'taken-for-granted' basis of historical materialism is challenged in its subtlest formulations by the 'always-to-be-validated' Nietzschean critique. Deconstruction is inimical to Marxist thought at the point where it questions the validity of *any* science or method set up in rigid separation from the play of textual meaning. Jameson and Eagleton represent the opposite faces of a common dilemma. Jameson assimilates history and meaning to an open-ended free play where, as we have seen, historical method becomes little more than an optional gesture of commitment. Eagleton rejects this pluralist outlook and argues resourcefully for a knowledge of the text which would measure its distance from the effects of rhetorical duplicity and error. But for criticism to step outside the textual domain and achieve such knowledge in *other than figurative terms* is an objective beyond its reach. The end-point of deconstructive thought, as Derrida insists, is to recognize that there is no end to the interrogative play between text and text. Deconstruction can never have the final word because its insights are inevitably couched in a rhetoric which itself lies open to further deconstructive reading. Criticism can only be deluded in its claim to operate (as Eagleton puts it) 'outside the space of the text' on a plane of scientific knowledge. There is no metalanguage.

Althusserian Marxism is a form of deconstruction, but one that seeks to halt the process at a point where science can extract the hidden message of ideology. This movement of arrest in the name of some determining system or structure is the strategy that Derrida dismantles in his essay 'Force and Signification'. It involves a crucial blindness to elements of rhetoric which – as in Eagleton's case – can be read deconstructively to bring out their figural evasions. Marxist criticism invites such a reading when it assumes a post-structuralist theoretical standpoint. Jameson and Eagleton share this assumption in so far as they treat the text as a rhetorical construct which 'works' ideology into new, problematic formations accessible to scientific reading. They accept, that is, the structuralist divorce between text and reality, regarding 'the real' as an *effect* produced by certain culturally privileged codes of representation. With Jameson, indeed, it is hard to distinguish the Marxist case for a 'productive' textuality from the Barthesian ecstasy of liberated meaning. Eagleton avoids this total abandonment to rhetoric, but only by constraining his text to ignore what would otherwise call its method into question. His metaphors hypostatize an image of the relation between text, ideology and science which in turn depends upon figurative detours conspicuously open to deconstructive reading.

Once criticism enters the labyrinth of deconstruction, it is committed to a sceptical epistemology that leads back to Nietzsche, rather than Marx, as the end-point of its quest for method. Nietzschean 'method' is no more perhaps than a lesson in perpetual self-defeat, but a lesson more rigorous and searching than the compromise assurances of post-structuralist Marxism. Pierre Macherey exhibits the same crucial blindspot in his efforts to preserve the 'scientific' status of criticism against the various beguilements and obfuscating rhetorics of the text. 'The real, as it is formulated in the discourse of the work, is always arbitrary because it depends entirely on the unfolding of this discourse' (Macherey 1978, p. 37). Deconstructionist readings take the same line of argument to show how narrative discourse typically produces a kind of paradoxical logic which undercuts its own referential or realist pretensions. Macherey goes on to insist that 'the themes immediately extracted from literary works can have no initial value as concepts' (ibid., p. 21). This would seem to accord with Nietzsche's sceptical injunction against passing too easily from image to concept. But Macherey still thinks of critical 'science' as a discourse which can so completely free itself from textual constraints as to see right through to the underlying conflicts of literary ideology. (For a fuller account and critique of Macherey's thinking, see Belsey 1980.) He takes it as axiomatic that criticism can break with the whole delusive rhetoric of textual representation. What this axiom suppresses is the knowledge that criticism also constructs itself as a discourse of tropes and analogies all the more beguiling for its scientific claims.

FOUCAULT AND SAID: THE RHETORIC OF POWER

This conflict of interpretations is at the heart of current post-structuralist debate. Michel Foucault has gone furthest toward spelling out the implications of Nietzschean thought for the project of Marxist and historical-interpretative method. In the following passage he describes the rift between these two competing orders of knowledge:

> In appearance, or rather, according to the mask it bears, historical consciousness is neutral, devoid of passions, and committed solely to truth. But if it examines itself and if, more generally, it interrogates the various forms of scientific consciousness in its history, it finds that all these forms and transformations are aspects of the will to knowledge: instinct, passion, the inquisitor's devotion, cruel subtlety, and malice.
>
> (Foucault 1977, p. 162)

Nietzsche's challenge to Marx (an issue Foucault strategically skirts) goes along with this radically textual or figurative mode of understanding the ruses of history. It disrupts all those metaphors of access-to-truth by which 'scientific' method sustains its immunity from question. Foucault, like Nietzsche, adopts what he calls a 'dissociating view' of historical meaning, one that sets out to shatter 'the unity of man's being through which it was thought he could extend his sovereignty to the events of his past' (ibid., p. 154).

Foucault's Nietzschean rhetoric amounts to an activist rewriting of Derrida's text on Hegel. It sets out to create a maximum disturbance in the charmed circle of exchange where history, consciousness and meaning coincide in the mastery of knowledge. Foucault's critique would equally apply to a Marxist 'science' convinced of its power to escape the figurality of language and achieve a perspective atop all the conflicts of textual signification. It is no longer, he argues, 'a question of judging the past in the name of a truth which only we can possess in the present'. History writing on Nietzschean terms involves a surrender of the privileged claim to knowledge once entertained by a sovereign consciousness. It becomes a question, in Foucault's words, of 'risking the destruction of the subject who seeks knowledge in the endless deployment of the will to knowledge' (ibid., p. 164). Such is the effect of applying a Nietzschean or deconstructive rhetoric of tropes to the self-possessed categories of Marxist-structuralist thought.

What might come of this postponed encounter between Marxist and Nietzschean theories of the text? Jeffrey Mehlman's *Revolution and Repetition* (1979) gives a brief but trenchant example of how deconstruction can press upon the strategies of Marxist discourse and draw out its textual aberrations. Mehlman shrewdly latches his argument to 'The Eighteenth Brumaire of Louis Bonaparte', one of Marx's most eccentric and anomalous texts (Marx 1968). The republic of the Nephew is seen as an absurdity defeating all the laws of dialectic, a clownish repetition of historical events which utterly disrupts the Marxist categories. History repeats itself as farce; reason is confronted with images of a prodigal stupidity which numb its powers. Mehlman shows how this bafflement infects the very texture of Marx's prose, erupting into metaphors and fantastic processions of senseless but colourful detail. Bonapartism is the 'scandal' of Marxian thought, the 'systematic dispersion' (as Mehlman reads it) of any theory attempting to link historical events with a logic of *representation*. The sheer descriptive relish of Marx's text — its listing of absurd, unassimilable detail — works perversely to undermine dialectical reason. *Napoléon le Petit* becomes not merely a parody of the Uncle but the instance of a 'generalised parasitism' gnawing at the bases of Marxist-historical thought. 'Revolution' as the term of dialectic gives way to a grotesque 'repetition' voiding the significance of history.

Foucault has described these effects of textual repetition in his essay on Gilles Deleuze. What they bring into play is an undifferentiated, non-categorical surplus of meaning which mocks and destroys the putative laws of thought. Dialectic depends upon categories that 'organise the play of affirmations and negations, establish the legitimacy of representation, and guarantee the objectivity and operation of concepts' (Foucault 1977, p. 186). Repetition, on the other hand, breaks down all those explanatory systems of history and knowledge which presuppose a logic of identity and non-contradiction. It takes hold (as in Mehlman's reading of Marx) where 'the barely-launched mediation falls back on itself . . . when it constantly returns to the same position, instead of distributing oppositions within a system of finite elements' (ibid.). Such irruptions of uncontrolled meaning are the points at which textuality asserts itself against any form of absolute methodical constraint.

This is not to condemn critical theory, as some would suppose, to an endless play of self-occupied textual abstraction. Rather it is to recognize, with Foucault, that texts and interpretative strategies compete for domination in a field staked out by no single order of validating method. Foucault follows Nietzsche in deconstructing those systems of thought which mask their incessant will to power behind a semblance of objective knowledge. His analysis of these various 'discursive practices' constantly points to their being involved in a politics none the less real for its inextricably textual character. Edward Said, in his book *Orientalism* (1978), has offered a very practical example of how deconstruction can engage cultural history on its own textual ground and contest its claims to objectivity. The image of 'the Orient' constructed by generations of scholars, poets and historians is shown to be governed by an ethnocentric discourse secure in the power of its superior wisdom. Occidental reason is confirmed point for point in its mythography of oriental laziness, guile and 'exotic' irrationalism. To combat this discourse by exposing its ruses of metaphor is not to set up as a 'science' unmasking the confusions of ideology. It is an act of challenge which situates itself on rhetorical ground the better to meet and turn back the claims of a spurious objectivity.

Said has argued the case for this approach in his recent essay 'The Text, the World, the Critic' (1979). Texts are irreducibly 'worldly' in the sense that they acquire an unpredictable reception-history and lead a varied afterlife of readings and interpretations which place them squarely in the public domain. Discourse is incapable of sustaining itself in what Said calls 'a hermetic, Alexandrian textual universe, having no connection with actuality'. Texts are in and of the world because they lend themselves to strategies of reading whose intent is always part of a struggle for interpretative power. It is a similar impulse – according to Said – that induces the novelist to weave into her fiction details of circumstance and context that insist on its narrative veracity. Fiction has always involved this sense of an 'unwillingness to cede control over the text . . . to release it from the discursive obligations of human presence' (Said 1979, p. 177). The control may indeed be illusory, a wishful projection of authorial power; but it reflects an awareness that texts are always subject to competing strategies with their own 'worldly' interests and motivating values.

It is surely no coincidence that one of Said's examples is the same text of Marx ('The Eighteenth Brumaire') that Mehlman singles out for deconstructive treatment. Said's observations are similar up to a point. He notes the disruptive effects of 'repetition', the way in which the text 'inserts' Louis Bonaparte into a sequence of outrageous roles and correspondences which elude any rational account. Said, however, reaches a conclusion rather different from Mehlman's, and one that supports the thrust of his argument for understanding texts as bearers of a 'worldly', practical meaning. Mehlman interprets 'The Eighteenth Brumaire' as a kind of rhetorical affront to history, a monstrous and proliferating discourse which takes on its own absurd narrative power. Said sees all this, but is struck more forcibly by the strange *correspondence* between this egregious text and the order of historical events. Like the novelist – but to an even higher pitch of obsession – Marx fills in every circumstantial detail to underline the Nephew's role as 'farcical repetition' of the Uncle. The text's sheer density of documentation is oddly reinforced by a pattern of narrative links that lends it a kind of perverse authenticating logic. Textual strategies become, paradoxically, a means of explaining the absurd contingencies of historical happening. That this explanation issues in parodic or 'repetitive' form is precisely a measure of its power to convince.

What really challenges understanding, in Said's view, is the question of how a text, 'by being a text, by insisting upon and employing all the devices of textuality, preeminent among them repetition, historicizes and problematizes all the fugitive significance which has chosen Louis Bonaparte as its representative' (ibid., p. 178). There is no room here for that too simple contrast between 'the world' and 'the text' which Said regards as a falsification of deconstructive thought. His approach to these problems is persuasive in its power to combine a rigorous textual awareness with a practical commitment to the politics of reading as a force for social and historical change. It is not, like so much post-Althusserian Marxist theory, locked in the problems of a discourse fixated upon its own formulations and unable to recognize their figurative nature. Only by following through the logic of deconstruction, rather than meeting its challenge halfway, can theory escape this imprisonment by the metaphors of its own frozen discourse. Thus Nietzche's challenge retains its power to provoke and unsettle the discourse of Marxist criticism.

6

THE AMERICAN CONNECTION

For the past thirty years or so Derrida has been dividing his time between Paris and America, mainly through his regular visiting appointments at Yale, Irvine and other universities. His following among American critics has grown apace, and it is now safe to say that he exerts a greater influence on them than any of his fellow French post-structuralists. This is evident from the sheer volume of critical writing that nowadays bears the deconstructionist imprint, whether openly acknowledged or (more often) betrayed by certain character-istic turns of argument or phrase. Derrida himself has entered with alacrity into the various discussions sparked off by his writing. To disciples and opponents alike he has responded with a number of prolix and mind-wrenching texts designed for translation and wittily exploiting the inherent ambiguities of the medium. In some of these essays the playful inclination – already well developed in his writing on Nietzsche – seems to outrun any content of serious argument. But one needs to exercise a good deal of caution when applying such con-ventional measures of worth to texts that explicitly put them in ques-tion. Perhaps the most radical effect of Derrida's writing has been to transform the very notion of what counts as 'serious' critical thought.

Individual critics have responded very differently to Derrida's example, so that even to speak of a deconstructionist 'movement' is already to blur some vital distinctions of emphasis and style. In Chapter 5 I pointed to one such divergence, the debate that has lately sprung up between the purist deconstructors and those (like Edward Said) who wish to restore the text to a 'worldly' or political dimension of meaning. In broadly institutional terms, Yale and Johns Hopkins have done most to disseminate Derridean theory in its resolutely textual – and largely apolitical – form. The Marxist or activist challenge has hitherto come from outside, though now, with Frederic Jameson teaching at Yale, the debate is being pressed nearer home. But even within the group of critics most closely identified with Derrida's thinking – Geoffrey Hartman, Paul de Man and J. Hillis Miller – differences emerge which suggest a certain ambivalence about the aims and priorities of deconstruction. This ambivalence is also more marked in the texts Derrida has produced at the bidding (or provocation) of his American colleagues.

A passage from *Of Grammatology* may help to focus the issue. Deconstruction, Derrida writes,

> always in a certain way falls prey to its own work. This is what the person who has begun the same work in another area of the same habitation does not fail to point out with zeal. No exercise is more widespread today and one should be able to formalize its rules.
>
> (Derrida 1977a, p. 24)

The 'exercise' is very much more widespread now than when Derrida wrote these words. The zeal for deconstruction has not, on the other hand, always gone along with the kind of argumentative rigour Derrida calls for here. Indeed, its appeal for some critics rests very largely on the promise of an open-ended free play of style and speculative thought, untrammelled by 'rules' of any kind. This response has characterized much of what passes for American deconstructionist criticism, at least in its more publicized varieties. With the notable exception of Paul de Man – whose texts display an early-Derridean incisiveness and rigour – the Yale critics have mostly opted for deconstruction on its dizzy, exuberant side. This is not to say that the two can be firmly distinguished, or that one side merits less 'serious' attention than the other. It points, rather, to a choice between rigour and freedom to which Derrida's texts have themselves responded in very different ways.

DECONSTRUCTION 'ON THE WILD SIDE': GEOFFREY HARTMAN AND J. HILLIS MILLER

We have seen how deconstruction 'arrived' in America at just the right moment to attract those critics, like Geoffrey Hartman, who had begun to fret under the various constraints of New Critical method. It offered the enticing prospect of a criticism free to explore whatever stylistic possibilities it chose, without observing any strict demarcation between 'creative' and (merely) 'critical' writing. Hartman makes the point most exuberantly in his essay 'The Interpreter: A Self-Analysis' (in Hartman 1975, pp. 3–19). The piece begins with a forthright confession: 'I have a superiority complex vis-à-vis other critics, and an inferiority complex vis-à-vis art.' He then proceeds to dismantle both these burdensome conditions by playing them off in a style of paradoxical argument which brings 'the interpreter' out on a level (of inventiveness, cunning, rhetorical power) with the text he interprets. Like Derrida, he argues that origins are delusive, that texts are always 'belated' with regard to the tradition they inhabit, just as critics feel themselves humbly confined to a secondary role of mere explication. For Hartman, the only way out is for the critic to throw off his 'inferiority complex' and enter wholeheartedly – with a Nietzschean swagger – into the dance of meaning.

> I think that is where we are now. We have entered an era that can challenge even the priority of literary to literary-critical texts. Longinus is studied as seriously as the sublime texts he comments on; Jacques Derrida on Rousseau almost as interestingly as Rousseau.
>
> (ibid., p. 18)

Or, for that matter, Hartman on Derrida on Rousseau . . . the argument is at no pains to conceal its self-interested character. Quite simply, for Hartman, 'writing is living in the secondary, knowing it is the secondary. That is the curse, or the blessing.'

Hartman often taxes the reader's patience with his virtuoso style and his use of interpretative problems as a sounding-board for his own private struggles. All the same, his writing does convey the exhilarating spirit, the glimpse of new horizons, brought about by Derrida's influence. He and Hillis Miller have been the readiest to follow Derrida's ideas to the limit of interpretative freedom. Miller presents his own self-defence in an essay that cunningly deconstructs the oppositional semantics of the words 'host' and 'parasite' ('The Critic as Host', 1977). He traces a mazy route through the twin etymologies, showing how their meanings cross and redouble until both seem to partake of an ambivalent, almost symbiotic relationship where the 'host' (text) is at least as parasitic as the 'parasite' (critic). Miller's etymological procedures and his ploy of strategically reversing a traditional metaphor are both powerful tactics borrowed from Derrida. They lead to the upshot of his argument: that critics are no more 'parasites' than the texts they interpret, since both inhabit a host-text of pre-existent language which itself parasitically feeds on their host-like willingness to receive it. Such arguments can clearly be put to a great variety of tactical uses. Miller extends his semantic juggling to the question of whether deconstructionist readings are 'parasitic' (as M. H. Abrams had claimed) on normal or conventionally 'faithful' interpretations. He is able to demonstrate, once again, that the norm not only presupposes but in some sense *contains* whatever deviations it is required to exclude.

Miller puts these ruses to work in a style that emulates, though it doesn't fully match, the rigour of Derrida's arguments. He is ultimately concerned, like Hartman, to justify this new-found interpretative freedom by seeking out twists of linguistic figuration that suit his paradoxical purpose. Miller's receptiveness to deconstruction can be traced back to problems raised but only partially answered in his previous criticism. During the sixties and early seventies his thinking was much influenced by a group of critics – the so-called 'Geneva School' – who saw interpretation as an effort to grasp the *modes of consciousness* expressed in literary texts. Most prominent among them were Jean Starobinski, Jean-Pierre Richard, Georges Poulet and Jean Rousset. Their general approach was set out by Miller in an article ('The Geneva School', 1966) which offered a useful introduction to the group for most English-speaking readers. Poulet and his colleagues thought of criticism 'as beginning and ending in a coincidence of the mind of the critic and the mind of the author'. The aim was always 'to re-create as precisely as possible the exact tone which persists in a given writer throughout all the variety of his work'.

For Miller this clearly represented a welcome break with the doctrines of American formalism. It also provided a promising alternative to the various rival theories – Freudian, Marxist and others – which had not yet succeeded in challenging the pedagogic rule of New Criticism. By rejecting such methods and focusing instead on the forms of *consciousness* evoked by literary texts, the Geneva critics were helping to free interpretation from the dead hand of critical abstraction. Most importantly for Miller, they had no use for the *spatialized* concepts of form and structure which had gained such a hold on American criticism. Literature was not to be reduced to 'an objective structure of meanings residing in the words of a poem or novel'. Neither was it 'the unwitting expression of a writer's unconscious', nor indeed 'a revelation of the latent structures of exchange which integrate a society'. Texts were primarily there to be experienced, their meanings 'brought into the open' through a process of ideally sympathetic re-creation on the critic's part.

This dream of a perfect, unimpeded communion of minds goes deep in Miller's 'pre-deconstructionist' writing, as it does for Hartman and other American critics whose temperamental homeground is Romantic poetry. Romanticism holds out the utopian idea of a merging between mind and object, a state of awareness so finely attuned to experience that all such distinctions drop away and the knower is at one with the known. Wordsworth's poetry was a constant search for these privileged moments or 'spots of time', while Coleridge pursued a similar theme through the toils of idealist metaphysics. The inherent pathos of this attempt – the fact that the mind can never achieve such perfect communion – is often manifest in Hartman's moments of chastened self-reckoning. In 'The Interpreter: A Self-Analysis' he recalls how his criticism at first aspired to a direct, 'unmediated' communing with the text; then, as the ideal receded, how he found ambiguous comfort in the speculative byways opened up to thought by its own self-conscious operations (Hartman 1975, pp. 3–19). The pattern for Hartman's confessional narrative is clearly Wordsworth's *Prelude*, where the poet looks back to the rapturous intensity of his childhood vision with a sense of belatedness and well nigh unbridgeable distance. For Hartman this is the impasse encountered by all Romantic and post-Romantic thought. The 'unmediated vision' lies beyond reach of language, because language brings along with it a mediating structure of awareness which can never coincide with its object in a moment of pure, self-authenticating knowledge. This was the burden of Hartman's criticism long before he met with its powerful formulation in the texts of Derrida. All the same, one can see what impact those texts must have had on a critic already prone to meditate on the delusiveness of origins, the myth of self-presence and the mediating agency of language.

There is much the same development visible in Hillis Miller's shift from a 'criticism of consciousness' to a mode of deconstructionist thought. His faith in the Geneva critics was pinned to their assumption that mind could be somehow present to mind in a purely intuitive transfer of meaning and awareness. In his 1966 essay Miller quotes (approvingly) the view of Georges Poulet that language at its most expressive is a perfectly *transparent* medium, allowing the critic to enter fully into the author's state of mind. By the time of his *Thomas Hardy: Distance and Desire* (1970), this position is already coming under strain from Miller's use of *textual* images in place of those metaphors drawn from consciousness itself. The critic's mode of entry, Miller writes,

> is language, a medium within which he already dwells. He can insert himself into the text because both he and it are already interpenetrated by their common language. The means of his interpretation is also language, those words of his which even in the most passive act of reading he adds to the text as he understands it . . .
>
> (Miller 1970, p. 36)

This passage can perhaps be made to square with the Genevan ideal of a criticism wholly given up to the interplay of mind with mind through the perfect transparency of language. But, whatever his intentions, Miller's terminology now insists on the endlessly *textual* nature of all understanding, the way in which meanings are deferred and multiplied as soon as one begins to interpret.

In fact Miller goes on from this passage to pick up a metaphor from Hardy which has since become something of an *idée fixe* in his

deconstructionist writing. Indulging his penchant for riddling etymologies, Miller reminds us of the affinity between 'text', 'texture' and
the 'tissue' of associative links which relate writing to the language of
weaving and tapestry.

> The critic adds his weaving to the Penelope's web of the text, or
> unravels it so that its structuring threads may be laid bare, or re-
> weaves it, or traces out one thread in the text to reveal the design it
> inscribes . . .
>
> (ibid.)

This labyrinthine imagery and play on language are typical of Hillis
Miller's way with deconstruction. For him, as for Hartman, it combines
a certain devious rigour of explanation with an even more attractive
strangeness of result. It also manages to solve at a stroke those problems
of consciousness vis-à-vis the text which beset Miller's earlier criticism.
If interpretation is always caught up in a chain of proliferating sense
which it can neither halt nor fully comprehend, then the critic is
effectively absolved of all responsibility for limiting the play of his own
imagination. This means a total break with the notions of fidelity and
disciplined awareness enjoined by Miller's Genevan mentors. By
replacing the rhetoric of consciousness with a rhetoric of textuality,
deconstruction – at least as Miller conceives it – obliterates the line
between text and interpretation.

In their day the New Critics would have stigmatized such talk as a
bad case of the 'personalist heresy', the mistake of treating criticism as
a vehicle or platform for displays of interpretative brilliance. W. K.
Wimsatt, philosopher-elect of the movement, played on this theme in a
rearguard defence of New Critical precepts (Wimsatt 1970). Unless it
preserved some sense of the poem as an autonomous object – in
Hegel's terms, a 'concrete universal' – interpretation would always be
tempted to run wild in games of its own inventing. Hence the title of
Wimsatt's essay ('Battering the Object'), and hence his choice of Hillis
Miller, among others, as an influence to be held at bay.

At the time it was Miller's Genevan connections and his subjectivist
approach which seemed to Wimsatt a dangerous sign of critical malaise. And in a sense his predictions were accurate enough, as Miller and

Hartman went on to prove. Wimsatt's essay makes every attempt to counter the threatened dissolution of boundaries between text and criticism. The idea of 'organic form', he observes, was 'a very material subject-matter (as in Erasmus Darwin's "Botanical Garden") . . . before it became the rarified metaphysics of a theory of aesthetic knowledge and form' (ibid., p. 63). By this rather offbeat comparison Wimsatt clearly means to defend the New Critical idea of the poem as a self-contained 'organic' form, as opposed to those critics – like Hartman and Hillis Miller – who were busily deconstructing such claims. He is even prepared to welcome those aspects of structuralist thought that can be turned to advantage in propping up the notion of textual autonomy. Thus Wimsatt quotes approvingly Jakobson's famous statement that poetic language 'projects the principle of equivalence from the axis of selection onto the axis of combination' (ibid., p. 78). This has the merit, in Wimsatt's eyes, of focusing attention on the self-sufficient formal attributes of poetry, rather than trying to dissolve them (like Miller) into the play of interpretative consciousness. The fact that he can enlist Jakobson as an ally for 'the ontological approach' is evidence of the deep affinity between New Critical poetics and structuralism in its classic, conservative form.

The Yale deconstructors reject this ontological constraint and happily embrace all the dangers Wimsatt so strenuously sought to avoid. Hartman makes a virtue and even a vocation of pushing his critical style to the edge of sheer self-indulgence. His recent collection of essays (Criticism in the Wilderness, 1980) is a plea for critics to 'come out' and stake their claim to an answerable style released from the old New Critical conventions of sobriety and tact. Behind Hartman's case is a rootedly American dislike of what he calls 'the Arnoldian concordat', the view of criticism as at best a humble handmaid to creative endeavour. He sees this attitude as having passed down through Eliot to the American New Critics, enforcing an orthodox code of interpretative manners which reflects the continuing dominance in America of British tradition. For Hartman the problem of critical style is closely bound up with the question of cultural identity and the need, as he sees it, to establish a distinctively 'American' voice for criticism. This is turn goes along with an openness to continental European sources – Heidegger, Derrida, Walter Benjamin, and others – not so much for their specific ideas as for the fact that they fly in the face of everything 'British' and post-Eliotic.

Hartman's enterprise takes courage, as well it might, from Derrida's deconstructive merging of origin and supplement, or text and commentary. Criticism is now 'crossing over' into literature, rejecting its subservient, Arnoldian stance and taking on the freedom of interpretative style with a matchless gusto. Theory becomes, in Hartman's hands, a tactical weapon of provocative intent against all those self-imposed restrictions that critics have hitherto embraced. The result is a striking but rather promiscuous line-up of names and philosophies. Hartman is even ready to defend the obfuscating rant of Thomas Carlyle, finding it a salutary antidote to the suave complacencies of Arnold. In the Yale revisionists (especially Harold Bloom) he perceives the same hankering for a language true to its prophetic lights and possessing the courage of its metaphors. Oscar Wilde's twists of paradox in 'The Critic as Artist' are set alongside the deconstructionist statements of Nietzsche, Heidegger and Derrida.

Hartman is not concerned to accommodate these thinkers to any kind of ordered or consistent philosophy. Indeed, the 'accommodating' style in criticism – the stress on good sense, rationality and order – is Hartman's main target in most of his recent essays. There has now grown up, he suggests,

> a new isolationism masking under the name of Common Sense and characterizing what it opposes as Skywriting. The Skywriters march under the banner of Hegel and continental philosophy, while the Common Sense school is content with no philosophy, unless it be that of Locke and a homespun organicism.
>
> (Hartman 1978, p. 409)

The pretence of even-handedness here is shrewdly undermined by the choice of metaphors. Hartman himself is a confirmed Skywriter, drawing all his sources behind him in the same meteoric orbit.

This is deconstruction 'on the wild side', a criticism that thrives on Derrida's example but rarely seeks to emulate his rigour of argument. Hartman can defend his all-embracing rhetoric by invoking Derrida's powerful deconstructions of philosophic texts. From here it is a short step to the general idea that philosophy is simply another variety of literature, a text pervaded by the same ruses of figuration. In which case, Hartman concludes, 'It is not a matter of "knowing" Derrida or Heidegger but of reading and steeping oneself in a corpus of critical, philosophical, and literary texts that they incorporate and revise' (ibid., p. 411). Thus Hartman justifies his attempt to wrench criticism away from its humble destiny by exposing it to all the buffeting philosophic winds he can raise. Taking the rigorous work of deconstruction largely for granted, Hartman frolics in the aftermath with great stylistic verve and a thankful sense of having moved, for his part, decisively 'beyond formalism'.

Yet nagging doubts remain about Hartman's breezy assurance that 'knowing' Derrida or Heidegger is less important than bathing in their heady rhetorical wake. His strategies, even more than Miller's, run up against a sticking-point which recalls – ironically – Wimsatt's principled stand on the question of objectivity. Hartman's essay 'The Interpreter' closes on the following typically extravagant but queasy note:

> Things get mixed up in this jittery situation. It should be the inter-preter who unfolds the text. But the book begins to question the ques-tioner, its *qui vive* challenges him to prove he is not a ghost. What is he then?
>
> (Hartman 1975, p. 19)

The reference, of course, is to *Hamlet*, and Hartman obligingly goes on to transpose the dialogue:

Interpreter: Who's there?
Book: Nay, answer me; stand, and unfold yourself.

Hartman clearly enjoys these perplexities and exploits them, as here, to paradoxical effect. On the other hand they do remain fixed at a level of self-occupied rhetorical juggling which never really breaks with the old antinomies created by formalist dogma. Hartman's impressionistic style is trapped in an endless rehearsal of gestures which raise the 'personalist heresy' to a high point of philosophic principle. In the last analysis his criticism moves not so much 'beyond formalism' as round and about its ambiguous fringes.

PAUL DE MAN: RHETORIC AND REASON

If Hartman represents deconstruction in its ludic or libertarian vein, Paul de Man exemplifies the opposite qualities of hard-pressed argument and high conceptual rigour. In his Preface to the collective volume *Deconstruction and Criticism* (1979), Hartman divides the Yale revisionists into two broad categories of 'canny' and 'uncanny' critics, the latter being those (Paul de Man among them) who pursue deconstruction to its ultimate, unsettling conclusions. In fact one could argue that these terms cross over and exchange implications in truly Derridean style. De Man is in a sense the 'canniest' of all, since he exerts a firm argumentative grasp, even at the furthest reaches of paradox, and never permits himself anything like Hartman's style of rhapsodic philosophizing.

We have already seen how de Man's rhetorical strategies were applied to the 'old' New Criticism and its organicist metaphors. Unlike Hartman, he is not content with a skirmishing engagement, a mode of deconstruction that lives on its wits and offers no hold for theory. De Man's readings draw out the innermost logic of the text, showing how rhetorical tensions develop to a point where that logic is implicitly confounded by its own implications. For de Man this discrepancy between reason and rhetoric is endemic to all literary texts, and to criticism also wherever it passes from mere explication to theory and self-conscious method: 'Critics' moments of greatest blindness with regard to their own critical assumptions are also the moments at which they achieve their greatest insights' (de Man 1971, p. 109). This leads on to the argument that texts always generate a history of partial or 'aberrant' readings, the blindspots of which can be deconstructed but never so completely demystified as to bring criticism out on a level of perfect clarity and truth. 'Criticism' and 'crisis' are linked not only by a punning etymology but by the very nature of interpretative thought. 'The rhetoric of crisis states its own truth in the mode of error' (ibid., p. 16). This is to say that criticism thrives on an ultimate *aporia* which it may not recognize but which everywhere marks its performance.

De Man's most recent collection of essays (*Allegories of Reading*, 1979) started out, he says, as an 'historical study' but transformed itself along the way into a 'theory of reading'. How this came about can be seen most clearly in the chapter on Proust. Taking a passage from *Du Côté de chez Swann* which treats expressly of the pleasures of reading, de Man mounts an intricate critique which shows how the metaphors of 'inward contemplation' (literature as escape) are subtly intertwined with those of referential (or 'real-life') experience. This has the effect of breaking down the conventional assumption that draws a firm line between private and public activities, the world of thought and the world outside. Despite Proust's manifest intention, his images of solitary pleasure give way to a jostling crowd of apparently *external* sense-impressions. Perception and imagination are strangely confused, along with the normative logic that tries to hold them apart. Such 'static polarities', as de Man explains, are 'put into circulation by a more or less hidden system of relays which allows the properties to enter into substitutions, exchanges and crossings that appear to reconcile the incompatibilities of the inner with the outer world' (de Man 1979, p. 60). De Man pursues these figurative detours with a rigour of argument none the less 'logical' for its end result in paradox and *aporia*. The reading thus produced is unthinkable, he admits, in terms of a straightforward logic 'dominated by truth and error'. Yet the power of figurative language is such as to command our provisional assent to the 'totalizing world' that Proust's metaphors create.

De Man is all the same a 'canny' enough critic to glimpse, behind these metaphors, a kind of inbuilt textual unravelling which declares their subterfuge even in the act of rhetorically passing it off. Though there may be, as he says, 'no limit to what tropes can get away with', still there is an element of self-deconstruction involved in all such figurative language. Proust's metaphorical epiphanies always dissolve, under close inspection, into chains of 'literal' (or metonymic) detail which undercut the claim to a unified world of inward and outward perception.

Metaphor and metonymy are singled out by Roman Jakobson, and by many structuralist critics, as the two most pervasive and powerful devices of rhetorical language. Metaphor involves the perception of a similarity between otherwise strikingly distinct semantic attributes, such that the sense of distance is preserved in the act of imaginatively leaping across it. The 'wind of change' is by now a metaphor staled by habit, but which still carries a sense of vaguely 'poetic' suggestion. For this reason metaphor has come to be regarded as the hallmark of 'creative' language, the means by which it breaks with the normal run of day-to-day 'literal' usage. Metonymy, meanwhile, works by substituting part for whole, 'the name of an attribute or adjunct . . . for that of the thing meant' (e.g. 'all hands on deck', where 'hands' refers metonymically to the men who have and use them). Thus in Yeats's lines from 'Leda and the Swan'—

> A shudder in the loins engenders there
> The broken wall, the burning roof and tower
> And Agamemnon dead.

the language involves both metaphor *and* metonymy, each sufficiently signalled by context. The 'broken wall' and 'burning roof and tower' are aspects of a mind's-eye image of Troy which the reader supplies, as it were, to fill out the picture. To interpret 'a shudder in the loins' requires a larger stretch of imaginative reason, connecting the 'literal' sense (the rape of Leda) to various Yeatsian themes of historical catastrophe and violent rebirth. Metonymy is in this sense closer to what we think of as straightforward referential language. It has therefore been devalued by many rhetoricians as a device either subservient to metaphor or simply not requiring detailed explanation. The importance of Jakobson's distinction – as David Lodge argues in *The Modes of Modern Writing* (1977) – is that it treats metaphor and metonymy as equally resourceful but organized according to opposite schemes of production. Thus Lodge proposes a new kind of literary history, based on Jakobson's bi-polar model and tracing the periodic shifts of emphasis from strongly metaphorical (modernist) to markedly metonymic (or 'realistic') writing.

Lodge is perfectly at ease within the broad structuralist limits of applied theory and description. He is not concerned to deconstruct either his own working concepts or the texts that provide their testing-ground and justification. De Man's reflections on metaphor and metonymy follow a very different path. Where Lodge treats the two devices as mapping out the field of modern writing – as if in a kind of amicable rivalry – de Man finds them everywhere locked in rhetorical combat. For him it is not enough to challenge traditional prejudice by placing metonymy on an equal footing with the claims of metaphor. Their relationship needs to be totally reversed, so that metaphor displays a delusory, at times almost furtive, attempt to conceal its own textual workings. Hence the demystifying power that de Man seeks out in texts, like those of Proust, which lay bare the sources of illusion. The seductions of metaphor cannot, in the end, disguise the figural means by which their effects are attained. A close enough reading always reveals the constitutive gap between intention and signification. The actual workings of Proustian description are always at bottom metonymic, though 'motivated by a tendency to pretend the opposite'.

This suspension of language between metaphor and metonymy – or 'symbol' and 'discourse' – is the crux of de Man's interpretative theory. In *Blindness and Insight* it pointed the way towards deconstructing the organicist metaphors, the images of self-sufficient unity and form, prevalent among the American New Critics. The same oppositions are at work in de Man's various essays on the concepts of metaphor and symbol advanced by the Romantics (mainly Wordsworth and Coleridge) in their quest for a unified order of perception (see de Man 1969). Typically, de Man finds these concepts undone by a reading that interrogates their figures of encompassing vision – the symbol as a pure, intuitive merging of subject and object – and that sets in their place an open-ended 'allegory' of thought in the process of reflective understanding. This is the outcome of his essay on the German poet Rilke (in de Man 1979, pp. 20–56), where de Man explores the limits of a poetry devoted (as he reads it) to a rhetoric of 'pure figuration'. The failure to achieve this exemplary status – to redeem language from every last taint of its referential function – appears in the ruses and detours of meaning which Rilke is forced to exploit. It amounts to a virtual undoing of the perfect correspondence (implied but unachieved) between 'the semantic function and the formal structure of language'. Poetry succeeds in sustaining such high-Romantic themes 'only at the cost of a subterfuge to which it finds itself necessarily condemned'.

One is left in effect with a choice of readings, naïve or

deconstructionist. Deconstruction suspends the persuasive (or meaningful) force of language in the interests of a purified logic of figure.
The naïve reading yields itself, more or less consciously, to what de
Man calls 'a normative pathos or ethical coercion'. While he admits
that there must always be room for this latter possibility, de Man loads
his terms so as to leave no doubt that deconstruction is the preferred
alternative. To submit unresistingly to a 'normative pathos' or 'ethical
coercion' is clearly not the way of critical intelligence as de Man conceives it. At times, indeed, there seems a kind of ethical compulsion
behind the zeal with which he prosecutes the vagaries of symbol and
metaphor. Frank Lentricchia has recently suggested (Lentricchia 1980)
that de Man's criticism bears the marks of a lingering Sartrean influence, the existentialist concept of 'bad faith' being surreptitiously
transposed into textual-rhetorical terms. Metaphor and symbol would
then correspond to the *mauvaise foi* of accepting human nature as something fixed and self-determined, its meaning given in advance. Deconstruction would set itself to prove, on the contrary, that meaning is
produced (like Sartrian authenticity) only through a constant self-
critique which always *defers* the sense of achieved identity. Certainly de
Man is the fiercest of the Yale deconstructors, with a rigour not easily
explained unless in ethical terms.

Yet de Man himself would be the last to claim that deconstruction
carries on at an altitude of thought removed from all persuasive or
ethical drives. His readings of Nietzsche make this point over and again.
Nietzsche may dismiss the traditional idea of 'rhetoric as eloquence',
and concentrate instead on the business of critically unravelling the
tropes, revealing their false and presumptive claims to truth. But this
enterprise itself requires a style of persuasive presentation which can
scarcely elude the traps laid down by its own self-critical awareness.
Nietzsche's critique of metaphysics, like Derrida's after him, has to be
conducted in a language that partakes of both conceptual and
persuasive elements. Its rhetoric belongs as much to 'literature' as to
'philosophy', so far as that distinction still holds up.

In fact, it is de Man's central argument here that 'literature' is precisely what results from philosophy's inability to think through its own
constitution in textual-rhetorical terms. Nietzsche is a stylist, a 'literary' writer, to the extent that he acknowledges the ultimate complicity

of thought and rhetoric, the fact that his critique of philosophy is itself 'structured as rhetoric'. Nietzsche in the end 'rehabilitates persuasion' by showing that language in its performative aspect both pervades and delimits the project of philosophy. The term 'performative' is taken from the philosopher J. L. Austin, who applied it to those forms of utterance (or 'speech-act') which are meant to produce effects – to persuade, promise, etc, – as opposed to purely assertive or 'constative' utterances. Nietzsche's rhetoric, according to de Man, 'earns a right' to its own inconsistency by pursuing the work of deconstruction to a point where knowledge encounters the absolute *need* for performative expression. (See pp. 108ff. for more detailed discussion of Austin and speech-act philosophy.)

Allegories of Reading can therefore be seen as an effort to negotiate – though not simply to conflate – the rival claims to knowledge of philosophy and literature. The habit of treating them as separate disciplines is one that, in de Man's view, 'deprives the reading of philosophical texts of elementary refinements that are taken for granted in literary interpretation'. But this is not merely – as it can seem with Hartman – a game of critical oneupmanship, a takeover bid on behalf of literary theory. De Man's 'canny' qualities of disciplined argument are sufficient guarantee against the kind of self-supporting intellectual romp that deconstruction sometimes seems to invite. Nietzsche, he remarks – and the same might be said of de Man's own writing – 'advocates the use of epistemologically rigorous methods as the only possible means to reflect on the limitations of those methods' (de Man 1979, p. 115). In the end it is only by confronting its limits – by forcing analysis to the point of *aporia* or self-contradiction – that thought comes up against the gap between itself and the aberrant 'logic' of the text.

DECONSTRUCTION AT THE LIMIT?

Along with this respect for the protocols of reason, de Man shows an unusual willingness (unusual, that is, by deconstructionist standards) to credit the text with some implicit grasp of its own rhetorical strategies. This question first posed itself in the chapter on Rousseau in *Blindness and Insight*, where de Man effectively argued, as against Derrida, that a text must in some sense contain or *prefigure* its own deconstructive reading. It may be as Jonathan Culler has argued (1972), that de Man's was itself an oddly partial reading, one that ignored those passages where Derrida insists on the close and reciprocal exchange between text and deconstruction. However de Man has a real case to argue, and takes it up again, more resourcefully, in *Allegories of Reading*.

His contention is that rhetoric considered in the suasive (or performative) mode must finally escape the rigours of deconstruction. 'A statement of mistrust', as he puts it, 'is neither true nor false: it is rather in the nature of a permanent hypothesis.' Deconstruction can sustain its sceptical position only to the point where its findings have to be argued in more or less persuasive terms. And at this point, as Nietzsche perceived, it will always elude or outflank its own most vigilant scepticism. The interpreter faces the same dilemma. On the one hand, he can adopt a thoroughgoing sceptical line which detects and discounts every last vestige of a suasive rhetoric – in which case (as de Man shows of Derrida) his reading must open up an endless series of further deconstructions, each latching on to those rhetorical aspects that can never be expunged in its own performance. On the other hand, the critic can acknowledge, with de Man, that there must be an end-point to this dizzying regress. It is reached at the moment when scepticism encounters a figural will to power beyond reach of further deconstruction.

This is not, of course, the kind of 'intentionalist' reading which the old New Critics – and the structuralists after them – so firmly rejected. Without wishing to claim that Rousseau intended, or consciously grasped, any such latent possibilities of meaning, de Man puts the case that his *texts* in themselves provide the only starting-point for deconstructive treatment. This position is maintained against considerable odds in the chapters on Rousseau in *Allegories of Reading*. The odds are stacked by de Man himself, who goes to quite remarkable lengths to demonstrate the gap between Rousseau's apparent topics of discourse – culture, politics, his own life-history – and the textual dynamics that govern and (most often) undermine them. It is a case, once again, of the tropes taking over the business of narrative or logical argument, substituting a play of figural language that obeys its own laws of inverted cause-and-effect.

De Man is at his most 'uncanny' when describing the *Social Contract* (for instance) as a text that refers not *outside itself* to some real political order but entirely to its own 'constitution' as a network of rhetorical codes and devices. As he puts it at one point,

> The tension between figural and grammatical language is duplicated in the differentiation between the State as a defined entity (État) and the State as a principle of action (Souverain) or, in linguistic terms, between the constative and the performative aspect of language.
>
> (de Man 1979, p. 270)

As the *Contract* is itself both 'statutory and operative', so the language that describes it shuttles incessantly between constative and performative modes. The 'double perspective', in this case, involves an understanding that Rousseau's text both deconstructs its own argument and saves itself – like Nietzsche's – by a kind of preemptive rhetorical strike. Writing survives and transcends the process of figural reduction.

There is a similar, redemptive turn of argument in de Man's final chapter on Rousseau's *Confessions*. Here it is the nature of narrative 'excuses' – the fiction masquerading as honest self-scrutiny – which provides a handle for deconstructive reading. To 'confess' is to indulge in a series of self-justifying utterances which claim to be 'sincere', or to offer direct access to the writer's memories and the workings of his moral conscience. Yet confessions are always, in some sense, a strategy designed to 'excuse' the penitent by placing his guilt in a narrative context that explains it, and thus absolves him from responsibility. Such excuses run the danger that 'they will indeed exculpate the confessor, thus making the confession (and the confessional text) redundant as it originates' (ibid., pp. 278–301).

Again, there is a gap opened up between the claim to truth and the way in which the text deconstructs that claim as a merely rhetorical or *post hoc* rationalization. Guilt – including the 'guilty pleasure' of writing – can always be seen as a product of textual contrivance, re-created by a narrative cunning that evades, while ostensibly parading, the causes that engender it. Once embarked on his narrative, Rousseau is caught in a chain of signifying episodes that substitute their own devious logic for the truth-telling virtues of autobiography. So much so, indeed, that 'Rousseau's text, against its author's interest, prefers being suspected of lie and slander rather than of innocently lacking sense' (ibid., p. 293). The imperatives of writing subdue those of truth or candour, reducing the *Confessions* – from a deconstructive viewpoint – to 'a product of textual grammar or a radical fiction'.

This would seem to press as far as possible towards discounting intentions, or involving them in a web of textual significations beyond all conscious control. For de Man, however, the point is to recognize the fundamental urging of a rhetoric which nevertheless persists in the text when deconstruction has employed all the means at its disposal. Rousseau's 'excuses' may not function in the way he explicitly intends, but they still lead back to a conflict of motive and logic where the subtlest critic meets his match. Language itself, in de Man's words, 'dissociates the cognition from the act'. What the text *performs* is in the last analysis immune from further sceptical attack. Deconstruction is not a matter of mere critical gamesmanship precisely because it uses – *can* only use – the figural leads and devices advanced by the text itself. In reading, as de Man insists, we are 'only trying to come closer to being as rigorous a reader as the author had to be in order to write the sentence in the first place'. It is to this end of saving the text that de Man so carefully stakes out the limits of deconstruction and the gap that persists between the reductive grammar of tropes and the rhetoric of textual performance.

'ORDINARY LANGUAGE': THE CHALLENGE FROM AUSTIN

Derrida himself – it must be said – gives little sign of accepting any such 'performative' check to the free play of deconstruction. His treatment of speech-act philosophy, in the essay 'Signature Event Context' (Derrida 1977b), sparked off an exchange with the American philosopher John Searle, in the course of which Derrida made it plain that his intent was to baffle and provoke, rather than to reach any common ground of discussion. The essay itself (first published in French) is rigorously argued and takes up many of the themes familiar from *Of Grammatology*. The rejoinder to Searle is in a very different vein, playing all manner of mock-solemn games with Searle's line of argument and no doubt indulging the Yale deconstructors in their taste for such verbal jousting. It is clear from this exchange that Derrida has absorbed more than a little of the ludic propensity shown by his American disciples (Paul de Man excepted). His encounter, first with speech-act philosophy and then with Searle as its living representative, offers a measure of this tactical-cultural shift.

'Signature Event Context' is mainly concerned with Austin's theory of performative utterance, as briefly described above. According to Austin, language serves a great variety of purposes, not all of which are accountable as statements of fact or logical entailment (see Austin 1963). It can be used to *perform* certain kinds of rhetorical act like promising, declaring a couple man and wife, or ritually naming some object or other. Such performative functions may be explicitly marked ('I *hereby* declare . . . '), or they may depend on context for their special meaning. What sets them apart from statements of fact is the *intention* or 'illocutionary force' (Austin's term) which goes along with their utterance. Performatives involve an intention and a commitment, on the speaker's part, to stand by his words and acknowledge (at least as he utters them) all the obligations they entail.

Austin introduces various refinements and distinctions by way of explaining the different kinds of illocutionary force. Common to them all, however, is the idea that performative speech-acts are somehow guaranteed and authenticated by the present good faith of whoever utters them. Austin expressly rules out such 'etiolated' or 'parasitic' instances as promises spoken in jest, on the stage, or as part of a quotation from some source other than the speaker. These utterances are void of commitment, merely aping the conventions and in no sense possessing genuine performative status. The conditions of producing a 'felicitous' speech-act – on Austin's terms – can be summarized as sincerity, correctness of form, and propriety of context. To fail on any of these counts is to fall into idle talk or other, more insidious kinds of linguistic delinquency.

Derrida finds in Austin's notion of 'speech-act' a classic restatement of the philosophic stance that privileges 'speech' at the expense of 'writing'. Austin's conditions of performative felicity require that the speaker 'mean what he says' in the sense of being presently involved with his utterance and faithfully *intending* its import. Yet it is in the very nature of performatives, Derrida argues, that they hold good for various occasions and contexts where the supposed original force of intention is no longer present. Performative speech-acts derive their operative meaning from the fact that they embody *conventional* forms and tokens of utterance which are always already in existence before the speaker comes to use them. This 'iterability', or power of being trans-ferred from one specific context to another, is evidence that speech-acts cannot be confined to the unique self-present moment of meaning. They partake of the *différance* or distancing from origin that marks all language in so far as it exceeds and pre-exists the speaker's intention. Austin's criteria for speech-act felicity are therefore inconsistent with what his performatives are actually required to do. They manifest the same metaphysical hankering for presence and origins that Derrida discerns in the texts of Saussure or Husserl. The 'iterability' of per-formatives means that they can be explained and located only within a larger system of non-self-present signification. They belong to writing in Derrida's sense of the word: an economy of difference nowhere coinciding with the present intentions of individual speech.

This gives Derrida his hold for deconstructing those loaded oppositions that Austin requires in order to separate 'felicitous' from 'infelicitous' speech-acts. Does it not follow, Derrida asks,

> that what Austin excludes as anomaly, exception, 'non-serious', *citation* (on stage, in a poem, or a soliloquy) is the determined modi-fication of a general citationality – or rather, a general iterability – without which there would not even be a 'successful' speech-act?
>
> (Derrida 1977b, p. 191)

The same applies to signatures, including Derrida's own, artfully appended to this essay. Signatures confer an authenticity which, depending as it does on *repetition* – on the capacity for being detached from 'the present and singular intention' of the signatory – always lies open to doubt. The 'felicitous' signing of a cheque, for instance, depends on certain agreed preconditions of trust, mainly the signa-tory's knowledge – or conviction – that the bank will honour her requirement. Yet the very conventionality of such transactions leaves them perpetually exposed to fraud and double-dealing, just as language may often not 'mean what it says'.

Of course, Derrida concedes, we get along normally without entertaining such doubts, accepting the conventions of authenticity as if they belonged to a natural order of truth. Their 'effects' in day-to-day discourse can hardly be questioned. But to build a whole *philosophy* on the conventions of language, as Austin does, is to invite a more rigorous scrutiny – one that uncovers contradictions in the nature of speech-act commitment. As Derrida argues, these 'effects' are only made possible by a repressed knowledge that the opposite could always obtain, that they may be grounded in nothing more than an empty or fallible convention. The underlying metaphors of Austin's philosophy – 'pure' versus 'impure' speech-acts, 'parasitical' variants, and so forth – are highly susceptible of deconstruction.

Searle responds to the effect that Derrida has confused the issue, mainly by ignoring the communicative ground-rules that give performative language its particular force (Searle 1977). His argument rests on the Chomskian assumption that speakers possess an innate linguistic competence by which they are enabled to produce and comprehend a potentially infinite variety of well-formed utterances. From this point of view the conventionality of speech-acts is precisely the means of their being understood and preserving their force *despite* the vicissitudes of context. Searle thus reverses Derrida's argument, maintaining that the 'iterability' of linguistic forms 'facilitates and is a necessary condition of the forms of intentionality that are characteristic of speech-acts' (ibid., p. 208). He further objects that Derrida's concept of 'writing' ignores the basic intelligibility that attaches to most written texts irrespective of whether the author's 'intentions' are there to consult. Communicative competence plays the same role in written as in spoken language, allowing the reader – if he is not intent upon wilful obfuscation – to apply the standard interpretative rules and arrive at the intended conclusion. Searle thus rejects the Derridean claim that speech-acts are invaded by a 'generalized citationality' (or writing) which renders them just as 'parasitic' as the deviant cases proscribed by Austin.

Clearly this exchange held out small promise of agreement or concession on either side. Searle presupposes what Derrida denies to begin with: that language is properly adapted to communicate meaning, and – as a corollary to this – that whatever obstructs communication is either deviant or somehow beside the point. Derrida opens his essay by deconstructing the very concept of 'communication', arguing that it opens into regions of undecidability where no appeal to context or convention can possibly arrest the disseminating free play of language. The sheer distance of thought between Derrida and Searle can be gauged by an example the latter gives to support his view of communicative competence. 'On the twentieth of September 1793 I set out on a journey from London to Oxford' (ibid., p. 20). Now here, Searle argues, is a straightforward communication which comes across plainly, despite the fact that the author and his 'intentions' are long since dead. Searle puts this example forward as a knock-down case which presumably even Derrida could hardly controvert.

However such sentences are favoured 'texts' for deconstruction, not only by Derrida but by others (like Barthes) who share his fascination with the slippages of everyday referential meaning. Barthes quotes the merest of telegraphic greetings: 'Monday. Returning tomorrow. Jean-Louis.' He then makes play with all the possible ambiguities that lurk behind even such a simple and practical piece of language. (Which Jean-Louis? Which of the various Mondays on which the message might have been penned?) From this point Barthes takes off into one of those flights of strange but meticulously argued fantasy that characterize his later writing. Society, he reflects, tries to bar such pleasurable vagaries by insisting on specific memoranda of dates, places, patronymics, and so forth. But can we not imagine

> the freedom and, so to speak, the erotic fluidity . . . which would speak only in pronouns and shifters, each person never saying anything but *I, tomorrow, over there*, without referring to anything legal whatsoever, and in which the *vagueness of difference* (the only fashion of respecting its subtlety) would be language's most precious value?
>
> (Barthes 1977, pp. 165–6)

What Barthes is imagining here is the utopian equivalent of Derrida's *différance*, a pure textuality redeemed from every last taint of referential meaning. It is a view of language undreamt of in Searle's philosophy because it totally rejects the normative constraints of effective communication. Where Searle rests squarely on commonsense assumptions about how words are *used* in everyday practical terms, Derrida and Barthes see language as everywhere revealing its potential aberrations and never coming to rest in a stable order of meaning.

In his subsequent rejoinder, 'Limited Inc abc' (Derrida 1977c), Derrida exploits every possible means of subverting the logic and tacit assumptions behind Searle's argument. He makes great play with the notion of copyright, incorporating large chunks of Searle's text – indeed, during the course of his argument, quoting nearly all of it! – and turning them against their own purpose by manifold sleights of cunning. In what sense can Searle have proprietory interest in a text that claims to be founded on truths universally implicit in the nature of language? Derrida even renames his opponent 'SARL', the spelling of which is meant to indicate 'Société à responsabilité limitée', or 'Limited' (company) or 'Inc', as the title has it. Searle/Sarl is thus set up as a convenient butt for Derrida's attack on the notion that texts can be owned, controlled, 'limited' or appropriated in the name of some sovereign authorial source. The exchange becomes, for Derrida, an elaborate cross-play of textual strategies and in no sense an encounter of two selfpossessed philosophical views. He goes on to exercise a shrewd deconstructive leverage on all those concepts and protocols of argument that Searle accepts as a basis for 'serious' discussion. What is left of speech-act philosophy if one chooses to question the ethics of sincerity and speaking-in-earnest which it has to presuppose? Searle's passing reference to the 'suspect status of the "non-serious"' gives Derrida an opening for much delighted play with the solemn conventions of Anglo-American academic discourse. Searle adopts a sternly proprietory tone in pointing out Derrida's 'misunderstandings' of speech-act philosophy, his 'falsification' of the issues involved and the fact that 'Derrida's Austin . . . bears almost no relation to the original'. Such arguments fall plump into Derrida's hands, assuming as they do that 'Austin' is not just the name attached to a certain body of texts but that Austin's presence – and that of his disciple – continues to exercise a juridical power over how those texts are to be read.

Derrida is under no illusion that he has 'taken Sarl seriously' or met his arguments with reasoned opposition at any point. The object of 'Limited Inc' is to stage a confrontation which never really takes place, but the very *avoidance* of which is a kind of tactical triumph. Derrida's aim throughout is to manoeuvre Searle on to textual ground where speech-act conventions run up against absurdity or limiting cases of their own application. As he archly suggests at one point.

> a theoretician of speech-acts who was even moderately consistent with his own theory ought to have spent some time patiently considering questions of this type: Does the principal purpose [of 'Signature Event Context'] consist in being *true*? In appearing true? In stating the truth?
>
> And what if *SEC* were *doing something else?*
>
> (Derrida 1977c, p. 178)

That 'something else' is deconstruction in the 'uncanny' or vertiginous mode Derrida has often exploited when writing for a mainly American readership. Its themes are certainly continuous with his earlier texts, but its strategies more artfully contrived, more roundabout and circumstantial.

It would clearly be rash in the extreme, after Derrida's exchange with Searle, to suppose that these ludic elements exclude any 'serious' intent. On the other hand it is interesting to see how Derrida's texts have been drawn and provoked by their involvement with American debates. A striking example is Derrida's contribution to the volume *Deconstruction and Criticism*, published as a kind of manifesto for the Yale deconstructionists (Hartman et al 1979). The topic is ostensibly Shelley's poem 'The Triumph of Life', which serves as a focus for the other contributors but which barely manages to peep through the tangles and cunning indirections of Derrida's text. He makes no pretence of 'interpreting' the poem but uses its title and random associative hints as a springboard into regions of giddying uncertainty, where details merge and cross in a joyful breakdown of all proprietory limits. Any talk of meaning or structure is ineluctably 'caught up in a process which it does not control', which for Derrida signals the total dissolution of those boundaries that mark off one text from another, or that try to interpose between poem and commentary. 'The Triumph of Life' is teasingly played off against Blanchot's narrative *L'Arrêt de mort*, producing a series of figural crossings, swerves and substitutions which abolish all sense of textual autonomy. This gambit is pushed to the limit by a footnote, addressed to the translator, which runs the full length of Derrida's text and constantly adverts to the impossible nature of the whole undertaking – the way in which translation exemplifies the 'abysmal' slippages and detours of all understanding.

Derrida's strategy here has more in common with Hartman or Hillis Miller than with a 'purist' deconstructor like de Man. It is a virtuoso exercise of writing which assumes all the textual freedoms granted by an underdetermined or radically ambiguous context. Translation, like criticism, reaches a point where it has to abandon the manageable rhetoric of 'polysemia' (or multiple meaning, New Critical style) and embrace the 'free play' of textual dissemination. In his recent productions Derrida has used all the means at his disposal to project and dramatize this process, as distinct from the kind of rigorous argumentation at work in Of Grammatology or Writing and Difference. Of the critics at Yale it is de Man who has done most to sustain that early-Derridean insistence on the need for deconstruction to remain, in some sense, a discipline of close reading. Hartman's has been the more typical reaction, taking Derrida's texts as a cue for simply throwing off all the old, irksome restraints of method and style. To sort out the two-way 'influence' here would be a fruitless undertaking, given the degree of intertextual penetration and exchange which these writings consciously exploit. At any rate it is clear by now that deconstruction in America is not a monolithic theory or school of thought but a gathering-point for critics who are otherwise divided on many central questions of technique and style. Resistances and tensions are building at Yale, as they did during the waning of the 'old' New Criticism, presided over by Hartman and his colleagues. One of the most eloquent dissenting voices is that of Harold Bloom, whose strategies in the face of deconstruction have a strange heroic grandeur of their own.

HAROLD BLOOM

We have seen how the challenge to formalist dogma went along with a revived interest in the poetry and ethos of Romanticism. Bloom devoted his first book to Shelley (Shelley's Mythmaking, 1959), who had long been the target of critics (Eliot and Allen Tate among them) who argued implicitly from Shelley's romanticized politics to what they considered his failings of imaginative nerve and moral immaturity. Shelley became the standard example of a poet who consistently over-stepped the limits of answerable style and sacrificed his craft to the attractions of a vague pantheistical uplift or ersatz religion. T. E. Hulme had indeed stigmatized Romanticism as 'spilt religion', and laid down that poetry must not concern itself with ultimate issues beyond its proper scope and command. It was left to the New Critics to work out the systematic rules and sanctions of this moral embargo.

Bloom conducts a defence of Shelley which is also a principled rejection of the classicist poetic and everything that flowed from it. He develops an idea from the Jewish theologian Martin Buber, that human experience divides into two kinds or qualities – expressed in terms of the 'it' and 'thou' attitudes – which between them stake out the great moral choices of existence. Bloom sees Shelley as having tried over and again, in the best of his poetry, to reassert the value of human relation-ships, the 'thou'-saying attitude which creates a world of mutual rec-ognition and sympathy, whether between one human being and another or humanity and the living universe. This amounts to an aes-thetic philosophy opposed point for point to the formalist idea of the poem as an impersonal object or 'verbal icon' for detached contempla-tion. To Bloom's way of thinking, it is only in moments of emotional defeat – or satirical bitterness – that Shelley is forced back into such an impersonal mode. His case against Shelley's modern detractors rests on a neo-Romantic belief that the poet is indeed, as Wordsworth expressed it, 'a man speaking to men'. Critics who condemn the poetry on that account – under cover of formalist dogma – are simply closing their minds to any possibility of a world redeemed from the 'it-ness' of routine perception.

In Bloom's more recent writing the personalist heresy is pushed even further in the direction of a full-blown Romantic myth of cre-ation. *The Anxiety of Influence* (1973) laid the ground-work of Bloom's revisionist poetic. There exists, he argued, a complex and fascinating tension between the 'strong' poets in any tradition – those with a powerful drive to preserve their own identity – and the predecessor poets whose influence they have to cope with and somehow turn to advantage. The poet suffers with peculiar anguish that guilt-ridden hatred of the father that Freud ironically described in terms of the typical 'family romance'. His will to expression is pursued through cunning forms of displacement, or defensive 'tropes', which at the same time disguise and elaborate the will to be self-begotten, to acknowledge no previous authority or influence. The strong poet has the courage to recognize his own belatedness vis-à-vis the tradition he inherits, and the strength to subvert it by 'troping' his predecessors. How this theory might apply to the woman poet — since its terms are on the face of it so exclusively Oedipal — remains very much an open question, and one which Bloom never addresses.

From Spenser, through Milton to Blake, Shelley and such modernists as Lawrence and Yeats — the tradition Bloom stakes out is a line very different from that proposed by Eliot and the New Critics. Bloom's is a dissident tradition which he traces back largely to the radical Protestant stirrings of the English Civil War, and which then reaches forward to the young Romantics and their thwarted hopes for the French Revolution. As Bloom points out, it is a line strategically ignored by Eliot and his followers, whose version of literary history — Donne, Herbert, Pope, Dr Johnson, Hopkins and Eliot himself — represents a distinctly Anglo-Catholic and conservative scheme of values. Bloom makes no bones about his preferences: 'One line, and it is the central one, is Protestant, radical and Miltonic-Romantic: the other is Catholic, conservative and, by its claims, classical.' There is a clear enough alignment between the latter tradition, with its emphasis on poetic self-discipline, and the working methods of formalist criticism. Bloom sets out not only to revise the whole modern estimate of poets such as Blake and Shelley but to reinstruct critics in the calling to which — as avatars of the same tradition — they are bound eventually to return.

Criticism for Bloom is itself a kind of poetic re-enactment, and he shows small patience with the modest conventions of critical address. *The Anxiety of Influence* presents an exotic terminology and system of 'revisionary ratios' by which to plot the labyrinthine ruses of poetic self-invention. In *Kabbalah and Criticism* (Bloom 1975) the esoteric tonings are yet more insistent and the claims more defiantly pitched. Drawing on the kabbalistic mysteries of Creation, and all the attendant apparatus of hermetic commentary, Bloom sets out a programme for criticism which could scarcely be further removed from the orthodox

Eliotic standpoint. The inspirational detours of kabbalistic wisdom are equated with the acts of creative 'misprision', or swerves from origin, which Bloom sees at work in all great poetry. Whether or not these far-fetched analogies are really worth the carriage depends on one's willingness to accept his extraordinary claims for the saving power of poetic imagination.

Poetry and Repression (1976) finds Bloom once again on the hallowed revisionary ground of Romantic and post-Romantic poetry. 'Repression', for Bloom, is a word that moves across suggestively from its Freudian sense of sublimated motive to a meaning that also involves the sublime, but in a context more familiar from Romantic philosophies of mind and nature. The theme of a natural innocence regained is one that haunted the imaginations of all those poets, from Blake to Wallace Stevens, whose 'belatedness' Bloom sets out to interpret. The Romantic sublime is a quest for lost origins which the strong poet always engages in, though aware that his belated condition puts it beyond reach of any but the subtlest revisionary tropes and displacements. Repression is a knowledge of perpetual self-defeat, yet at the same time a power of somehow retrieving the sublime through the crises and conflicts of sublimated influence.

Up to a point there is much in common between Bloom's 'revisionary ratios' and the practice of deconstruction. Both start out from the idea that literary history, in so far as it exists in any genuine sense, has to deal with texts in their relationships one with another, through a process of perpetual displacement which can only be described in rhetorical terms. Both dismiss the subjectivist illusion of the poet as self-possessed creator of meaning, an individual subject expressing the truths of his or her own authentic vision. To interpret a text is to seek out the strategies and defensive tropes by which it either confronts or evades the texts that precede it. Bloom is in accord with Derrida when he insists that textual origins are always pushed back beyond recall, in a series of hard-fought rhetorical encounters that make up the line of descent in poetic history. Where the difference emerges is in Bloom's countervailing argument that 'strong' poets must always strive to create at least a working-space of presence for their own imagination. In other words, Bloom wants to halt the process of deconstruction at a point where it is still possible to gauge a poet's creative stature in terms of his overriding will to expression. It could hardly be otherwise, given Bloom's intense involvement with Romantic poetry, and his efforts to rescue that tradition from the classicizing canon of Eliot and his followers.

It is therefore not surprising that in his recent books Bloom should seem torn between a defence of poetry which holds to the ethos of Romantic individualism, and a deconstructive poetics which tends to dissolve such themes into something approaching an abstract system of tropes and relationships. In the last resort, however, Bloom is always willing to invoke the terminology of 'voice', 'presence' and authorial selfhood which Derrida so persistently calls into question. Bloom's arguments are mustered in his methodological 'coda' to *Wallace Stevens: The Poems of Our Climate* (1977). The book sets out to place Stevens's poetry in the great Romantic line of descent, which Bloom wants to claim as a modern American home-ground, since Eliot effectively broke with that tradition for English poets of a modernist sympathy. Behind this rejuvenated Romanticism stands the figure of Ralph Waldo Emerson, the Concord philosopher and sage whom Bloom regards as the great precursor of everything strongest and most vital in American poetry. Emerson becomes the mediating presence in a mode of pragmatic idealism which transplants the 'sublime' of Wordsworth and Shelley to a climate of belatedness and strenuous new beginnings. Emerson is shrewdly beforehand with the modern deconstructors by accepting from the outset the absence of comforting illusions – the bankruptcy of Idealism – and setting in their place a radical will to imaginative power. Stevens enters this picture as a poet of intense moral vision and 'humanizing pathos', whose relation to the American sublime involves him in a rhetoric of crisis, a sequence of urgently redemptive tropes and misprisions.

Bloom is here conducting a complex and many-levelled strategy of argument. He stands in much the same relation to his 'deconstructing' colleagues as Stevens to Emerson, or to that side of Emerson which wanted to reduce the expressiveness of language to the inbred tropes of rhetoric. 'Deconstructing Emerson is of course impossible, since no discourse has ever been so overtly aware of its status as rhetoricity' (Bloom 1977, p. 12). Faced with this impasse, Stevens adopts the only possible adequate response, a rhetoric strong enough to 'trope' or wilfully transfigure the Emersonian reduction. As Bloom most succinctly puts it:

> In Stevens, we will see Emersonian Fate turning into . . . the First Idea. Transcendental Freedom in Stevens becomes the refusal to bear so dehumanizing a reduction. Power or Will in Stevens' mature poetry is the reimagining of a First Idea.
>
> (ibid., p. 27)

Bloom clearly sees himself as doing for present-day criticism what Stevens achieved for American poetry. His closing chapter confronts the deconstructors with an account of what it is to move *through* and *beyond* their sceptical epistemology, to a concept of rhetoric that would reinstate the poet as a seeker after truths of his own strong imagining. Bloom still admits the power of deconstruction, the force of what he calls 'this advanced critical consciousness, the most rigorous and scrupulous in the field today'. But he sees no way beyond such a reductive outlook, except by readmitting the will to expression which animates not only the poet's tropes but the critic's rhetorical motives when he comes to interpret them. There has to be a leap from the knowledge that *all* interpretation is a network of superimposed tropes, to the faith that something might yet be achieved to clear a space for the modern imagination.

This is where Bloom parts company with de Man and the purist deconstructors. He sees them as having reached the point where scepticism must give way to a redemptive or reconstructive 'troping' aware of its own liabilities.

> The issue of the limits of deconstruction will be resolved only if we attain a vision of rhetoric more comprehensive than the deconstructors allow, that is, if we can learn to see rhetoric as transcending the epistemology of tropes and re-entering the space of the will-to-persuasion.
>
> (ibid., p. 387)

This act of willed reversal is the key-point of Bloom's poetics, and the crux of his difference with Hartman, Miller and the others. Powerful and convincing though their arguments are, it is still possible to 'trope' them in turn by seeing their negative stance as one stage only in a double movement of interpretative thought. Bloom stakes his readings on a concept of 'misprision', or masterful troping, which strives to attain this Nietzschean transvaluation of values. If the 'strong' poet is one who creatively misreads and reinterprets the precursor, then the strength of criticism is likewise its power to invest the strategies of reading with a sense of hard won significance. This leads Bloom back to the crisis-laden rhetoric of *Kabbalah and Criticism*, the argument of which he resumes in his closing pages on Stevens. Kabbalistic tradition is quarried as a source of figurative ploys sufficiently strange and powerful to confront the reductive tropes of deconstruction.

One could hardly wish for a wilder and stranger language than the rhetoric of 'crossings', or defensive encounters, which Bloom brings to bear in his grappling with Stevens's poetry. It is a language torn between the abstract register of post-structuralist thought and the high prophetic tone of which Bloom is both master and (occasionally) near-comic victim. He takes the line of maximum resistance in straddling the ground between thought and vision, concept and trope, philosophy and poetry. His defence for this outlandish style is that it answers to the strangeness and taxing rhetoric of poetry itself. Poets, he argues, are first and foremost 'masters of misprision', and only incidentally (or at a great remove of theory) the 'conceptual rhetoricians' that deconstruction would make of them. To read them 'more truly and more strange' we need in the end 'a wilder definition of trope' than anything offered by the current deconstructors.

Bloom's real quarrel with his Yale colleagues is that they fail to understand the conflicts and antagonisms engendered by the poet's 'belated' encounter with tradition. The New Critics invented various ways of sealing the poem off within a timeless, self-sufficient realm of interlocked meaning and structure. Internal 'tensions' (of irony, paradox, etc.) were there to validate the techniques of criticism as a disciplined and *sui generis* form of knowledge. Deconstruction abandons this fenced-off critical estate when it speaks of the 'intertextuality', or rhetoric of endlessly shuttling allusion, which makes up the history of writing. For Bloom, however, this notion is too generalized and neutral to convey the complex rivalries between poet and poet. If the New

Critics sought to contain those tensions within the formalist limits of the poem as 'verbal icon', deconstruction seeks to dissolve them entirely by an open-ended rhetoric of figural displacement.

Bloom's invocation of kabbalist hermeneutics is a means of countering both these reductions. At the heart of his project is the guiding assumption 'that a Kabbalistic or Gnostic theory of rhetoric must deny that there can be any *particular* semantic tension in language, because in the Kabbalistic vision all language is nothing but semantic tension raised to apocalyptic pitch'. (ibid., p. 394). The 'particular tension' to which Bloom here refers might be glossed as the kind of specialized inbred rhetoric of poetry devised by the 'old' New Critics. At the same time his argument shrewdly undermines the deconstructionist position by insisting on the conflict of individual wills to expression behind the encounter of text with text. This struggle, he urges, must not be lost sight of in the undifferentiated merging or 'free play' supposedly envisaged by Derridean deconstruction.

DERRIDA AND BLOOM ON FREUD

Bloom is equally un-Derridean in the use he makes of Freudian motifs and analogies. Derrida's reading of Freud ('Freud and the Scene of Writing', in Derrida 1978, pp. 196–231) is yet another parable of deconstruction, a reading aimed at eliciting the metaphors of writing and psychic 'inscription' to which Freud resorts at crucial points of explanation. The upshot is to show that these 'metaphors' are in fact nothing of the kind. Though Freud always uses them by way of analogy or descriptive convenience, they become so enmeshed in his texts as to offer the most cogent and finally *inescapable* account of unconscious working. 'Physical content will be represented by a text whose essence is irreducibly graphic' (ibid., p. 199). When Freud envisages the unconscious as in some sense structured like a language, his terms of description are borrowed from the economy of *writing* rather than of speech. As Derrida shows, the entire Freudian topology of unconscious meaning depends on such notions as 'trace', 'spacing', 'difference' and others whose place can be found only within a graphic system of representation. In his early work, Freud held to the belief that these were merely metaphors pointing toward a mature neurological science which would finally dispense with such figurative props. Derrida argues, on the contrary, that Freud's indelible figures of writing are his chief contribution to a knowledge of the unconscious and its effects, in comparison with which his 'neurological fable' must itself be seen as a species of sublimated metaphor. Freud thus stands, with Husserl and Saussure, as a thinker whose texts uphold the tradition of Western metaphysics, yet which yield – through a deconstructive reading – critical motifs at odds with that tradition. Writing asserts itself despite Freud's will to restrict it to a figural and secondary status. As Derrida predicts, 'it is with a graphematics still to come, rather than with a linguistics dominated by an ancient phonologism, that psychoanalysis sees itself as destined to collaborate' (ibid., p. 220).

Derrida's reading of Freud gives some idea of what Bloom most objects to in the practice of deconstruction. It is a reading that totally discounts the psychic drama, the conflicts of will and motive, which Bloom seizes on by way of analogy with the poet's 'anxiety of influence'. Freud himself is for Bloom one of the master-spirits of modern interpretation, a 'strong' wrestler with unconscious meanings whose pattern he projects into powerful new myths of explanation. If Bloom, like Derrida, has little use for the 'scientific' side of Freudian theory, he is equally opposed to a deconstructive reading that would dissolve psychoanalysis into an undifferentiated play of textual meaning. 'The theoreticians of deconstruction in effect say, "In the beginning was the trope", rather than "In the beginning was the troper"' (Bloom 1977, p. 393). If the concept of trope is in itself a species of metaphor, a 'figure of figures', then it is up to the strong-willed interpreter (poet or critic) to assert the possibility of meaning over against an otherwise meaningless chain of reductions. Derrida's Freud is the producer of texts which everywhere reveal their unwitting dependence on a rhetoric that self-deconstructs into tropes and yet further tropes of writing. Bloom's Freud is a strong precursor who resists such readings through the power to convert them to his own imaginative end.

His deconstructing colleagues are by no means blind to the dangers and temptations Bloom perceives. Even Hartman sounds the occasional cautionary note when he contemplates the giddying prospects opened up by a pure rhetoric of tropes and intertextuality. His sense of excitement at the new-found freedoms offered to interpretative style goes along with a certain mistrust of the blurring of distinctions between 'text' and 'commentary' entailed by Derrida's approach. The problem is bound up with that move 'beyond formalism' which also dissolves the authority of 'the book'.

> By diminishing the book-centeredness of literary discourse you bring it closer to philosophical discourse and run the risk of homogenizing it. True, you may still have 'texts' rather than 'books' – but what constitutes a text is a slippery thing to define . . .
>
> (Hartman 1975, p. 13)

In Derrida Hartman notes the use of a 'highly repetitive and snippety canon', a habit of mixing text and citation which produces in the end 'a highly frustrating *clair-obscur*'.

Hartman's doubts are not serious enough to prevent him from rising to Derrida's challenge with a consciously Nietzschean stylistic verve. Bloom and de Man, in their different ways, represent a more powerful inward check on the centrifugal energies of deconstruction. Bloom's is a frankly rhetorical summons to arrest and reverse what he sees as a movement of 'serene linguistic nihilism', bent upon reducing poetry to a random play of unmotivated tropes or textual figuration. His style is embattled and his arguments pitched at a sometimes desperate level of urgent pleading. De Man writes from the opposite standpoint of a critic completely given over to the rigours of deconstruction. He is by far the toughest-minded of those 'conceptual rhetoricians' whose thinking and influence Bloom is at such pains to confront. Yet his readings most often come out, as we have seen, at a point where deconstruction has to acknowledge the 'performative' dimension of language that eludes its subtlest endeavours. Bloom and de Man can be said to arrive at similar conclusions from radically different premises. They both stand apart from what they see – Bloom quite explicitly, de Man by implication – as a facile misuse of deconstructionist theory.

7

CONCLUSION: DISSENTING VOICES

Bloom sets up as the opponent from within, meeting the deconstructors point for point on rhetorical ground of their own choosing. He thinks it impossible to answer a thoroughgoing scepticism except by fearlessly taking its measure and then responding with an equal and opposite will to persuade. Others would see Bloom's tactics as wholly misconceived, an uncalled-for yielding of hostages where a straightforward offensive is the proper response. Others again, like Murray Krieger, have tried to coax deconstruction down by arguing that its 'methods' are not, after all, so very different from those of the old New Criticism (see Krieger 1979). Much of this debate has been ephemeral and fruitless, a virtual repetition of the quarrels that surrounded the first obtrusions of structuralist thought on the American scene.

On the other hand there have been serious attempts to grapple with deconstruction on alternative philosophic ground. These mostly start out from the view that scepticism is *not* (as even Bloom seems forced to admit) irrefutable on its own terms of argument. Indeed, it may turn out to be self-refuting if one asks the sceptic by what special privilege his or her own arguments are exempt from doubt or mistrust (see Abrams 1978). The deconstructors clearly expect that their texts will be read with care and attention, their arguments weighed and their conclusions discussed in a decently responsible manner. Yet how can this be squared with their own professed scepticism towards meaning, logic, truth and the very possibility of communication? Their case might seem open to what the philosopher Jürgen Habermas, in a slightly different context, has called the 'transcendental *tu quoque*'. That is, they demand that their texts be properly understood – or at least intelligently read – while ostensibly denying the power of language to encompass any such end.

These objections have little force against a critic like de Man, whose extreme scepticism paradoxically creates a scrupulous regard for the text he interprets. The approach may be condemned as perverse – a sheer technique for creating trouble – but it remains closely argued and never gives way to a relativistic 'anything goes' approach. Derrida is likewise too canny a sceptic to be caught with his textual defences down. Even while 'playing old Harry' (as the translation puts it) with Searle's intentions, he can argue that his opponent has misread (or misquoted) certain passages of his (Derrida's) text and thus laid himself open to a stern rejoinder. His disregard for the conventional pieties of interpretation goes along with a meticulous attention to detail and a stubborn insistence on the letter of the text, its refusal to be explained away by any convenient means. Derrida's scepticism is not what some of his interpreters would make of it, a passport to limitless interpretative games of their own happy devising. This applies even to the latest texts in translation where the ideas of free play and intertextuality are pushed to a provocative extreme. The point is that Derrida, unlike some of his disciples, has arrived at this position through a long and strenuous process of deconstruction. It may seem quaintly moralistic to say that he has 'earned' this right by actually thinking through the problems his followers have picked up, as it were, ready-made. Yet this was already Derrida's contention in *Of Grammatology*: that thought can break with its delusive presuppositions only by constantly and actively rehearsing that break. Otherwise deconstruction remains an ineffectual gesture, a theory confined by the very oppositions it seeks to overthrow. It is here, Derrida warns, 'that the concept and above all the work of deconstruction, its "style", remain by nature exposed to misunderstanding and nonrecognition' (Derrida 1977a, p. 28)

Derrida's is not, in other words, a knock-down scepticism easily arrived at and just as easily refuted by a simple *tu quoque*. It is a hard-won position sustained by arguments that merit the same close *textual* scrutiny Derrida brings to his own best readings. On the other hand there are opposing views of language, truth and meaning which cannot be dismissed as merely naïve or philosophically bankrupt. Derrida implicitly acknowledges their force in his text on Austin. Deconstruction neither denies nor really affects the commonsense view that language exists to communicate meaning. It *suspends* that view for its own specific purpose of seeing what happens when the writs of convention no longer run.

Scepticism in philosophy has always borne this ambiguous relation to the 'natural' or commonsense attitude. Its proponents have never pretended that life could be conducted in a practical way if everyone acted consistently on sceptical assumptions. What would such 'consistency' amount to, indeed, if one denied every last standard of reason and logical coherence? This is not to say that the sceptics' questions are trivial or totally misconceived. They are – as I have tried to show with Derrida – questions that present themselves *compulsively* as soon as one abandons the commonsense position. But language continues to communicate, as life goes on, despite all the problems thrown up by sceptical thought.

Richard Rorty has stated the issue most adroitly in his essay 'Philosophy as a Kind of Writing' (Rorty 1978). There are, he suggests, two 'traditions' of philosophy which exist in a state of perpetual rivalry, but which can never properly *confront* one another because their aims and idioms are so disparate. On the one hand are those thinkers who share the conviction that philosophy is a rational dialogue of minds pursued from age to age in the quest for communicable truth. Scepticism is allowed a place in this philosophy, but only so long as it serves to eliminate various sources of error and establish more firmly the indubitable bases of truth. Opposed to this tradition is another, more diverse company of minds, one that carries out periodic raids and incursions into 'mainstream' philosophy. These thinkers reject any normative appeal to consensus values or beliefs and thrive on their fissiparous energies of paradox and style. Philosophy as 'writing', in Rorty's sense, uses language not as a more or less efficient means of rational exchange but as a fighting-ground on which to conduct its major campaigns. The self-conscious practice of philosophic *style* goes along with a rooted scepticism about ultimate truth and method. These two traditions have grown up through various historical shapes and guises. In current Anglo-American perception the line seems to fall between commonsense reason and the 'continental' strain descending from Hegel, through Nietzsche, to the current French 'excesses'. From the other side things look very different, as may be gathered from Derrida's quizzical dealings with Austin and Searle.

To see these philosophies as locked in dispute, or as both competing for the same objective, is according to Rorty a plain misapprehension. Their sporadic skirmishing is really nothing more than the result of chance encounters. The distance between them is expressed by Derrida in his closing reflections on the exchange with Searle:

> I ask myself if we will ever be quits with this confrontation.
> Will it have taken place, this time?
> Quite?

> (Derrida 1977c, p. 251)

This sense of non-encounter is what Rorty perceives as the gulf between commonsense-rationalist philosophies and those that drive beyond the limits of plain-prose reason. 'Writing' is in this sense the symptom and accomplice of a radical linguistic scepticism.

WITTGENSTEIN: LANGUAGE AND SCEPTICISM

The counter-arguments to deconstruction have therefore been situated mostly on commonsense, or 'ordinary-language' ground. There is support from the philosopher Ludwig Wittgenstein (1889–1951) for the view that such sceptical philosophies of language rest on a false epistemology, one that seeks (and inevitably fails) to discover some *logical correspondence* between language and the world. Wittgenstein himself started out from such a position, but came round to believing that language had many uses and legitimating 'grammars', none of them reducible to a clear-cut logic of explanatory concepts. His later philosophy repudiates the notion that meaning must entail some one-to-one link or 'picturing' relationship between propositions and factual states of affairs. Language is now conceived of as a repertoire of 'games' or enabling conventions, as diverse in nature as the jobs they are required to do (Wittgenstein 1953). The nagging problems of philosophy most often resulted, Wittgenstein thought, from the failure to recognize this multiplicity of language games. Philosophers looked for logical solutions to problems which were only created in the first place by a false conception of language, logic and truth. Scepticism, he argued, was the upshot of a deluded quest for certainty in areas of meaning and interpretation that resist any such strictly regimented logical account.

Wittgenstein's philosophy of language clearly has its anti-deconstructionist uses. If our ways of talking about the world are a matter of tacit convention, then scepticism is simply beside the point, a misplaced scruple produced by a false epistemology. Wittgenstein sees the history of philosophic thought as both bedevilled and largely sustained by such self-created puzzles. His line of reply is understandably attractive to those who reject deconstruction and seek a philosophy of meaning to put in its place. From a Wittgensteinian viewpoint, there is a basic and persistent error of thought in the post-Saussurian textual theory which makes such a startling phenomenon of the split between 'signifier' and 'signified'. To see this as a problem or paradox is to repeat the traditional mistake, that which comes of expecting language to relate directly to objects or ideas. Such, according to Wittgenstein and his disciples, is the root of all sceptical philosophies. They are driven into bewilderment and paradox by failing to notice the variety of possible 'fits' between language, logic and reality.

This argument would seem to offer an alternative, if not a full-scale rejoinder, to post-structuralist textual theories. The appeal to 'ordinary language', with its implicit sanctions and conventions, is seen as a more sensible way of coming to terms with the arbitrary nature of the sign. Structuralism – it might be argued – is fixated on the age-old delusion which, in one form or another, has always preoccupied philosophy. This gave rise to those attacks on 'realist' fiction (by Barthes among others) which seemed to assume that author and reader were incapable of telling narrative verisimilitude from straight reportage. The rift between sign and referent became a high point of radical theory; it was forgotten that fiction has always been more or less aware of its own fictionality, even if the symptoms were not always there on the surface, as in some post-modernist texts. A Wittgensteinian approach would reject such paradoxical 'readings' (like Barthes's S/Z) as based on a perverse and myopic idea of how language actually adapts to the flexible conventions of narrative.

Other objectors have taken a flatly moralistic line. Gerald Graff, for one, has denounced deconstruction as a culpable retreat from the problems of modern society, a kind of textual fiddling while Rome burns (see Graff 1979). Graff thinks that the new rhetoricians have much more in common with the 'old' New Criticism than they like to believe. What both movements come down to, he argues, is a form of sophisticated escapism, denying literature any power to engage with 'real' experience. Where modernism had started out (with Eliot, Joyce and their contemporaries) as a genuine protest against the reductive monopoly of old-style realist convention, it has now taken hold as a kind of institutional escape-route, totally divorced from any sense of social engagement.

Graff sees the same debilitating influence at work in the 'post-modernist' style of fiction practised by writers like Thomas Pynchon and Donald Barthelme. If realism is merely a matter of dominant convention, with no more claim to truth than other, more self-conscious modes of writing, then the way is clearly open to a wholesale scepticism which acknowledges only the infinite play of textual inscription. The trouble with Graff's toughminded stance is that it doesn't engage with his opponents in any real argumentative way. He lumps them all together, critics and novelists alike, as self-condemned enemies of reason, without seeing – or allowing himself to see – the force of their case. Thus Frank Kermode is taken to task for his argument (in The Sense of an Ending) that we always interpret texts in humanly satisfying ways, despite our awareness that such meanings are tentative and provisional, not to be confused with the truths of everyday practical experience. Graff treats this as yet another case of last-ditch critical manoeuvring, an attempt to reclaim vital ground which should never have been yielded in the first place. Yet Graff argues to much the same effect as Kermode when he appeals to Wittgenstein on the communal sense-making role of conventions in language and fiction. His appeal is more assertive than Kermode's – not so much hedged about with qualifications – but presents a similar tactical line of defence.

Wittgenstein is always at hand with a knock-down argument against thoroughgoing scepticism: that 'if you tried to doubt everything you would not get as far as doubting anything. The game of doubting itself presupposes certainty' (quoted by Graff 1979, p. 195). But this, once again, is to throw the whole argument back to a level of flatly commonsense assertion which hardly meets the deconstructionist challenge. There is a dead-end to Graff's line of argument where he simply ignores – rather than thinking through – the issues raised by deconstruction. His mistake is to believe that these problems can be neatly cleared away by tracing them back, explaining where they came from historically and why they have continued to exert such an influence. In this case, according to Graff, the line can be followed via the New Critics to Kant and his Romantic descendants, with their puzzling over mind and its relation to 'objective' reality. But the puzzles remain, and indeed provide critics like de Man with a rich prehistory for their deconstructive arguments.

It is the same with Graff's halfway redemptive readings of postmodernist novelists like Pynchon and Barthelme. On the one hand, Graff condemns their lack of intellectual fight in (supposedly) endorsing the hopelessness, 'anomie' and defeatist scepticism of modern society. On the other, he wants to wrench them away from this collective despair by offering hints of an alternative, 'adversary' reading. Thus Barthelme's stories 'call attention to their own inability to overcome their imprisonment in the artifices of language and the solipsism of consciousness, though it should not be forgotten that this very strategy itself makes a statement' (Graff 1979, pp. 236–7). Well, one or the other, but surely not both, unless – as Graff seems otherwise unwilling to admit – the 'meaning' of a text is open to all manner of strategic (mis)interpretations. Here, as with his anti-deconstructivist thrusts, Graff seems to offer not so much a worked-out critique as a kind of desperate moral imperative, eloquently stated but nowhere argued beyond a sticking-point of commonsense assumption.

There is more force to the argument from Wittgenstein when applied to some of the recent, stereotyped versions of deconstructive theory. A glance at the current American journals will show how deconstruction has taken hold, not only in new publications like *Glyph* and *Diacritics* but even in the august pages of *PMLA*. The rate of production is now such that all the canonical poems and novels will soon have a deconstructionist 'reading', to place alongside the New Critical, Marxist and other competing approaches. Abrams views this proliferating output − not without reason − as a sign that deconstruction is falling prey to mere ingenuity and academic oneupmanship.

The truth is that deconstructionist theory can only be as useful and enlightening as the mind that puts it to work. Some current applications, especially in the field of narrative analysis, do bear the marks of a certain routine ingenuity. They mostly take the form of paradoxical 'double readings', intended to show how novels display their own artifice even when exploiting the realist mode. The peculiar logic of narrative is such that 'effects' are no longer related to 'causes' in a straightforward sequence of temporally unfolding events. Rather, it is the nature of fictional form − the demands of plot and construction − which operate a kind of logical reversal, an affront to commonsense reason. 'Causes' in the novel are brought into play by the need for some solution or (apparently) antecedent fact which explains and unravels a complicated plot. In this sense causes are really *effects*, since they spring from a given complex of events which creates them, as it were, in pursuit of its own coherence. Effects are likewise transformed into causes by the same curious twist of logic (see Jonathan Culler, 'Story and Discourse in the Analysis of Narrative', in Culler 1981, pp. 169–87).

George Eliot's *Daniel Deronda* is a favoured example, inviting such treatment for several reasons. First, it stages a virtual confrontation between the realist mode of the 'Gwendolen Harleth' chapters (the parts Leavis signally approved of) and the visionary strain of the mysteries surrounding Deronda's Jewish identity and sense of mission. From this point of view it can be said to 'deconstruct' the commonsense assumptions linking the ideology of nineteenth-century realism to the judgements of modern conservative critics like Leavis. Moreover, it throws into sharp relief the paradoxes about cause-and-effect which deconstruction is resolved to uncover. The novel represents Deronda as finding out the truth of his racial origin through a series of episodes and 'chance' encounters which seem to point back to some mysterious pre-existent meaning. But the absent 'cause' is itself brought about, in narratological terms, by the events and portents it ultimately serves to explain. Cynthia Chase has hit upon a letter in the novel (from Hans Meyrick to Deronda) which underlines the paradox rather neatly. 'Here at home', he writes,

> the most judicious opinion going as to the effects of present causes is that 'time will show'. As to the present causes of past effects, it is now seen that the late swindling telegrams account for the last year's cattle plague – which is a refutation of philosophy falsely so called, and justifies the compensation to the farmers.
>
> (quoted by Chase 1978, p. 225)

On the face of it a sample of Meyrick's puckish humour, the passage clearly lends itself to deconstructive reading. That effects should 'cause' causes, and causes be construed as 'effects' of effects, is a Nietzschean paradox that runs nicely athwart the usual logic of causal explanation.

But these ideas about narrative, though strikingly formulated, are after all not so remarkable. That novels are *constructed* in a certain way – and to that extent reorder the 'logic' of contingent events – is known upon a moment's reflection to every reader. The corollary that the two narrative 'logics' are inherently at odds is by no means so obvious, and it suggests a certain effort to seek out self-supporting puzzles and paradoxes. In fact it amounts to what philosophers would call a 'category mistake', a confusion of logical realms or orders of discourse. Structuralist theory was clear enough about the basic distinction between 'story' and 'plot', the one an implied (and imaginably real-life) sequence of events, the other a pattern imposed by the requirements of narrative form. They represent two different kinds of reading: the latter is attentive to structure and device, while the former rests on a willing – but not necessarily naïve – suspension of disbelief. To see them as locked in conflict or paradox is to mistake the conventions of narrative for the rigours of logical discourse. The tactics of 'double-reading' automatically generate the kind of paradoxical impasse they set out to find. Like the structuralist attack on that ubiquitous chimera the 'classic realist text', such strategies ignore the variety of possible relations between language, text and reality.

However this is not for one moment to deny the vigour and sheer argumentative power of Derrida or de Man at their best. Of course it is too early as yet to predict what effects deconstruction will have on the wider practice of critical and philosophic writing. For de Man the deconstructive opening is a summons not to be ignored: criticism, he says, will have its work cut out for years to come, that is if it wishes to measure its strength against this new and rigorous textual awareness. Others may dismiss such claims or view them with frank alarm. What is clear already is that critics very largely out of sympathy with deconstruction have registered its impact and felt the need to argue their case with circumspect care. Denis Donoghue, for one, has taken issue with Derrida in his book *The Sovereign Ghost* (1976). Donoghue comes out, as one might expect, for the saving power of poetic presence – or 'imagination' – as against Derrida's supposedly nihilist assault on all such notions. Murray Krieger likewise, as a rearguard defender of the old New Criticism, challenges Derrida on the grounds that poetry partakes of a vitalizing presence that eludes the abysmal textuality of tropes (Krieger 1979).

Neither of these is an 'answer' to Derrida, in the sense of posing an obstacle to the activity of thought and the process of displacement that deconstruction has set in train. Both, on the other hand, bear witness to the unsettling power of Derrida's texts. Deconstruction has marked out a new domain of argument for the age-old quarrel between 'literature' and 'philosophy'. The claims of analysis have never been pressed so far as by conceptual rhetoricians like de Man. Nor has criticism ever taken on such courage, intellectual and stylistic, in asserting its claim as an autonomous and self-respecting discipline of thought. To ignore that claim is to close one's mind to something other, and more, than a short-lived swing of literary-critical fashion.

AFTERWORD (1991): FURTHER THOUGHTS ON DECONSTRUCTION, POSTMODERNISM AND THE POLITICS OF THEORY

In the ten-or-so years since I wrote this book, 'deconstruction' has reached out beyond the specialized enclave of a few elite academic institutions and become something of a buzzword among commentators on the postmodern cultural scene. It is a term that now comes readily to novelists, politicians, media pundits, pop journalists, TV presenters, newspaper columnists (up or down-market) and others with an eye to intellectual fashion or a taste for debunking such pretentious jargon. What they mostly have in mind (so far as one can tell) is a vague idea of 'deconstruction' as the kind of thing that academics typically get up to when they question commonsense truths and values that everyone else takes pretty much for granted. And when the word is applied with non-derisory intent – as by writers of a left-liberal persuasion or those with a more sophisticated readership in view – then it tends to mean simply 'criticism of received ideas', or (a slight improvement) 'thinking that systematically challenges consensus values from a sceptical, dissenting or oppositional standpoint'. But these usages all have one thing in common, namely their suggestion that a term like this, however arcane its origins, must be available for purposes – or adaptable to contexts – which require little or nothing in the way of 'specialized' critical grasp. Perhaps this explains the otherwise mysterious popularity of novels and TV serializations which are largely given over to the shop-talk of literary intellectuals, characters for whom 'deconstruction' figures (along with 'post-structuralism', 'postmodernism' and the rest) as an item of everyday casual parlance, one whose knowing deployment in the right situation can be relied upon to produce all manner of benefits, from academic tenure to erotic intrigue. And I had better admit – as this book goes into its second edition after a good many interim reprints – that similar factors may well be at work in the widespread demand for 'accessible' primers like the volume you are presently reading.

Meanwhile the word has enjoyed a comparable vogue among literary critics and those whose job it is to know what they think about the latest intellectual and cultural trends. Often it is used with a strongly negative connotation: thus 'deconstruct' = 'take things apart (literary texts, philosophical arguments, historical narratives, truth-claims or value-systems of whatever kind) in a spirit of game-playing nihilist abandon and without the least concern for constructing some better alternative'. On this view it is merely one more symptom of a deep-laid cultural malaise which no doubt set in during the 'permissive' 1960s and whose other manifestations include the breakdown of traditional moral values, the ascendance of fashionable relativist doctrines across various academic disciplines, and the concomitant desire among literary critics to revise the 'canon' of acknowledged great works for the sake of promoting their own pet ideological agenda. Or again, somewhat less prejudicially: 'to deconstruct', an ambivalent or middle-voice verb, one that hovers between the active sense 'to read texts with an eye sharply trained for contradictions, blind-spots, or moments of hitherto unlooked-for rhetorical complication' and the alternative (non-interventionist) account according to which it is always *the texts themselves* that undermine more traditional, naive ways of reading, so that criticism has only to keep track of this process – i.e., remain alert to the telltale signs of inbuilt textual resistance – and thereby demonstrate its non-complicity with an otherwise ubiquitous Western 'logocentrism' or 'metaphysics of presence', a mystique that runs (in Terry Eagleton's words) all the way 'from Plato to Nato'. As we have seen, it is difficult – maybe impossible – to decide between these two interpretations when faced with readings at the level of rhetorical complexity produced (or discovered) by adepts like Derrida and Paul de Man. But if one thing is certain it is the fact that these readings bear no resemblance to the popular idea of deconstruction as a species of out-and-out hermeneutic licence, a pretext for critics to indulge any kind of whimsical, free-wheeling or 'creative' commentary that happens to take their fancy.

All the same it strikes me now – coming back to this book with some measure of critical detachment – that I might have explained more exactly what I meant by distinguishing the 'rigorous' deconstructors (e.g. Derrida and de Man) from those others, Geoffrey Hartman among them, who practised what I called 'deconstruction on the wild side', and who showed little interest in following out its more philosophical implications. Several reviewers took issue with this line of argument and I can see why they found it less than satisfactory. For one thing, it left me in the awkward position of suggesting – or sometimes appearing to suggest – that Derrida's own productions could be seen as falling into two distinct categories, on the one hand writings (like *Speech and Phenomena* or the essays in *Margins of Philosophy*) that argued their case in a rigorously consequential manner, and on the other those texts – written mainly for a 'literary' readership – where he exploited all manner of stylistic or performative effects for the sake of deconstructing the type-cast distinction between 'literature' and 'philosophy', along with those between reason and rhetoric, concept and metaphor, literal and figural meaning, etc. For it hardly needs saying that one cannot get far with a work like Derrida's *Glas* – his extraordinary intertextual commentary on passages from Hegel and Genet – if one attempts to sort out the 'philosophical' content (i.e., those passages that engage *seriously* with Hegel's arguments, truth-claims, ethical values, historical theses, etc.) from another, flamboyantly 'textual' dimension where argumentative validity is beside the point, and where writing takes on the kind of freedom denied it by a long line of sternly disapproving philosophers, from Plato to the modern analytical school. My critics were surely right to point out that Derrida's whole enterprise was aimed squarely against the notion that philosophy somehow had access to truths — innate ideas, a priori concepts, primordial intuitions, structures of prelinguistic understanding or whatever — which could find no place in literary texts on account of their mimetic, metaphorical or fictive character. For it is precisely when his readings attain their highest degree of argumentative rigour and subtlety — as in essays like 'White Mythology', 'Plato's Pharmacy' and 'The Double Session' — that Derrida is most successful in drawing out that anomalous 'logic of the supplement' that inhabits philosophical discourse from the outset, and that makes it impossible finally to assert the truth-claims of philosophy over against the dissimulating wiles of rhetoric, literature, or writing. At any rate one would need to ignore a high proportion of Derrida's most significant work in order to make out a case for regarding him as first and foremost a 'philosopher' of rank and secondarily a writer or 'literary' stylist whose gifts in this direction — however striking or brilliant — shouldn't be allowed to obscure his primary achievement.

But having said all this I should still want to claim that we won't even begin to take the measure of that achievement unless we attend closely to Derrida's arguments and assess them, moreover, against the highest standards of philosophical accountability. For it is only on account of a longstanding prejudice — and one still current among many of Derrida's detractors — that the practice of an artful, allusive or 'literary' style is taken to be somehow incompatible with the interests of serious, truth-seeking thought. This prejudice assumes its most elaborate and systematic form in a work like Jürgen Habermas's The Philosophical Discourse of Modernity (trans. 1987), where Derrida is cast — along with various other 'postmodern' enemies of reason — as just another latter-day sophist, a skilful rhetorician whose literary gifts are placed in the service of a wholesale Nietzschean-irrationalist creed, a betrayal of that 'unfinished project of modernity' which Habermas regards as our last, best hope in an age of distorted mass-media values and inert consensus politics. Where Habermas goes wrong is in basing his account on a partial (often second-hand) acquaintance with Derrida's texts, and in taking it for granted — again on the strength of deconstructionist primers, my own (unfortunately) included — that the gist of those texts is to elevate rhetoric above reason, 'literature' above 'philosophy', and stylistic play above the serious business of thinking constructively about issues in the realms of epistemology, ethics and socio-political critique. What Habermas simply cannot entertain – for reasons connected with his analysis of the modern 'public sphere' of differential truth-claims, discursive practices, languages 'specialized' for the various purposes of argument, critique, normative value-judgment, aesthetic expression, etc. – is the notion that philosophy can *both* engage seriously with these issues *and* conduct its arguments in a style that on the face of it belongs more to 'literature' than to 'philosophy'. In fact, as I have argued at length elsewhere, Habermas is virtually predestined to misread Derrida in so far as he makes it a requirement for enlightened or emancipatory thought that criticism should respect this *de jure* separation of discursive regimes, and not allow itself to become mixed up with the poetic (or 'world-disclosive') function properly served by metaphorical or literary language (see Norris 1989a).

The same standing prejudice would appear to be at work in recent attacks on Derrida from within the broadly analytical tradition of Anglo-American thought. These include John Ellis's *Against Deconstruction*, a book which (quite properly) requires that deconstructors give cogent, articulate and logically accountable reasons for advancing their more controversial claims, but which also (quite wrongly) takes it as read – on the basis of a limited acquaintance with their texts – that no such arguments are forthcoming (see Ellis 1989). What is particularly irksome about these polemics is the fact that they engage only with isolated passages from Derrida taken out of context – or with the writings of 'literary' acolytes lacking Derrida's philosophical acumen – and then make this their platform for a wholesale dismissal of 'deconstruction' as a topic that scarcely warrants serious attention. Hence the importance, as I would still maintain, of respecting the distinctive philosophical valencies of Derrida's work, and not going along with the pseudo-deconstructive, pan-textualist or levelling view of philosophy as just another 'kind of writing', one where interpretation goes all the way down, where concepts invariably prove to be metaphors in disguise, and where rhetoric at last wins out in its age-old quarrel with the truth-claims of philosophic reason. For this would be to yield the main point at issue for critics like Habermas and Ellis. That is to say, it would effectively sidestep their charge that deconstruction is 'irrational', that it fails to respect the basic protocols of logic, argumentative consistency, enlightened discourse, etc., but only by means of an evasive tactic that leaves those criticisms firmly in place *from any but a counter-enlightenment or irrationalist standpoint*. And this tactic should satisfy nobody who has read at all extensively in Derrida's work, in particular those essays (early and late) where he engages the 'unthought axiomatics' of philosophers like Plato, Husserl and Austin, exposing their ideological blind-spots, their moments of complicity with a naive or pre-critical attitude, but doing so always – as I hope to have shown – with the utmost attentiveness to matters of argumentative detail and philosophical accountability.

I might have put the case more strongly in this book, as for instance by pressing further with Derrida's arguments – in his essay 'White Mythology' – about the strictly *undecidable* relation of priority between metaphor (or figural language in general) and the claims of philosophy, from Plato and Aristotle down, to delimit or contain the effects of such language by subjecting them to its own, more rigorous order of literal, self-evident truth. On the one hand Derrida follows Nietzsche *up to a point* in remarking how every last concept and category of Western philosophical thought – including the terms 'concept' and 'category' – can be traced back to some effect of sublimated metaphor, some figural expression whose root meaning philosophy must needs forget or repress if it is to keep up its own constitutive self-image as a discipline specialized for adjudicating issues of argumentative warrant, truth and falsehood, knowledge and belief, the intelligible *versus* the sensible, and – subsuming all these – its claim to determine the very 'conditions of possibility' for separating erroneous from 'clear and distinct' (or philosophically valid) ideas. For, as Derrida remarks, '[this] appeal to the criteria of clarity and obscurity would suffice to confirm . . . [that] the entire philosophical delimitation of metaphor already lends itself to be constructed and worked by "metaphors". How [otherwise] could a piece of knowledge or a language be properly clear or obscure?' (Derrida 1982, p. 252). And again, more generally: 'there is no properly philosophical category to qualify a certain number of tropes that have conditioned the so-called "fundamental", "structuring", "original" philosophical oppositions: they are so many "metaphors" that would constitute the rubrics of such a tropology, the words "turn" or "trope" or "metaphor" being no exception to this rule' (p. 229).

Among literary critics such passages have mostly been read as a knock-down argument against the truth-claims of philosophy. Or – more cynically – as a handy device for cutting the philosophers down to size by showing that their talk of reason, truth, *a priori* concepts and so forth was always just a species of self-deluding rhetoric, one that ignored all the lessons to be learned from a reading of Nietzsche or Derrida. But this argument unfortunately comes back like a boomerang, since Derrida's purpose in 'White Mythology' is precisely to *deny* that we could ever effect such a straightforward reversal of priorities, a turning of the tables on 'philosophy' (or reason) in the name of 'literature' (as commonly equated with metaphor, rhetoric, or style). For, quite simply, there is *no possibility* of discussing metaphor – or defining its attributes, its difference from 'literal' usage, or its problematic role within the texts of philosophy – without falling back on some *concept* of metaphor, a concept that will always have been 'worked' or elaborated in advance by the discourse of philosophic reason. Thus 'each time that a rhetoric defines metaphor, not only is *a* philosopy implied, but also a conceptual network in which philosophy *itself* has been constituted' (Derrida 1982, p. 230).

Hence the most difficult, or indeed (as Derrida sees it) the strictly undecidable question: 'can these defining tropes that are prior to all philosophical rhetoric and produce philosophemes still be called metaphors?' (p. 230). An affirmative answer, such as Nietzsche provides – at least on the reading of Nietzsche's texts most favoured by the adepts of 'literary' deconstruction – will then have to cope with the further problem of just what constitutes 'metaphorical' language, aside from the various theories, definitions and accounts of literal *versus* figural meaning produced by philosophers from Aristotle to the present day, and then taken up (with no matter what shifts of evaluative priority) by poets, rhetoricians or literary theorists who *necessarily* work with those same ubiquitous concepts and categories. But this doesn't mean that 'philosophy' has the last word, or that any such genealogical enquiry will always reach a point where some concept of metaphor – or generalized philosophy of rhetoric – will henceforth command the field. For it is still the case, as Derrida has shown, that 'the entire philosophical delimitation of metaphor lends itself to be constructed and worked by "metaphors" ' (p. 252). And this argument holds *as a matter of demonstrable fact,* i.e. on all the evidence drawn from the texts and privileged key-terms of philosophic discourse, despite the equally compelling argument that we cannot advance a single proposition on the nature and workings of metaphor without invoking categories that belong to the domain of philosophic reason.

Now it should be clear, even from this brief account, that Derrida's mode of argument in 'White Mythology' is very far from endorsing the vulgar-deconstructionist view that 'all concepts come down to metaphors in the end', or that philosophy is just another 'kind of writing', one that enjoys no distinctive status *vis-à-vis* literature, rhetoric, or the human sciences at large. On the contrary: what Derrida brings out with such exemplary force is the need to think these questions through with the utmost philosophical precision and care, even if – at the limit – they produce antinomies (or aporias) which cannot be resolved in one or the other direction. This point is made most emphatically in Derrida's recent (1989) 'Afterword' to his notorious debate with John Searle on the topic of Austinian speech-act philosophy, a debate that has occasioned widespread misunderstanding among philosophers and literary theorists alike. The standard line on this exchange – a line which the present volume doubtless did something to promote – was that the whole thing amounted to a slightly farcical (but instructive) breakdown of communications, a non-encounter where the two parties were arguing at cross-purposes. Thus Searle played the role of a typecast straight-man or earnest 'philosophical' seeker-after-truth, while Derrida (especially in *Limited Inc*, his near book-length rejoinder) elected to indulge in all manner of rhetorical games at Searle's expense, with the purpose of showing that speech-act theory self-deconstructed at precisely the point where it tried to distinguish *serious* (or authentic) from non-serious ('deviant' or 'parasitical') instances of speech-act performance. this account of the episode had harmful effects, it seems to me now, since it lent some credence to the prevalent view among Anglo-American philosophers (i.e., that Derrida was a tricksy rhetorician whom one needn't even bother to read, since his texts simply flouted all the protocols of 'serious' philosophical debate), while it also encouraged literary critics to adopt a blithely dismissive view of philosophy as a discourse still hung up on old problems which Derrida had now 'deconstructed' to such brilliant effect that they simply dropped out of sight. And this reading fitted in all too neatly with the reception-history of Derrida's work in North American academic circles, a history marked by the massive indifference (or uninformed hostility) evinced by most philosophers, and the equally massive (though not always much better informed) enthusiasm shown by disciples in departments of English or Comparative Literature.

In his 'Afterword: Toward an Ethic of Discussion' Derrida attempts to clear away some of the sources of confusion by insisting on four main points: (1) that his essay on Austin had revealed certain *crucial and logically inescapable* difficulties in the project of speech-act theory; (2) that Searle had *misread* Derrida's essay, and done so moreover for reasons bound up with his own proprietary interest in Austin's work; (3) that it is Searle, not Derrida, who plays fast and loose with 'philosophical' distinctions; and (4) that his own (Derrida's) reading of Austin is in fact more rigorous, more philosophically adequate, and more attentive to the nuances (including the moments of self-professed perplexity) in Austin's text than anything offered by Searle's more confidently orthodox account. Thus Searle perceives it as a central weakness in Derrida's argument that he tends to adopt a rigidly binary (either/or) mode of reasoning, so that speech-acts must be conceived *either* as falling under the truth/falsehood distinction *or* as wholly conventional, fictive or non-truth-conditional forms of utterance; that performatives are *either* intentional and sincerely-meant *or* simply products of this or that 'iterable' speech-act convention that excludes all reference to speaker's intentions; and again, that any appeal to contextual criteria — to the question of 'who says what, under what circumstances, and with what juridical or *de facto* warrant?' — will *either* settle the issue once and for all *or* leave it entirely unresolved, since one can always invent any number of imaginary or hypothetical contexts where this criterion just wouldn't work. Hence the major fallacy of Derrida's essay, as Searle sees it: that 'unless a distinction can be made rigorous and precise, it isn't really a distinction at all' (Searle 1977, p. 205).

Derrida's response is worth quoting at length since it goes clean against the idea of deconstruction as a sophistical exercise entirely unconcerned with issues of right reason or logical warrant.

> If Searle declares explicitly, seriously, literally that this axiom (i.e. the true/false distinction and its various speech-act correlatives) must be renounced ... then, short of practising deconstruction with some consistency and of submitting the very rules and regulations of his project to an explicit reworking, his entire philosophical discourse on speech-acts will collapse. ... To each word will have to be added 'a little', 'more or less', 'up to a certain point', 'rather', and despite all this, the literal will not cease to be somewhat metaphorical, 'mention' will not stop being tainted by 'use', the 'intentional' no less slightly 'unintentional', and so forth. Searle knows well that he neither can nor should go in this direction. He has never afforded himself the theoretical means of escaping conceptual opposition without empiricist confusion.
>
> (1989, p. 124)

One could hardly wish for a stronger statement of Derrida's unconditional adherence to those standards of argumentative rigour, consistency and truth which characterize the discourse of philosophy at its best, and which cannot be abandoned – or notionally 'deconstructed' – without giving up any claim to competence in the realm of philosophical debate. After all, as Derrida writes,

> What philosopher ever since there were philosophers, what logician since there were logicians, what theoretician ever renounced this axiom: in the order of concepts (since we are speaking of concepts and not of the colours of clouds or the taste of certain chewing gums), when a distinction cannot be rigorous and precise, it is not a distinction at all.
>
> (pp. 123–4)

This passage will most likely come as a surprise to readers – some present company no doubt included – who think of deconstruction as a project whose aim is always to subvert such value-laden binary oppositions as those between truth and falsehood, reason and rhetoric, fact and fiction, or philosophy and literature. Nor can it be said that they are entirely wrong in this belief, since after all – and despite the seeming disclaimers cited above – it is among the chief aims of Derrida's work to show that these distinctions always give rise to problematical, anomalous or marginal cases (as in Austin's texts) where *at the limit* such categories prove inadequate. But his argument against Searle still holds: that it is only by respecting the exigencies of philosophic thought right up to those limits that we are enabled to perceive the constitutive blind-spots, the moments of 'aporia' or undecidability which mark the point of philosophy's encounter with deep-laid problems in its own pre-history or 'unthought axiomatics'.

Over the last few years there have been welcome signs that philosophers (or literary theorists with an adequate grounding in philosophy) have started on the long overdue task of assessing Derrida's work in relation to thinkers like Kant, Fichte, Hegel, Husserl, Wittgenstein and Austin. My own subsequent books have been largely devoted to this same undertaking, especially in the area of present-day analytical philosophy, where despite the ritual show of hostilities (sadly typified by responses to the Derrida/Searle 'debate') there is much to be gained from an ecumenical approach that seeks out genuine points of contact while avoiding any kind of reductive or premature synthesis. All the same, one comes to feel − as Frank Kermode once remarked in a slightly different connection − like one who ventures out on to no-man's-land offering cigarettes as a good-willed gesture and then, for his pains, gets shot at by both sides. In this case the fire comes from several quarters, among them: (1) analytical philosophers who refuse to believe that serious thinking could ever be conducted in Derrida's 'extravagant' style, or arrive at such wildly counter-intuitive conclusions; (2) traditionalist literary critics who have no time for philosophy (or 'theory') of whatever kind; (3) literary deconstructors of a thoroughgoing 'textualist' persuasion who reject the idea that Derrida is in any sense engaged with 'philosophical' questions, or conceptual issues that lend themselves to treatment in the form of argued exposition and critique; and (4) postmodernists for whom 'deconstruction' is fine just so long as it doesn't make deluded claims of theoretical cogency and rigour. It would take more space than I have at my disposal here to offer even a half-way adequate response to each of these opposing viewpoints. Suffice it to say that objection (2) simply misses the mark, since Derrida is not in the business of producing traditional (interpretive) literary criticism, while objections (1) and (3) both take rise from the erroneous supposition that a due regard for the textual (or 'writerly') aspect of Derrida's work will necessarily preclude any attempt to make his arguments available for reasoned analysis and debate. In short, there is a curious convergence of views between 'analytical' opponents of Derrida who take him to be just a super-subtle rhetorician with nothing of serious import to communicate, and purist deconstructors who reject any notion that there might be *philosophical* arguments and truth-claims present in Derrida's texts.

So it is hardly surprising that the issue has stalled around a typecast set of traditional antagonisms – reason *versus* rhetoric, philosophy *versus* literature, etc. – which simply reproduce the inherited structures of a quarrel whose starting-point is Plato's case against the poets, sophists, professional rhetoricians and other such purveyors of a false (non-philosophical) wisdom. What most needs stressing in face of this absurdly polarized debate is that Derrida is *both* a writer or stylist of extraordinary power *and* a thinker whose work (or some of whose work: let me instance 'White Mythology' and the essays on Plato, Kant, Husserl and Austin) will bear comparison with the finest achievements of modern analytical philosophy. Of course this is a crude way of stating the issue since Derrida so effectively challenges the traditional viewpoint that would treat philosophy as somehow belonging to a realm of thought ideally exempt from the vagaries of rhetoric, writing or so-called literary 'style'. Such is indeed his chief objection to Searle's idea that one can extract a generalized theory of speech-acts from a text like Austin's *How To Do Things With Words*, a text that very often works to undermine its own categorical or systematic claims by coming up with all manner of linguistic evidence – jokes, quotations, anecdotes, literary allusions, odd turns of metaphor or idiomatic usage – which cannot be fitted into any such tidy scheme of things (see also Felman, 1983). But Derrida's point is certainly not to argue that we should therefore, in reading Austin, suspend all the usual (properly philosophical) criteria of truth and falsehood, logical rigour, consequential argument, etc., and henceforth treat his writings as belonging to a realm of generalized 'undecidability' where those standards can no longer be taken to possess the least relevance or critical force. On the contrary: the chief virtue of Austin's text is the fact that its keenest insights derive from a willingness to follow up the occasional abnormalities of 'ordinary language' while *at the same time* maintaining a scrupulous regard for the protocols of reasoned argument. Where Austin most strikingly resembles Derrida – and differs from Searle – is in not giving way to the systematizing drive (or the desire for an all-purpose explanatory paradigm) that would classify speech-acts as 'proper' or 'deviant', 'genuine' or 'parasitical', etc., in keeping with a preconceived normative model. And the same applies to Derrida's writings in so far as they operate simultaneously at two levels, that is to say, a performative (or 'writerly') level where philosophic truth-claims are constantly brought into question, and a level of none the less rigorous argument and critique where issues of validity (or truth and falsehood) are always inescapably raised, even if – as often happens – the emergent criteria for what counts as valid argument are complicated beyond any straightforward appeal to well-established procedural constraints. (See Staten 1984 for a treatment of Wittgenstein's linguistic philosophy that makes out a similar case for deconstruction as possessing its own, apparently wayward but in fact highly consequent logic.)

I have stressed this point mainly with a view to contesting the widespread (but erroneous) idea that deconstruction is basically just another variant of the current 'postmodernist' turn across various fashion-prone areas of thought. The adepts of this persuasion – Jean Baudrillard chief among them – argue that enlightenment is a thing of the past, that criticism (or theory) is likewise a dead or dying enterprise, and that henceforth there can be no question of separating truth from falsehood, knowledge from consensually warranted belief, socio-political reality from its ideological appearances, or other such time-honoured terms of distinction adumbrated by thinkers from Plato to Kant, Hegel, Marx, Husserl and Adorno. Elsewhere – as in the writing of 'post-analytical' philosophers like Richard Rorty – deconstruction has come to figure as a handy cover-term for everything that points beyond the old dispensation of reason, knowledge and truth; that is to say, the long-cherished but sadly deluded idea that philosophy could ever come up with adequate answers to a range of well-defined problems in the realms of ethics, epistemology, aesthetics, political theory, etc. Thus Derrida plays the role of an arch-debunker, a latter-day sophist or wily rhetorician whose special gift it is to dance rings around

those earnest seekers-after-truth – especially 'constructive' philosophical thinkers in the Kantian or present-day analytic tradition –
who still make believe that such problems exist, or that theirs is the
discipline best equipped to solve them.

Hence the title of Rorty's best-known essay on Derrida, 'Philosophy
as a Kind of Writing' (1978), where he urges that we give up thinking
of philosophy as in any sense a specialized activity of thought, an
activity (that is to say) with its own distinctive standards of rigour,
validity and truth. We should think of it rather as just another voice in
the ongoing cultural 'conversation of mankind', one that is always
liable to hog the conversation – to set up as a privileged truth-telling
discourse – but which can then most effectively be cut down to size by
a quick reminder, such as Derrida provides, that all its most basic
concepts and categories are in fact nothing more than optional items in
some purely contingent 'final vocabulary', some preferential idiom
with no genuine claim to get things right or (in Plato's phrase) to 'cut
nature at the joints'. From this point of view Derrida is just the latest
(though probably the most resourceful and ingenious) in a line of
'strong-revisionist' sceptics and dissenters which runs – broadly speaking – from the ancient Greek sophists, via 'scandalous' apostles of
unreason like Nietzsche, to current (postmodern or neo-pragmatist)
thinkers who have likewise perceived the delusive character of all such
philosophical truth-claims. In which case nothing could be more futile
– or less in keeping with the spirit of Derrida's work – than the attempt
to annex him to an outworn 'enlightenment' tradition that still finds
room for those otiose values of reason, truth and critique.

The reader can scarcely have failed to notice a very marked shift of
emphasis (or evaluative tone) from my basically approving discussion
of Rorty's essay in Chapter 7 to the above paragraph of less-than-
sympathetic summary exposition. What accounts for this shift is my
growing conviction, not only that Rorty has *got Derrida wrong* – misread
him in certain crucial respects – but also that one couldn't intelligibly
raise such questions (i.e., questions of interpretive validity and truth) if
the postmodern-pragmatist argument won out, if philosophy found
itself effectively demoted to just another 'kind of writing', and deconstruction took on its likewise sharply diminished role as a source of
rhetorical fun and games at philosophy's expense. Of course this puts

me in the position of needing arguments – philosophical arguments – with which to back up my case, unlike Rorty who remains true to his pragmatist lights in rejecting the idea that such differences could ever be settled by invoking criteria of right reason, interpretive truth, or fidelity to the text in hand. I have presented such arguments at length elsewhere (see for instance Norris 1989b) and Rorty has responded pretty much along the expected lines: why bother with all this talk of truth-claims, transcendental deductions, 'conditions of possibility', etc. when Derrida provides us with a welcome escape-route from those bad old Kantian habits of thought? (Rorty 1989b). I hope that the answer will have come across clearly enough from various sections of this book, in particular Chapter 5 (on 'the politics of deconstruction'), where I counterpose Marx and Nietzsche as the two great precursors of that widespread modern 'hermeneutics of suspicion' that questions all received currencies of knowledge, value and belief. But I am now more doubtful as to the purport of deconstructive arguments – like mine in that chapter – which score rhetorical points off some typecast 'theoretical' position (in this case Althusserian structuralist Marxism) by claiming to show how its whole apparatus of enabling concepts and categories rests on a covert tropological dimension or a series of sublimated metaphors. For there is no good reason to suppose that the manifest presence of figural elements in a piece of argumentative writing must in any way impugn its theoretical adequacy or undercut its philosophic truth-claims.

So Chapter 5 is where I would want to make the largest changes if this were a full-scale revision of the book in the light of subsequent developments. There is something to be said for the position arrived at in my penultimate sentence, i.e. that 'only by following through the logic of deconstruction, rather than meeting its challenge half-way, can thought escape this imprisonment by the metaphors of its own frozen discourse' (p. 69). But the closing flourish ('Nietzsche remains at the last a disturbing threat to the taken-for-granted rhetoric of Marxist theory') now strikes me not only as a somewhat facile triumphalist gesture but also as deriving from a false – or very partial – reading of Derrida's arguments in 'White Mythology' and elsewhere. For it is precisely his point in that essay that one has said nothing of interest on the topics of metaphor, writing and philosophy if one takes it as read (whether on Nietzsche's or Derrida's authority) that all concepts are a species of disguised metaphor, or that all philosophical truth-claims come down to a play of ungrounded figural tropes and displacements. What this reading necessarily leaves out of account is Derrida's further (and equally forceful) demonstration that every such thesis on the name and nature of metaphor is structured according to a set of strictly *philosophical* oppositions whose logic cannot be grasped – much less 'deconstructed' – by adopting the postmodern–pragmatist line and simply declaring them obsolete or redundant. Ten years on, it is easier to see how some passages of this book – including the elaborately staged 'confrontation' between Marx and Nietzsche – might have seemed to fit in with the emergent strain of anti-enlightenment (and specifically anti-Marxist) thinking that has lately enjoyed such a runaway success among politically jaded 'postmodern' intellectuals. (See Sloterdijk 1988 for a splendidly vigorous and well-documented account of how this cultural malaise took hold.)

Honesty – along with certain practical constraints – requires that I let those passages stand. But I should also want to point to other sections of the book, particularly those on Derrida's *Speech and Phenomena* and de Man's *Allegories of Reading*, where it is made very clear that deconstruction involves absolutely no slackening or suspension of the standards (logical consistency, conceptual rigour, modes of truth-conditional entailment, etc.) that properly determine what shall count as a genuine or valid philosophical argument. One major source of confusion here is the idea that deconstruction always makes appeal to some *other*, wholly unfamiliar (though indeed ubiquitous) species of textualist 'logic', an appeal whose upshot is supposedly to license all manner of wild interpretive games. Such would be the 'logic of supplementarity' which Derrida discovers everywhere at work in the texts of Rousseau, and which seems to controvert the express meaning of everything that Rousseau has to say about nature, culture, civil society, sexual politics, the origins of language and so forth. But in fact – as Derrida is at pains to point out – his reading is meticulously faithful not only to the details (including the 'marginal' details) of these various texts of Rousseau, but also to the order of *logical* necessity which constrains those texts to mean something other than Rousseau (or his mainstream exegetes) would manifestly wish them to mean. I wish that

I had cited the following passage, since it might have prevented some misunderstanding on the question of Derrida's supposedly extreme anti-intentionalist stance.

> This brings up the question of the usage of the word 'supplement', of Rousseau's situation within the language and the logic that assures to this word or this concept sufficiently *surprising* resources so that the presumed subject of the sentence might always say, through using the 'supplement', more, less, or something other than what he *would mean* [*voudrait dire*]. . . . The reading must always aim at a certain relationship, unperceived by the writer, between what he commands and what he does not command of the patterns of the language that he uses. . . . To produce this signifying structure obviously cannot consist of reproducing, by the effaced and respectful doubling of commentary, the conscious, voluntary, intentional relationship that the writer institutes in his relationship with the history to which he belongs thanks to the element of language. This moment of doubling commentary should no doubt have its place in a critical reading. To recognize and respect all its classical exigencies is not easy and requires all the instruments of traditional criticism. Without this recognition and this respect, critical production would risk developing in any direction at all and authorize itself to say almost anything. But this indispensable guardrail has always only *protected*, it has never *opened*, a reading.
>
> (Derrida 1977a, pp. 157–8)

That this is not just a piece of self-justifying argument but a claim repeatedly borne out in the reading of Derrida's texts will I hope be evident to anyone who has followed my book thus far. And the same applies to de Man's practice of hard-pressed rhetorical exegesis, an approach that may indeed produce many instances of heterodox or counter-intuitive argument – witness his readings of Rousseau, Nietzsche and Proust – but which none the less refers back *at every point* to specific details of the text in hand, and which never takes refuge in a generalized appeal to the non-availability of truth-values in criticism, the bankruptcy of classical reason, or the idea of rhetoric as an omnipresent dimension of language that makes it simply futile to invoke standards of argumentative rigour and consistency. In short, de Man's writings have nothing whatsoever in common with the kind of levelling neo-pragmatist view – espoused by thinkers like Rorty and Stanley Fish – which equates 'rhetoric' with language in its purely suasive or performative aspect, and which thus heads off any critical engagement with that other dimension of rhetoric (what de Man calls the 'epistemology of tropes') where reading can effectively go against the grain of a dominant interpretive consensus (see de Man 1986 and Norris 1988).

While I'm about it let me quote another crucial passage, this time from de Man, which may also do something to dispel false ideas of deconstruction as an all-licensing excuse for interpreters to make what they like of texts. For it is precisely Fish's argument – pursued in a number of brilliant set-piece essays – that if this is the case then interpretive conventions necessarily go all the way down, so that 'theory' is a pointless (or 'inconsequential') activity, and issues of right reading can only be settled on suasive-rhetorical grounds (Fish 1989). For de Man, on the contrary,

> reading is an argument . . . because it has to go against the grain of what one would want to happen in the name of what has to happen; this is the same as saying that reading is an epistemological event prior to being an ethical or aesthetic value. This does not mean that there can be a true reading, but that no reading is conceivable in which the question of its truth or falsehood is not primarily involved.
>
> (Preface to Jacobs 1978, p. xiii)

Taken together with Derrida's riposte to John Searle – and read (as I would hope) in conjunction with the texts where he and de Man make good these critical claims – such passages indicate something of the distance that separates deconstruction from other, more pliant or accommodating variants of the so-called 'postmodern condition'. Where this difference registers with maximum force is in currently fashionable talk of Marxism (or socialist politics in general) as yet another chapter in the failed project of 'enlightenment' thinking, a project wedded to obsolete values of *Ideologiekritik*, emancipation through the exercise of critical reason, or social progress as identified ultimately with 'truth at the end of enquiry'. That this book runs the risk of encouraging such talk through its setting-up of Nietzsche *versus* Marx as the ultimate deconstructive stand-off – or by sometimes appearing to suggest (like Rorty) that such issues come down to just a choice of rhetorical strategies or 'final vocabularies' – is my main reason for appending this postscript as a kind of *caveat lector*.

In part these reservations have to do with the changed political climate in Britain and North America over the past ten years. For this period has witnessed not only the emergence of a dominant right-wing consensus ideology at the levels of government policy-formation and public debate, but also a widespread failure of intellectual nerve on the left, signalled most clearly in the various forms of presumptively 'post-Marxist' theorizing that are now offered as the only way beyond the current 'crisis' of socialist values, a crisis brought on as much by events in Eastern Europe as by electoral trends nearer home. This book was written at a time when such changes were scarcely predictable, and when the left – although going through a pretty rough patch in prac-tical-political terms – could still lay claim to occupying the high ground of intellectual and cultural debate. Nowadays this situation has changed to the point where prominent 'left' commentators, writing in journals like *Marxism Today*, compete with each other in their willing-ness to dump all that old conceptual baggage ('base/superstructure', 'forces and relations of production', 'science/ideology', 'theoretical practice', etc.), and their zeal to embrace an alternative 'New Times' rhetoric that cheerfully acknowledges the chronic obsolescence of Marxist thought and the irrelevance of any *theoretical* project that would criticize currently prevailing consensus values. Hence (among other things) the present high vogue for postmodernist gurus like Baudril-lard who claim to have 'deconstructed' all those Marxist categories by showing that they amount to nothing more than a local variation on the old enlightenment paradigm, a set of imaginary distinctions – as for instance between 'use-value' and 'exchange-value' – which no longer make sense in an epoch when *all* values are determined *through and through* by the wildly fluctuating feedback mechanisms of advertis-ing rhetoric, mass-media simulation, opinion-polls, consumer market-research and so forth. From which point Baudrillard goes on to draw the now familiar Nietzschean lesson: i.e., that the entire prehistory of

Western philosophical thought – beginning with Plato's seminal oppositions between *doxa* and *episteme*, opinion and knowledge, artistic mimesis and the order of genuine (philosophical) truth – must henceforth be seen as just a series of self-promoting ruses in the service of a hegemonic will-to-power masquerading as pure, disinterested critical reason (Baudrillard 1988).

Thus it is no coincidence that the book in which Baudrillard first developed these arguments (*The Mirror of Production*, 1975) should bear a title that so closely resembles Rorty's *Philosophy and the Mirror of Nature*. For they are both engaged in this project of dismantling all the critical resources that have characterized the legacy of enlightenment thinking, whether in its Kantian (epistemological or ethical) mode or in the various forms of Marxist *Ideologiekritik* that acknowledge that legacy in so far as they claim to distinguish the 'real conditions' of social and political life from the realm of ideology, consensus-values, or taken-for-granted 'commonsense' belief. Of course – as Derrida would readily concede – there is no question of laying down stipulative limits on the usage of a term like 'deconstruction', criteria that would rule against its loose or promiscuous application to thinkers like Rorty, Baudrillard and other purveyors of a wholesale anti-enlightenment creed. But one should at least take note of passages like the following, again from his second-round response to Searle, where Derrida declares categorically that

> the value of truth (and all those values associated with it) is never contested or destroyed in my writings, but only reinscribed in more powerful, larger, more stratified contexts . . . and that within [those] contexts (that is, within relations of force that are always differential – for example, socio-political-institutional – but even beyond these determinations) that are relatively stable, sometimes apparently almost unshakable, it should be possible to invoke rules of competence, criteria of discussion and of consensus, good faith, lucidity, rigour, criticism, and pedagogy.
>
> (Derrida 1989, p. 146)

And one should also go back to essays like 'White Mythology' in order to see just how utterly *wrong* – or how resolutely partial and one-sided –

is the reading of Derrida (Rorty's reading) that takes him to have pretty much levelled the difference between concept and metaphor, philosophy and literature, or arguments respecting the above criteria and pseudo-arguments that mostly take rise from a simplified notion of 'rhetoric' that equates with language in its purely suasive or performative aspect. (In this connection, see also de Man's *Allegories of Reading* and *The Resistance to Theory*, texts that make a programmatic point of countering such reductive treatments of rhetoric, and which explain with great precision how rhetoric conceived as an 'epistemology of tropes' can itself put up a highly effective resistance to consensus-based models of textual understanding.) In short, deconstruction is *not* just one offshoot of a postmodern-pragmatist ethos whose chief desire is to get out from under all those old 'philosophical' concepts and categories.

Furthermore, this helps to show what is wrong with the idea of a deep-laid antagonism between Marxism and deconstruction, a hostility engendered – as this book rather tends to suggest – by the deconstructive drive to reduce all versions of the base/superstructure argument (or the notion of economic determination 'in the last instance') to so many sublimated tropes or metaphors, figures that claim a power of 'theoretical' explanation while in fact they rest entirely on concepts – like that of 'theory' itself – which can in turn be traced back to some effaced metaphor of visual or spatial perception. For it will be apparent to any attentive reader of 'White Mythology' that this essay conducts a running debate not only with the whole (post-Aristotelian) tradition of philosophy's attempts to come to terms with metaphor, but also with the Marxist (and Leninist) debate on questions of language, theory, representation, the modalities of knowledge and the status of dialectical-materialist thinking *vis-à-vis* the rival discourse of 'empirio-criticism' and its claim to scientific adequacy. What is more, these concerns relate back at every point to what Derrida has to say about metaphor and its place in the 'great immobile chain' of ontological theses and determinations descending from Aristotle's treatment of the topic, and requiring the utmost analytical vigilance if one hopes to do more than simply reproduce their implicit teleology and inbuilt self-valorizing logic. Nothing could be further from Baudrillard's *tout court* dismissal of philosophy and Marxism alike as mere episodes in a self-deluding history of thought whose final chapter is the dawning recognition that all concepts, truth-claims, categories of value, etc. come down to so many optional variants on an age-old (ultimately Platonist) delusion of epistemological grandeur.

Some readers will no doubt have realized by now that this 'Afterword' amounts to a summary rendition of arguments that have occupied my own writing in the period since *Deconstruction: Theory and Practice* first appeared. The political question has lately been given a sharper, more urgent focus by the discovery of Paul de Man's wartime journalism and the consequent debate – documented here in the latest (2002) supplementary bibliography – as to whether there exists anything describable as a 'politics of deconstruction' and, if so, how best to understand its bearing on those early and (as I would argue) utterly unrepresentative texts. But it is also a question that cannot be adequately dealt with aside from the issue of just how deconstruction relates to the long-term project of enlightenment critique and the fortunes of critical theory at a time of widespread disenchantment and 'postmodern' posturing on the intellectual left. And the first requirement here is that we not give credence to the idea of deconstruction as simply a more specialized, rhetorically sophisticated version of arguments that can also be found in the work of thinkers like Rorty, Baudrillard and Fish. It is largely on account of this erroneous idea that Searle can get away with his cavalier treatment of Derrida as a muddle-headed sophist or wilful perverter of speech-act theory, and also – even more regrettably – that Habermas can avoid any serious engagement with Derrida's texts by assimilating deconstruction to the currency of a Nietzschean irrationalist doctrine carried over into the discourse of postmodern – pragmatist thought.

Lest any doubt remain on this score let me cite one further passage from his rejoinder to Searle. 'The answer is simple enough', Derrida writes: 'this definition of the deconstructionist is *false* (that's right: false, not true) and feeble: it supposes a bad (that's right: bad, not good) and feeble reading of numerous texts, first of all mine, which therefore must finally be read or re-read' (Derrida 1989, p. 146). I can think of no better piece of advice for readers concerned to evaluate the various claims and counter-claims presented in this book.

POSTSCRIPT TO THE THIRD (2002) EDITION

I

Ten years ago I wrote an Afterword to the second edition which entered a few reservations and caveats with regard to the original (1982) text. Then came the suggestion that I write yet another post-script for this latest reissue offering some thoughts about the book, its reception-history, and various developments in the interim. This left me in something of a quandary since my thinking had now changed to the point where I didn't feel much inclined to undergo yet another bout of retrospective autocritique. That is to say, I had continued to write about deconstruction – in particular about Derrida and de Man – but from a standpoint that stressed the relevance of their work to issues in epistemology, philosophy of logic, and philosophical semantics rather than their impact on literary theory (Norris 1997a, 1997b, 2000a). Perhaps the wiser course would have been to go for a straight reprint in the hope that – given such a lapse of time – this wouldn't be taken to signal endorsement of whatever I had once written. On a quick read-through almost every sentence struck me as standing in need of revision or a footnote acknowledging the range of objections that rose up against it. But this would be to pile an absurd weight of significance onto what was, after all, a fairly basic deconstructionist primer written at a time when no such book had yet been published and when there did seem a useful job of work to be done in explicating some of these difficult texts for a readership mainly in departments of English and Comparative Literature.

This was at any rate the task assigned me by Terence Hawkes, the series editor, who made it very clear − when the first-draft typescript came in − that accessibility for students was the main thing and that I had better cut or rewrite any passages which didn't meet that require-ment. For the record: there is a nice example on p. 29 where I had written − lifting a phrase from Herbert Marcuse − that deconstruction involved 'a rigorous effort of conceptual desublimation'. Surely, Terry protested, there must be some way of making the point in decent, communicative English prose. Wouldn't the phrase 'waking up' do just as well? And so we hit on the perfect compromise: 'a rigorous effort of conceptual desublimation, or "waking up" '. I have no reason to doubt his editorial wisdom since the book has stayed in print for some two decades and now looks set for a fresh lease of life with this quarter-centennial *New Accents* relaunch. Besides, I am grateful to Terry for hav-ing trusted me to write it in the first place and for making more allowances than I (or he) probably realised during all those red-biro sessions in various pubs around Cardiff and Penarth. Also it would be a shame to spoil the party by not saying something to mark the event. So let me use this opportunity partly to reflect on more recent develop-ments and partly to offer the reader some advice on which bits of the book still provide what I take to be reliable commentary and which need treating with some degree of caution. Rather than append yet another supplementary bibliography − and thus make the textual apparatus even more top-heavy − I have decided to include paren-thetical references which are keyed to specific points of discussion and which readers can follow up if they wish *via* the list of 'Works Cited' at the end. Of course the sheer volume of relevant material published over the past ten years or so has prevented me from offering anything more than a selective and no doubt partial review. However I would hope that these references include (1) the most important of Derrida's texts to have appeared during that period; (2) the most significant of de Man's posthumously edited and published work; and (3) a good proportion of the 'secondary' literature on deconstruction which has a fair claim to present some original, provocative, or noteworthy contribution. Whether any of my own work merits that description is scarcely for me to say. Still I shall make some reference to it so as not to be accused of false modesty, along with reference to other sources where it comes in for hostile treatment, so as to appear invincibly fair-minded.

II

Jonathan Swift said somewhere that the time to pack up writing was when you read something that you had written x years ago and thought: 'that's good', or 'wish I could do that now!', or even 'not at all bad considering'. The last reaction is probably closest to what I feel now except that it implies a degree of complacency which Swift would surely have thought good reason not to provide yet another piece of oblique self-advertisement under the guise of honest self-reckoning. For those old-fashioned types who begin at the beginning and read right through to the end this will perhaps conjure memories of what I have to say in Chapter Six about Paul de Man on the ambivalent rhetoric of Rousseau's *Confessions*. According to de Man – who perhaps had reasons of his own for wishing to complicate matters – such narratives always turn out to exculpate the confessor and thereby provide a pre-text or excuse for some fine display of worked-up retrospective guilt. This is an extreme version of the cynical case which holds that *qui s'accuse, s'excuse*, or that anyone who owns up to past faults must be doing so mainly for the sake of appearing all the better (more courage-ous and un-self-deluding) for their willingness to make a clean breast of things (de Graef 1993; Norris 1998). Still it should give pause to anyone – like myself – who is tempted to exploit an occasion like this for claiming some new-found critical or moral 'insight' into their own earlier 'blindness'. On the other hand there is something highly implausible – as well as deeply depressing – in the de Manian idea that any such claim can only be yet another symptom of moral bad faith or a failure to see how the act of confessing to past faults, lapses, derelic-tions of intellectual conscience and so forth can amount to nothing more than a covert strategy for grabbing the moral high ground.

Not that I feel anything like so bad about this book and its various shortcomings as de Man must have felt about his memories of those now notorious articles he wrote for a Belgian newspaper during the years of Nazi occupation. (See de Man, 1989; Hamacher, Hertz and Keenan [eds.], 1989.) Of course the storm over de Man's 'collaboration' had not yet blown up when this book first appeared and so I was able to discuss his essays on Rousseau, Rilke, Yeats and others without taking on the difficult issue as to whether – or just how far – those essays should be read as a kind of tortuously disguised apologia for his own self-evasions and failure to acknowledge the plain facts of the case. There was much pious huffing and puffing by (mainly US) commentators who took this episode as a platform for advancing their blanket view of deconstruction as a nihilist enterprise bent upon covering the tracks of wartime collaborators (e.g., Hirsch 1991; Kimball 1990; Lehman 1991). The crudity of these 'readings' showed up in a much worse light than some of the often super-subtle attempts by de Man's colleagues and disciples to read between the lines and make out a case for his having preempted and obliquely resisted the 'vulgar' interpretation (Cohen, Cohen, Miller and Warminski [eds.], 2001). All the same it now strikes me that in 1982 I was much too ready to go along with the de Manian rhetoric of 'undecidability' and the idea that deconstruction had blocked any appeal to such naively 'positivist' notions as truth, fact, historical evidence, or present accountability for past actions, including such actions as having written certain texts in a certain set of historical and socio-political circumstances. To the extent that deconstruction has been taken by some as lending added 'philosophical' credence to this broader postmodernist trend – not to mention its unholy alliance with various forms of revisionist (mostly right-wing) historiography – I should now very firmly wish to disown any passages in this book that might have encouraged such a reading (Mehlman 1995). Chapters Four and Five (on the Nietzschean connection and the idea of rhetoric as 'deconstructing' such values as truth and critique) are the parts that would come in for heaviest revision. But, again, that would make it a different book altogether and go well beyond the publisher's brief for admissible changes and corrections. So I had better just hope that interested readers will have time to look up my later publications on Derrida and de Man and see what I have to say there concerning the issue of deconstruction and its complex relationship to the values of truth, critique, and the 'unfinished project of modernity' (Norris 1987b, 1990, 2000b).

In particular I should want to contest the claim of certain 'literary' deconstructionists – as well as postmodernists, 'strong' textualists, and advocates of a 'post-philosophical' culture – that the best thing about Derrida's work is its having so usefully pointed a way beyond those same enlightenment values. On this view – epitomised by Richard Rorty in the title of his essay 'Philosophy as a Kind of Writing' – we should take Derrida with a large pinch of ironic postmodernist salt when he goes on about *différance*-with-an-a, logocentrism, the Western 'metaphysics of presence', and suchlike deconstructive variants on the old idea of philosophy as a quest for ultimate (albeit in this case ineffable) truths (Rorty 1982; also 1989 and 1991). The same applies to earnest exegetes of Derrida like myself and Rodolphe Gasché who deludedly suppose that Derrida is in the business of providing philosophical *arguments*, or that he has somehow 'radicalised' the project of philosophy by showing that it generates conceptual problems beyond its own power to contain or comprehend (Gasché 1986, 1994). Maybe it is the case – Rorty concedes – that Derrida was himself once subject to this same unfortunate delusion, as for instance in his early work on Husserl and his *echt*-deconstructionist yet minutely analytic and (no doubt 'in its own way') distinctly *philosophical* body of writing on Plato, Aristotle, Rousseau, Kant, Hegel, Husserl, and others. That is to say, these texts can plausibly be read by commentators like Gasché as involving the deployment of 'quasi-transcendental' modes of reasoning, arguments which carry on the Kantian project of enlightened critique while also (very much in the same spirit) questioning that project with regard to its own values, presuppositions, or 'unthought axiomatics'. However this is just the aspect of Derrida's work which Rorty thinks we should ignore or pass over in tactful silence since it shows him regrettably falling back into habits of thought which he more than anyone can help us to escape. Rather we should view him as playing 'bad cousin Derrida' to 'honest old uncle Kant' and as making the point – in his later texts – that philosophy is indeed a 'kind of writing', one that can exploit the full range of literary tricks (fictive scenarios, apocryphal references, intertextual allusions, 'accurate' quotations though taken wildly out of context, etc.) in order to shake off its false self-image as a privileged discourse of reason and truth. So if we want to carry on reading 'early' Derrida then we had much better do so in the spirit of postmodern ironists who have picked up a lesson or two from 'late' Derrida, instead of supposing (like Gasché and Norris) that the late texts only make any kind of sense if one treats them as performative elaborations of themes first broached – to more convincing effect – in the work of Derrida's early period.

I shall not belabour this difference of views any further since I discussed it briefly in the 1991 'Afterword' and have aired my disagreements with Rorty at greater length elsewhere (Norris 1997b, 2000b). Still, it offers a useful way into some of the more significant debates in and around deconstruction over the past decade-or-so. What has chiefly marked those debates is a widening rift between the 'literary', textualist or postmodern take on Derrida's work and other approaches which – with whatever critical reservations – emphasise its relevance to issues in metaphysics, ontology, epistemology, and philosophy of mind and language. (See for instance Cavell 1995; Cumming 1991; Evans 1991; Garver and Seung-Chong 1994; Johnson 1993; Lawlor 1992; Lawlor [ed.] 1994; McKenna and Evans [eds.] 1995; Wheeler 2000; Wihl 1994; Wood 1991; Wood [ed.] 1992.) Some critics and reviewers of this book – purist deconstructors – took me to task for naively supposing that any such distinction could be drawn, or that philosophy could any longer lay claim to distinctive criteria of truth, validity, or adequate conceptual warrant (Bennington 1994). Still less could it be thought – by anyone who had read Derrida aright – that there existed certain logical constraints on what properly counted as a valid argument apart from the various textual manifestations that most often turned out (on his reading) to involve complications beyond the grasp of any classical logic grounded in the principles of identity, non-contradiction, and excluded middle. (Thus: 'x = x', 'not x and not-x', and 'either x or not-x'.) After all, was it not the whole *point* of deconstruction to problematise the logocentric claim of philosophers from Plato down that reason and logic enjoyed a rightful privilege over literature, rhetoric, and the duplicitous arts of language? (Burgass 1991; Caputo 1998; Nealon 1993; Royle 1995; Wolfreys 1998). Whence the idea – still put about by a good many hostile and some more admiring commentators – that Derrida's chief desire is to turn this ancient prejudice around by playing all manner of irreverent games with the texts of the great dead (plus a few living) philosophers. Anyway, as I have said, the book came in for some solemn tut-tutting and high-toned disapproval on the part of Derridean acolytes who thought it symptomatic of my failure to grasp the most basic principles of deconstruction that I should have carried on using (not just 'mentioning' or 'citing') such surely discredited binary oppositions as concept/metaphor, reason/rhetoric, or philosophy/literature. Indeed – as one reviewer was at pains to point out – the list of my errors would have to start with the book's subtitle 'theory and practice' which any self-respecting deconstructionist ought to have spotted a mile off.

At the time I blushed to read this review and resolved never to lay myself open to any such criticism in future. Then – a few years later – it struck me that this was just another kind of self-styled 'radical' but in truth thoroughly orthodox stance which had laid Derrida's texts wide open to assimilation on the terms laid down by a host of postmodern-textualist epigoni. For anyone who might be interested, this realisation occurred between *The Deconstructive Turn* (1983) where I pushed pretty hard on the textualist line as applied to Plato, Descartes, Frege, Wittgenstein, and Austin, and *The Contest of Faculties* (1985) where I argued against any such idea that philosophy could properly or adequately be treated as just another 'kind of writing'. By then I had come think of the present book as yielding too much ground to the textualists and not coming out strongly enough against the nascent postmodernist trend. On the other hand, re-reading it now, I did take a firm – some would say an overly dogmatic – line on the need to distinguish Derrida's more 'rigorous' deconstructive readings from the kinds of wholesale hermeneutic licence claimed by some of his (mainly American) literary-critical followers. Geoffrey Hartman entered a mild complaint on this score when he found himself corralled together with J. Hillis Miller as a practitioner of deconstruction 'on the wild side', or one who enlisted Derrida's support for a mode of free-wheeling textual exegesis which blithely disregarded all such normative constraints (Hartman 1985). Let me take this belated opportunity to acknowledge Hartman's point since there is no reason why literary critics of a strongly 'hermeneutic' or revisionist bent should be subject to the same criteria that apply when deconstruction engages philosophical issues on avowedly philosophic terms. However the Rortian-textualist line is amply refuted by a careful attention to Derrida's actual procedures of close-reading as distinct from those occasional pronouncements – taken out of context – which might appear to support it. I am glad to report that my book makes a fairly good job of expounding Derrida's 'logic of supplementarity' in a way that respects the ground-rules of logical thought – as Derrida does – even while showing how they come under strain in texts such as Plato's *Phaedrus*, Rousseau's *Essay on the Origin of Language*, Husserl's *Origin of Geometry*, or Saussure's *Course in General Linguistics*. That is to say, Derrida nowhere denies (and indeed goes out of his way to affirm) that we have to think in accordance with classical logic if we are not only to make adequate sense of those texts but also to locate the symptomatic stress-points – the moments of *aporia* or logical tension – where such thinking meets its limit. (See especially Derrida 1988a; Farrell 1988; Norris 2000a; Priest 1994; Wheeler 2000.)

III

I do wish now that I had devoted more space to those essays in *Margins of Philosophy* – especially 'The Supplement of Copula' – where Derrida comes out most explicitly against the idea that linguistics 'precedes' philosophy, or that the forms of accredited logical reasoning are nothing more than the forms bequeathed by a certain linguistic pattern (that of the subject-predicate structure) inherited from the ancient Greek (Norris 1997a). I should also have made it much clearer that when Derrida 'deconstructs' the received order of priority between concept and metaphor – as in the essay 'White Mythology' – he is careful to insist that such analysis can proceed only by means of certain basic *philosophical* distinctions and logico-conceptual resources which find their most elaborate and rigorous treatment in the work of philosophers from Aristotle to the present. (Cf. Harrison 1999; Lawlor 1991; Morris 1991; Norris 2000a.) Thus there are parts of this book – especially Chapter Four, 'Nietzsche: philosophy and deconstruction' – which fall in too readily with the postmodern-textualist idea that 'all concepts are metaphors', 'all philosophy a "kind of writing"', and so forth. Elsewhere

I am too keen on promoting the notion that a rhetorical close-reading of philosophic texts in the deconstructionist mode is sure to produce just the kinds of irascible response manifested by philosophers like John Searle since it shows up their blind-spots of 'logocentric' prejudice and failure to read with sufficient alertness to details of the text that don't fit in with their orthodox preconceptions. There is some truth in this where Searle is concerned but it scarcely does justice to those other philosophers of a broadly 'analytic' allegiance who have shown more willingness to engage seriously with Derrida's work and its bearing on their own fields of interest. (See for instance Cumming 1991; McDonald 1990; Morris 2000; Warner 1989; Wheeler 2000).

By 1991 ('Afterword' to the second edition) I was already inclining to think that the infamous Derrida/Searle exchange was a *dialogue des sourdes* which had done great damage to the prospects for better understanding across the two philosophical traditions. That I made so much of it in 1982 must have signalled a certain mischievous desire *pour epater les philosophes*, along with the more respectable aim of challenging certain fixed preconceptions where these have the effect – as with Searle on Austin – of enforcing a narrowly prescriptive view of what texts must or *should* be taken to mean according to orthodox fiat. Still if I were now re-writing this book from scratch it would contain less scandal-mongering rhetoric – less talk of deconstruction as a 'standing affront' to the norms of 'conventional' philosophic discourse – and more efforts to negotiate common ground between the two (roughly speaking: post-Kantian mainland-European and post-Fregean Anglophone analytic) traditions of thought. I suppose this reflects my 'institutional' position at the time as a literary theorist with strong philosophical interests who wanted to stake the claim for deconstruction as a new way of reading philosophic texts with potentially transformative implications. There was also a keen sense among literary theorists – a sense well caught by the earlier (pre-1990) 'New Accents' volumes – that existing disciplinary demarcations were very much open to challenge and that literary theory was the cutting-edge 'discourse' best equipped to mount such a challenge. Having since – ten years ago – moved across into the Philosophy Section at Cardiff I am now less inclined to adopt this adversarial stance and keener to emphasise the relevance of

Derrida's work to the kinds of issue that typically preoccupy philosophers of language and logic.

Thus it seems to me a very welcome development that writers on the topic of deviant, many-valued, or 'paraconsistent' logics – among them most notably Graham Priest – are now turning their attention to Derrida's writings on the 'logic of supplementarity' (Rousseau, Saussure, Lévi-Strauss), of *différance* (Husserl), or of 'parergonality' (Kant's Third Critique). (See especially Priest 1994, 1995; also Norris 2000a.) This in turn goes along with a wider shift from the idea of deconstruction as a vaguely 'philosophical' sub-branch of literary theory to the idea of it as squarely and centrally concerned with questions that are – or that ought to be – of interest to philosophers on both sides of the (so-called) 'continental'/'analytic' rift. To some extent, no doubt, this change in its institutional fortunes has to do with the notoriously fashion-prone nature of literary theory and the fact that deconstruction no longer enjoys the kind of high-profile academic success in mainly US departments of English and Comparative Literature that it acquired (perhaps luckily for me) soon after this book first appeared (Lotringer and Cohen [eds.] 2001.) The story has been told often enough elsewhere and has to do with the rise of other movements – New Historicism, Cultural Materialism, Feminism, Gender Studies, Gay and Lesbian Criticism, Post-Colonial Theory – all of which acknowledge some debt to deconstruction while each of them claims to be primarily engaged with matters of more pressing socio-political concern. (See especially Elam 1994; Deutscher 1997; Feder, Rawlinson and Zakin [eds.] 1997; Holland [ed.] 1997; Madison [ed.] 1993; Martin 1992; also – for a broader conspectus – Selden [ed.] 1995; Knellwolf and Norris [eds.] 2001). Thus deconstruction most often figures as a taken-for-granted thesis concerning the value-laden nature of certain binary terms (such as text/context, male/female, 'high' *versus* 'low' literary culture, 'normal' *versus* 'deviant' sexuality, or the colonial 'centre' as opposed to the 'margins') which are then subject to strategic reversal through a reading which stresses their inherent instability or self-subverting character. Hence the tendency for 'deconstruction' to turn up in the sub-title of books by prominent cultural theorists who pretty much assume that its claims no longer stand in need of detailed justification.

I should not for one moment wish to deny that this has been among the most significant and positive legacies of deconstruction. After all, it is one to which Derrida has been closely allied, not only through providing some of its basic conceptual resources but also – more recently – as a matter of explicit and often passionate commitment to gender equality, international justice, and human rights (especially those of refugees or asylum-seekers) in the context of present-day world political events. However it is sometimes hard to make out what exactly the relationship is between the kinds of close-focused deconstructive reading that occupied most of his 'early' work – as discussed in the foregoing pages – and the wholly admirable stance that he has taken on these ethical or socio-political issues. This applies, for instance, to his book *The Other Heading* (1992b) where Derrida discusses the prospects for a European community founded on equal respect for the values of cultural autonomy and wider federal allegiance; or his essay 'Force of Law' (1990) which proposes the idea of justice as inherently transcending any given set of legal provisions or enactments; or his reflections on friendship and hospitality as alternative (non-contractualist) modes of ethical being-with-others (1997a, 1997b, 1998); or again, his recent long-awaited *rapprochement* with 'a certain' Marxism, one that abjures any 'vulgar'-Marxist conception of actual progress toward some realisable goal but which instead holds out for the indefinite promise of that which by very definition eludes all possible attempts to achieve it (Derrida 1994; also Sprinker [ed.] 1999). I should add that these texts are immensely subtle and often powerfully evocative, as well as conveying a keen sense of moral outrage at the glib pronouncements of postmodern adepts and celebrants of the 'New World Order' – Francis Fukuyama (1992) chief among them – who blithely ignore all the day-to-day evidence of human misery and suffering on a massive scale brought about by the World Bank, the IMF and other instruments of Western (mainly US) economic and geo-political strategy. There is no doubt that Derrida is committed to exposing and resisting the kinds of rhetoric that would mask this drive for global domination through facile talk about the 'end of ideology', the 'end of history', or capitalism and liberal democracy (US-style) as our last, best hope for worldwide stability and peace. Still it is hard to see how such resistance could be mustered when the alternatives are sketched in so elusive a way as to place them in a realm of unredeemable promise – a realm of 'weak messianic' thought – whose very nature is such as to prevent their being specified in terms of practical action toward definite political ends.

This problem emerges most strikingly, I think, in Derrida's now-famous cryptic pronouncement that 'justice' (or the idea of justice) is 'not deconstructible', since it stands altogether above and beyond those various legal codes, sanctions, statutes, case-law precedents and so forth which apply in any given politico-juridical context (Derrida 1990). These latter may indeed be 'deconstructed' through the kind of analysis – lately much in vogue among critical legal theorists – which fastens on their various anomalies, aporias, performative contradictions, and suchlike failures to achieve that same (strictly unachievable) ideal. (For a critical survey of the field see Norris 1988b; also Kramer 1991.) Now granted there is a sense – a distinctly Kantian sense – in which justice is not so much a *determinate concept* as a *regulative idea*, that is to say, not something (a set of institutions, legal codes, or ethico-juridical provisions) that could actually be brought about through some massive reform to our existing practices and thereafter provide a practical embodiment of the highest moral and civic virtues. Rather it is that to which we aspire – individually and collectively – while acknowledging its unattainability in practice and also the fact that it cannot be gainsaid or rendered historically obsolete by the melancholy record of failures and setbacks to date. I have written at length elsewhere about these socio-political and ethico-juridical themes in 'late' Derrida so will not pursue them in any great detail here (Norris 2000b). Where the problem arises – once again – is with their tendency to take on a quasi-mystical tone, as in his idea of justice as a strictly ineffable non-concept that eludes all our efforts to define (let alone deconstruct) it, or of Marxism – since the events of 1989 – as a 'promise' of (unspecified) better things to come whose redemptive virtue could only be betrayed through the vulgar desire to say what such a promise amounts to in practical-political terms.

IV

Having said all this I should nonetheless acknowledge that there is now a large body of writing on the ethics (and the politics) of deconstruction and that other commentators clearly don't share my sense of unease. (See for instance Baker 1995; Bernasconi 1998; Bernstein 1987; Caputo 1993; Patrick 1997; Perpich 1998; Postone 1998.) This debate is often focused on Derrida's lengthy dialogue – going right back to his 1957 essay 'Violence and Metaphysics' – with Emmanuel Levinas, a Jewish-Lithuanian thinker for whom ethics was 'first philosophy' and who maintained that the history of Western thought had been largely devoted to concealing or evading that primordial truth (Derrida 1978 [first published 1957] and 1991a; Levinas 1969, 1981; also Critchley 1992 and 1999; Perpich 1998; Raffoul 1998). That my book contains no mention of Levinas – even in the second-edition 'Afterword' – is a fact that many readers will find distinctly odd and which others, more familiar with the recent literature, will take as dating it beyond hope of redemption. Here again I could wish that I *had* included some discussion of 'Violence and Metaphysics', not least because that essay is – among other things – a *critique* of Levinasian ethics which questions the idea of the ethical relation as somehow bringing us face-to-face with 'absolute alterity', that is, with the intransigent demand upon us of an Other who (for all that we can know) has nothing in common with ourselves. Thus, for Levinas, ethics *precedes and invalidates* the entire project of epistemology, the latter conceived as a purely 'egological' (first-person-centred) quest for grounds of certainty, knowledge, or truth. This tradition he sees as running all the way from Plato and Aristotle to Descartes, Kant, and (most recently) Husserl, a thinker who – according to Levinas – devoted his entire life's work to shoring up those same delusive epistemological foundations. What we should rather acknowledge is the bankruptcy of all such thinking and the need to lay ourselves open to an ethical encounter – a naked confrontation with the 'face' of the absolute other – which shakes our every last source of epistemological assurance. (See also Bernasconi and Critchley [eds.] 1991; Bernasconi and Wood [eds.] 1988.)

This claim seems to me – as it once seemed to Derrida – philosophically incoherent and based on a highly questionable reading of the various thinkers (Husserl in particular) whom Levinas 'violently' calls to account for their failure to meet the ethical challenge. Indeed Derrida's early (1957) essay goes a long and complex way around in establishing (1) that my relation to the other *cannot but* take place through some mediating reference to my own experience, physical embodiment, perceptual modalities, and way of being-in-the-world; (2) that Husserl *does* have much to say – especially in his Fifth *Cartesian Meditation* – with respect to the self-other relation and the intersubjective dimension of phenomenological enquiry; and (3) that Levinas, by founding ethics on the idea of 'absolute alterity', is in danger of denying those elementary ties of reciprocal trust and mutual obligation which alone offer some hope of achieving peaceful coexistence despite and across certain otherwise intractable conflicts of ethnic, religious, or political allegiance. (See also Norris 1994.) So perhaps it is not surprising that writers – such as Critchley (1992) – who urge that deconstruction is an ultimately ethical enterprise and, moreover, who see Levinasian ethics as its end-point and justification should have had rather little to say about Derrida's various doubts and misgivings as raised in that early essay. Rather they focus on more recent texts where Derrida largely abandons his critical stance and endorses the Levinasian idea of ethics as involving a relationship (but how? one is surely entitled to ask) with the 'absolute other' or that which transcends our utmost capacities of mutual understanding or reciprocal give-and-take (Derrida 1991a, 1997b). In 'Violence and Metaphysics' Derrida talks about the other as an *alter ego*, one whose alterity I can claim to respect while nonetheless conserving a sense of our common humanity, that is, a sense of what makes him or her – recognisably – a human being like myself. However this idea counts for nothing from the standpoint of an ethics that raises 'otherness' to a high point of abstract principle and which thereby excludes any possible appeal to such modes of intersubjective understanding.

Critchley and others arrive at this position through the idea that there must be something more to deconstruction than the negative rhetoric of 'différance', 'aporia', 'undecidability', and so forth that typified Derrida's early writing on the texts of philosophy from Plato to Husserl. If so, then it requires an ethical leap of faith which acknowledges the closure of (so-called) 'Western metaphysics' and which brings us to confront what lies altogether outside and beyond those inherited concepts and categories. Hence Derrida's recent interest in Kierkegaard as a thinker who pushed this idea to the limit – in a text like *Fear and Trembling* – by treating the moment of ethical decision (Abraham's willingness to sacrifice his son at God's inscrutable behest) as one that required a total rejection of all merely human ties, values, and moral obligations (Derrida 1993a; Kierkegaard 1954). Indeed Kierkegaard insists that this is the only adequate (i.e., authentically Christian) way to interpret the story, and that exegetes are simply missing the point – betraying their own lack of faith – when they offer some alternative, more humanly 'acceptable' gloss, such as God's having always intended to contrive a last-minute reprieve for Isaac, or Abraham's somehow having known all along that God would not require him to go through with so dreadful an act. On the contrary, he argues: what the tale brings home to anyone capable of reading it aright is the sheer *impossibility* of justifying God's ways to man, or the absolute gulf that exists between human ethical values (including those which comport well enough with the kind of respectable, Sunday-best religion that Kierkegaard despised) and the dictates of authentic Christian faith.

Now there are – to be sure – many reasons why Derrida should be fascinated by Kierkegaard's writings. Among them one might instance his use of multiple pseudonymous personae, of endlessly shifting narrative viewpoints, of repetition (cf. Derrida's 'iterability') as a key deconstructive trope, or of irony carried to the limits (and beyond) of assignable author's intent. Yet the one notable reference to Kierkegaard in Derrida's earlier work is a passage in 'Violence and Metaphysics' where he remarks on the disturbing resemblance between Levinasian ethics and Kierkegaard's conception of Christian faith as requiring a moment of ultimate existential choice which transcends (and invalidates) all merely secular notions of ethical accountability (Derrida 1978). It seems to me that Derrida was right about this and that the last thing we want when trying to think straight about moral and sociopolitical issues is some notion of a leap outside and beyond the value-sphere of shared human concerns. To put it plainly: *Fear and Trembling* is a morally repulsive text which could be taken to justify any amount of inhuman or barbarous conduct on the basis of a self-justifying appeal to religious or other transcendent sources of 'authentic' inward faith. Moreover there is the fact of Heidegger's having deployed just such a rhetoric in order to place his thinking at the service of an 'authentic' commitment to the cultural politics of National Socialism and the 'self-affirmation' of the German University in response to that epochal challenge. (See Wolin [ed.] 1993). There is no room here for an adequate discussion of Derrida's lengthy and complex engagement with the issue of Heidegger's politics in relation to his wider philosophical project, early and late. Sufficient to say that this engagement has been marked by some highly subtle argumentation and by a typically generous willingness, on Derrida's part, to make the very best of a bad case (Derrida 1989). All the same there is more than a hint of special pleading about the notion that Heidegger's period of forthright Nazi allegiance during the mid-to-late 1930s can be explained symptomatically by his using the word *Geist* (= 'spirit') with a full commitment to its range of metaphysical, political, and 'national-aestheticist' meanings rather than his merely 'citing' it or placing it 'under erasure' as was the case (so Derrida contends) in Heidegger's earlier and later texts. Nor is this argument for the defence much helped by those who interpret the 'ethics of deconstruction' as a matter of confronting some strictly undecidable choice between alternative courses of action and thus being forced to 'decide' at the limit through a Kierkegaardian leap of faith beyond any kind of reasoned ethical justification. For it would then be a decision taken in the absence of humanitarian concerns and in response to the call of an 'authentic' conscience whose virtue lay precisely in its paying no heed to such concerns.

There is a passage of somewhat inscrutable irony in Derrida's text *Aporias* where he remarks that even the choice to feed one's cat every morning involves the decision to feed just *that single* cat rather than all the other cats, near and far, that might be equally or more in need of sustenance (Derrida 1993a). Well yes, one is apt to say: it is painful to think about all those starving cats, and even more so to reflect – as Derrida does in some eloquent passages elsewhere – on the degree of unnecessary human suffering, misery and injustice that is caused, very often, by political and socio-economic arrangements which one can and should protest without being able to do much about them in immediate practical terms. Still there is a fairly obvious sense in which one had much better feed one's own cat and those within feeding distance rather than remain constantly suspended in an agony of existential choice or take some decision in the absence of justifying grounds. In Heidegger's case that decision might well have involved his idea that animals were *Weltarm*, i.e., that they were 'poor' (existentially deprived) in respect of the 'world' that human beings uniquely inhabit through their capacity to raise fundamental questions about their own (authentic or inauthentic) mode of existence. So perhaps times were tough for any stray cats around Heidegger's isolated Black Forest retreat. I should perhaps point out – lest these comments appear merely flippant or obtuse – that Derrida has written at length about this aspect of Heidegger's thinking and suggested (albeit obliquely) that it may connect with his dangerous willingness to segregate human beings into those capable of authentic response to the primordial 'question of Being' and those to whom such a question could never present itself (Derrida 1983a, 1983b).

However my general point is that this 'ethical turn' in recent deconstructionist debate has taken some strange directions and offered rather little in the way of useful or enlightening moral guidance. (For further discussion see Bernstein 1987; Harpham 1991; Lipovetsky 1992) To be sure there are cases – extreme cases – where agents are faced with a choice between starkly conflicting ('incommensurable') claims on their sense of what it is right to do in some given situation and where any decision will therefore be taken in that moment of 'abyssal' or 'dizzying' choice when no appeal to custom, precedent, generalised principles, or maxims of good behaviour can help them at all. This has long been recognised as a problem for deontological theories – like that of Kant – which seek to define moral virtue in terms of our acting in accordance with universal precepts whose very remoteness from the contexts of everyday, situated human choice is such as to render them pretty much irrelevant for most practical purposes. Also there is the point, much stressed by postmodernists, that if an ethical choice is thought of as proceeding from any principles or guidelines that are laid down in advance then it can scarcely be either a genuine 'choice' or in any sense properly 'ethical' (Bauman 1993). Still – as I have said – it is hard to see how an ethics of ultimate 'undecidability' can offer much help in this respect. Rather we should recognise that dilemmas of this sort most often give rise to a complicated process of weighing up reasons, principles, motives, conflicting interests, circumstantial factors, short-term probable and long-term possible consequences, etc.

No doubt this process goes on for the most part at some preconscious level of thought of which we are largely unaware at the time and which may well strike us – in the moment of choice – as lying beyond any reasoned or principled justification. Nevertheless, very often, once the choice has been made we are able to offer some articulate account of it in terms that don't always come down (as de Man would cynically argue) to just another piece of bad-faith confession or self-exculpating narrative 'excuse'.

Of course there is much room for such intricate evasions of moral responsibility when we think about these matters in retrospect and especially when – like de Man – we may be tempted to elaborate an 'ethics of reading' which raises the dilemmas of moral choice to a high point of textualist principle. Thus on his account any claim to own up to past acts or omissions is one that automatically lays the claimant open to a charge of moral bad faith since it involves author and reader alike in a collusive attempt to deny or ignore the complex (or strictly 'undecidable') character of all confessional discourse (de Man 1979). In which case any 'ethics of reading' that merits the name must focus on just those moments of rhetorical or narrative *aporia* where the text puts up maximal resistance to naive or self-deluding notions of moral agency and choice. Least of all should we suppose that a text such as Rousseau's *Confessions* may properly be read (as it asks to be read) in the mode of honest self-reckoning, or again, that had de Man at some point acknowledged having written those offensive articles during the period of Belgian wartime Nazi occupation then this might justifiably be taken as an act of genuine (if belated) moral conscience (de Man 1989; Hamacher, Hertz and Keenan [eds.] 1989.). As I have said already, the 'debate' that ensued when those articles came to light was itself a less than edifying spectacle, with opponents lining up to denounce deconstruction as a strategy for getting collaborationists off the hook (Hirsch 1991; Lehman 1991; Mehlman 1995) while de Man's ex-students, colleagues and friends – Derrida among them – went some lengthy and elaborate ways around in order to construct at least a partial case for the defence (Derrida 1988b). This in turn gave a handle for their critics to say in effect 'we told you so!' and repeat their argument – sometimes (not often) with specific reference to de Man's later writing – that a deconstructive approach to such issues was one that could always find excuses for condoning any amount of bad behaviour. Besides, they remarked, his defenders showed an odd willingness to abandon their textualist principles when it came to adducing facts, evidence, and eye-witness testimony to the effect that de Man had *not* been anti-semitic; that he had ceased writing for *Le Soir* (at some personal risk) when the truth about the Nazi deportations became public knowledge; and even – though this remains controversial – that he had been actively involved with certain elements of the Belgian resistance. It appears not to have struck those who adopted this 'having-your-cake-and-eating-it' line that the same applied to their own case, i.e., that they could hardly convict de Man (along with his followers) of a full-scale textualist cover-up while also – purportedly – catching them out in a 'naive' appeal to the factual evidence or grounds of moral judgement.

By now, some twelve years on, this controversy has gone sufficiently off-the-boil to allow for a critical assessment of de Man's work that is informed but not completely overshadowed by knowledge of his wartime writings. Where it does still surface – albeit in a somewhat muted form – is with regard to the question as to how we should interpret de Man's late texts on the topic of 'aesthetic ideology' (de Man 1997). That is, should they be read as a powerful (if oblique) warning against the kinds of delusion that once captured his own thought or do they constitute yet another strategy for avoiding any genuine attempt to engage with issues of real-world moral and political conscience? (See especially Bohrer [ed.] 1993; Caruth and Esch [eds.] 1994; de Graef 1993, 1995; Cohen, Cohen, Miller and Warminski [eds.] 2001; Felman 1989; Herman, Humbeeck and Lernout [eds.] 1989; Holdheim 1989; Johnson 1990; Loesberg 1991; Prendergast 1990.) My own view – arrived at (I should say) after many changes of mind – is that both claims have a measure of truth and that any reading which declares firmly on either side of the issue is one that will fail to make adequate sense of these strange, compulsive, often perverse and (at times) downright baffling texts. All the same this is no reason to endorse the idea of an 'ethics of reading' that would follow de Man all the way to that point where 'undecidability' becomes a kind of fetish for warding off anything so crude or reductive as talk about matters of substantive ethico-political concern. To the extent that deconstruction has invited this charge – as for instance when J. Hillis Miller defines the ethical 'moment' as that which brings judgement to a stand through 'the structural interference of two linguistic codes' – it is in danger of obscuring the very real force of ethical commitment that runs through much of Derrida's work (Miller 1987). Even so, I would suggest, it is more evident in those texts (like the early essay on Levinas) which argue their way through a close engagement with distinctively philosophic issues than in those later writings – such as 'Force of Law' and *Spectres of Marx* – where Derrida is responding to an overtly ethical or socio-political agenda.

V

Perhaps – as some readers will by now have concluded – this just goes to show that things have moved on since 1982 and that Norris has become sadly out-of-touch with these latest developments. They might also conjecture (fairly enough) that it has much to do with my resistance to certain theologically-inspired or religiously-oriented readings of Derrida's texts (Caputo 1997b; Coward and Foshay [eds.] 1992; Hart 1989; Pitstock 1998; Taylor 1987; Ward 1995). Such readings tend to pass over those passages in 'early' Derrida where he emphatically denies that deconstruction is in any sense a version of negative theology, or that *différance* and other such deconstructive key-terms should be seen as providing a philosophic gloss to present-day forms of 'advanced' speculative religious discourse. (See for instance Derrida 1973.) Since then Derrida has shown himself less inclined to disown such attempts to enlist deconstruction in the name of a postmodern 'atheology' with marked irrationalist, mystical, or counter-enlightenment leanings (Derrida and Vattimo [eds.] 1998). Here I can only direct readers to various texts published over the past decade-or-so where I try to address this complicated question of Derrida's relationship to the discourse of enlightenment critique or what Jürgen Habermas calls the 'unfinished project of modernity' (Norris 1996, 2000b). Thus there is a constant awareness, in his recent writing, of the way that this relationship parallels certain episodes in the history of German philosophical thought, in particular the quarrel between Kant and those contemporary critics of Kant (like Hamann and Jacobi) who invoked a power of intuitive insight or a privileged access to truth beyond the reach of plain-prose critical reason (Derrida 1984). It doesn't take too much subtle reading-between-the-lines to detect here a whole series of ironic and highly self-conscious allusions to Habermas's charge that he (Derrida) has betrayed the Enlightenment project by indulging in a kind of mixed-mode discourse, a 'poetico-metaphorical' perversion of reason that wilfully subverts the genre-distinction between philosophy and literature (Habermas 1987). This charge seems to me unjustified and one which tells us less about Derrida's recidivist tendencies than about Habermas's failure to read the relevant texts with sufficient attentiveness to matters of detail and argumentative structure. All the same it does strike uncomfortably close to some of the ideas that have lately been advanced in Derrida's name and with reference to certain passages – like those instanced above – that can plausibly bear such a reading.

Let me end this somewhat dyspeptic postscript by offering a few remarks which may help to offset any lingering negative impressions. Firstly I should say that Derrida is by far the most intelligent, percep-tive, resourceful and *imaginative* thinker among those who have elected – during the past half-century – to devote themselves chiefly to the reading of texts in the Western philosophical tradition. Indeed it is this singular combination of an acute (often unsettling) analytic intelli-gence with a flair for highly inventive modes of narrative or 'literary' treatment that has drawn such a hostile response from philosophers (like Searle and Habermas) who wish to uphold the genre-distinction between philosophy and literature. It is in this respect that Derrida most strikingly resembles Kierkegaard, that is, in his extraordinary gift for raising philosophical issues of the deepest import through a mode of oblique or indirect discourse which places uncommonly large demands on any reader willing to forego the assurance of straight-forward conceptual grasp. So just as there is a sense in which we sell Kierkegaard short by taking him directly at his word in a text like *Fear and Trembling* so likewise there is a sense which we ought to resist any straightforward interpretation of Derrida's (apparently) fideist com-mentary on Kierkegaard's edifying discourse. That is to say, this is a 'kind of writing' which cannot be consigned (as Rorty would have it) to some hybrid postmodern genre that has at last come out on the far side of all that pointless 'philosophical' talk. Rather it is a way of doing philosophy which still – at its best – exhibits the utmost degree of analytic rigour while not seeking refuge in orthodox ideas of what constitutes a 'faithful' or properly authorised reading.

Deconstruction exhorts us to treat with great suspicion any use of the term 'genius' that goes along with the romantic cult of the author as a source of imaginative truths vouchsafed through some unique, self-validating mode of intuitive access. This idea is the target of de Man's late writings on the theme of 'aesthetic ideology' and is also (more ambivalently) called into question by Derrida's dialogical re-staging of the issue between Kant and his various counter-enlightenment critics (Derrida 1984). Indeed the very notion of 'genius' is one that no self-respecting deconstructionist could nowadays afford to deploy except within quote-marks which are taken to imply that this is a *mention* rather than a *use*, or a means of citing some outmoded idea which no longer stakes any serious claim to credibility. However that term applies to Derrida in precisely the Kantian sense: one whose breaking of established rules (i.e., the rules for what properly counts as an acceptable mode of discourse) is such that it extends and redefines the very scope of human creative-intellectual endeavour. Nobody has written with greater intelligence, insight and subtlety about a range of issues which also preoccupy philosophers in the 'other' (mainstream analytic) tradition but which tend to be treated as so many set-piece topics of debate where the criteria for competent (professionally adequate) address are firmly laid down in advance. In so far as Derrida has challenged this proprietary ethos through the kinds of hermeneutically adventurous reading more often practised by literary critics, one can well understand why his work has provoked such hostility from that quarter. All the same he has managed to keep a critical distance from the various derivative trends or fashions that have grabbed the high ground of recent cultural and literary theory.

There are parts of this book which strike me now as falling in too readily with some of those nascent trends, among them the facile (and politically dangerous) Nietzschean-postmodernist idea that history is itself a textual construct where 'truth' is just the label currently attached to some favoured mode of narrative emplotment or discursive representation. So far as I recall, the term 'postmodernism' had not yet achieved widespread currency in 1982 and there seemed, at the time, no urgent need to make the case for deconstruction as *not* just a sub-branch of this wider, sceptical-relativist movement of thought. Since then things have changed to the point where it is rumoured that students on some degree-schemes in cultural theory have the course-option 'Postmodernism I' or 'Postmodernism II', if indeed they are not required to take both. Early contributors to the *New Accents* series had the double good fortune of writing at a time when there existed already a sizable readership keen to keep up with developments on the 'theory' front but when – as yet – those ideas were very far from acquiring institutional respectability, let alone orthodox status. Of course, that situation had its downside in the proneness of some (myself included) to take them eagerly on board without enough in the way of seasoned critical reflection. Much better if I had dropped all the fogey-baiting talk about 'waking criticism from its dogmatic slumbers', deconstruction as philosophy's belated come-uppance at the hands of literary theory, and so forth. Better also if I hadn't been quite so keen to carve out a space for my own contribution by scoring points off other writers – among them Jonathan Culler – from whose work I had learned a great deal. That my book soon came in for similar treatment was a cause of mild annoyance at the time but really no more than I deserved. It is a pity that the old, still simmering dispute between traditionalists and theorists in departments of literature so quickly gave way to the kinds of intra-theoretical skirmishing that have flared up at regular intervals over the past two decades. Thus the celebrants of difference, heterogeneity, and openness to 'the other' as a high-point of postmodern ethical doctrine seem oddly disinclined to tolerate any criticism of their views, or any suggestion (as in Derrida's early [trans. 1978] essay on Levinas) that such thinking might be philosophically and ethically questionable. Still I am glad to have been a part of Terry Hawkes's great project during years that now seem – from my no doubt fogeyish perspective – like a period of high intellectual adventure.

Cardiff
September 2001

Notes for Further Reading (1982)

These notes are intended to supplement the Bibliography (pp. 190–224), where the reader will find full details of works referred to in the text. For obvious space-saving reasons I have avoided duplicating entries, except in the case of Derrida and other primary sources (de Man, Hartman, etc.) whose omission would create an oddly lopsided effect. Needless to say this is a highly selective listing, a series of signposts the reader can follow up to a point before branching off into regions of his or her own special interest. Items are arranged under two main headings: (1) Derrida, (2) Deconstruction in America, the latter ranging more widely over various post-structuralist debates.

DERRIDA

Texts in English translation

Speech and Phenomena, and Other Essays on Husserl's Theory of Signs. Trans. David B. Allison, Evanston, Ill.: Northwestern University Press, 1973. First published in French 1967. (See above, Chapter 3.)

'White Mythology: Metaphor in the Text of Philosophy'. *New Literary History*, VI, 1 (1974), 7–74.

Of Grammatology. Trans. Gayatri Chakravorty Spivak. Baltimore, Md: Johns

Hopkins University Press, 1977. First published in French 1967. Contains lengthy but accessible discussions of Rousseau, Saussure, Lévi-Strauss and the problematic status of writing in Western tradition. Together with the detailed Translator's Preface, these texts make up the best introduction to Derrida's thought.

'Signature Event Context'. *Glyph*, 1 (1977), 172–97. This deconstruction of speech-act philosophy was followed up by John Searle's rejoinder, 'Reiterating the Differences', *Glyph*, I (1977), 198–208. The exchange was capped by Derrida, 'Limited Inc abc', *Glyph*, II (1977), 162–254.

Edmund Husserl's Origin of Geometry. Trans. Edward Leavey. Stonybrook: Hays, 1978. First published in French 1962. Argues that writing and its structures of *differance* are always already presupposed, even by the 'ideal' truths of mathematics. A difficult and specialized text, though closely related to *Speech and Phenomena*.

Writing and Difference. Trans. Alan Bass. London: Routledge & Kegan Paul, 1978. First published in French 1967. Contains, among other things, important essays on Hegel, Freud, Foucault and Lévi-Strauss. Also the most explicit of Derrida's reflections on structuralism and its discontents. Should be read as a sequel to *Of Grammatology*, though the essays were written during the same period and share many themes.

'Speculations – on Freud'. Trans. Ian McLeod. *The Oxford Literary Review*, III, 2 (1978), 78–97. Continues the deconstructive treatment of psychoanalysis taken up in 'Freud and the Scene of Writing' (in *Writing and Difference*).

Spurs: Nietzsche's Styles. Trans. Barbara Harlow. Chicago, Ill.: Chicago University Press, 1979. Parallel texts in French and English. Derrida at his most elusive and extravagant, shuttling from Heidegger to Nietzsche's umbrella and the 'question of woman' in philosophy. Best approached via the pages on Nietzsche in *Writing and Difference*.

'Living On'. In Geoffrey Hartman (ed.), *Deconstruction and Criticism*. London: Routledge & Kegan Paul, 1979. Derrida's contribution to the Yale critics' symposium, ostensibly focusing (like the others) on Shelley's poem 'The Triumph of Life', but soon launching out on to speculative paths of its own. Very much a case of deconstruction 'on the wild side'.

'The Supplement of Copula: Philosophy *before* Linguistics'. In Josué V. Harari (ed.), *Textual Strategies: Perspectives in Post-Structuralist Criticism*. London: Methuen, 1979. Deconstructs the 'grammar' of

Western philosophy (Aristotle to Heidegger), as determined by the predicative structure of language. A difficult but important text.

Positions. Trans. Alan Bass. London: Athlone Press, 1981. First published in French 1972. Contains the texts of Derrida's interviews with Henri Ronse, Julia Kristeva, Jean-Louis Houdebine and Guy Scarpetta. Not a handy short-cut to Derrida's ideas but an interesting gloss on some of their implications. The first interview (with Ronse) is the most accessible and lucid, while the third (Houdebine and Scarpetta) raises the thorny question of Derrida's attitude to Marxist textual theory.

Texts in French

La Dissémination. Paris: Seuil, 1972. Includes important essays on Plato, Mallarmé and Philippe Sollers. 'La Pharmacie de Platon' is especially crucial for Derrida's account of Greek philosophy and its ambiguously hostile attitude to writing.

Marges de la philosophie. Paris: Minuit, 1972. Essays on language, philosophy and writing, including the originals of 'The White Mythology' and 'The Supplement of Copula' (see above).

Glas. Paris: Galilée, 1974. Derrida's most graphic demonstration of how texts can invade each other's space and play havoc with the logic of meaning. Hegel and Genet are brought face to face in a kind of perverse interlinear gloss which exposes philosophic reason to the lures and obsessions of a homosexual thief-turned-writer. Through a barrage of puns and typographical devices Hegel's language is wrenched out of context and transformed into a mind-bending parody of itself. *Glas* is an endlessly fascinating text, though its brilliant wordplay will seem little more than that to a reader unfamiliar with Derrida's work.

La Vérité en peinture. Paris: Flammarion, 1978. Deconstructs the notions of expressiveness, truth and authenticity, as presupposed by most art criticism and aesthetics generally. Brings out the affinity between Derrida's thinking and certain ideas of the German-Jewish critic Walter Benjamin, especially his theme of the modern disappearance of cultural 'aura' in an age of mass-produced art.

La Carte postale de Socrate à Freud et au-delà. Paris: Aubier-Flammarion, 1980. Essays on Freud and Lacan, prefaced by a sequence of 'postcards' addressed not to anyone in particular but to the general proposition that 'truth' is a shuttling and homeless exchange of messages, a writing bereft of source or destination. Teasingly contests Lacan's claims for psychoanalysis as the ultimate truth of language, a debate taken up in Derrida's rereading of Poe's 'The Purloined Letter' (a *locus classicus* of Lacanian theory). Plato's 'letters' – which may be apocryphal – become the jumping-off point for Derrida's reflections on the 'forgery' of writing, its limitless capacity for doubt and deception.

Writings on Derrida

The following is necessarily a selective listing of the more important books and articles that have appeared up to 1981. The aim is to represent as many sides as possible of a debate which has often polarized opinion, so that some of these pieces are distinctly hostile to Derrida, while others attempt a variety of mediating stances. Readers in search of more detailed documentation may wish to consult John Leavey and David B. Allison, 'A Derrida Bibliography', *Research in Phenomenology*, VIII (1978), 145–60. This covers Derrida's writings (including those in English translation) up to early 1978, along with more than 200 secondary items, many of them marginal but showing the extraordinary range and resonance of Derrida's impact.

Allison, David B. 'Derrida and Wittgenstein: Playing the Game'. *Research in Phenomenology*, VIII (1978), 93–109.

Altieri, Charles. 'Wittgenstein on Consciousness and Language: A Challenge to Derridean Theory'. *Modern Language Notes*, XCI (1976), 1397–423. (See above, Chapter 7.)

Bass, Alan. ' "Literature"/Literature'. In Richard Macksey (ed.), *Velocities of Change*. Baltimore, Md, and London: Johns Hopkins University Press, 1974, 341–53.

Berezdivin, Ruben. 'Gloves Inside-Out'. *Research in Phenomenology*, VIII (1978), 111–26. Mainly on Derrida's *Glas*.

Brown, P. L. 'Epistemology and Method: Althusser, Foucault, Derrida'. *Research in Phenomenology*, VIII (1978), 147–62.

Cousins, Mark. 'The Logic of Deconstruction'. *The Oxford Literary Review*, III (1978), 70–7.

Culler, Jonathan. 'Jacques Derrida'. In *Structuralism and Since: From Lévi-Strauss to Derrida*, 154–80. London: Oxford University Press, 1979.

Culler, Jonathan. *On Deconstruction*. London: Routledge & Kegan Paul (1983).

Cumming, Robert Denoon. 'The Odd Couple: Heidegger and Derrida'. *Review of Metaphysics*, XXXIV (1981), 487–521.

de Man, Paul. *Blindness and Insight: Essays in the Rhetoric of Contemporary Criticism*. New York and London: Oxford University Press, 1971. Among the earliest American texts to register the impact of deconstruction; contains de Man's intricate critique of Derrida on Rousseau.

Ellman, Maud. 'Spacing Out: A Double Entendre on Mallarmé'. *The Oxford Literary Review*, III (1978), 22–31.

Garver, Newton. Preface to the English translation of Derrida's *Speech and Phenomena*, IX–XXIX. Evanston, Ill.: Northwestern University Press, 1973. Interesting on the relationship between Derrida's and Wittgenstein's philosophies of language.

Garver, Newton. 'Derrida on Rousseau on Writing'. *Journal of Philosophy*, LXXIV (1977), 663–73.

Grene, Marjorie. 'Life, Death and Language: Some Thoughts on Derrida and Wittgenstein'. In *Philosophy In and Out of Europe*, 142–54. Berkeley and Los Angeles, Calif.: University of California Press, 1976.

Hartman, Geoffrey. 'Monsieur Texte: On Jacques Derrida, His *Glas*' and 'Monsieur Texte II: Epiphany in Echoland'. *Georgia Review*, XXIX, 4, and XXX, 1 (1975–6).

Hartman, Geoffrey. 'Crossing Over: Literary Commentary as Literature'. *Comparative Literature*, XXVIII (1976), 257–76. Takes Derrida's *Glas* as a pretext for Hartman's critical-liberationist plea.

Hartman, Geoffrey. *Saving the Text: Literature/Derrida/Philosophy*. Baltimore, Md: Johns Hopkins University Press, 1981.

Hoy, David Couzens. *The Critical Circle: Literature and History in Contemporary Hermeneutics*. Berkeley and Los Angeles, Calif.: University of California Press, 1978. Useful chapter on Derrida's differences with Heidegger, Gadamer and current hermeneutics.

Johnson, Barbara. 'The Frame of Reference: Poe, Lacan, Derrida'. *Literature and Psychoanalysis, Yale French Studies*, 55–6 (1977), 457–505.

La Capra, Dominick. 'Habermas and the Grounding of Critical Theory'. *History and Theory*, XVI (1977), 237–64. Compares the relation between textual theory and historical understanding in Derrida, Foucault and representatives of the Frankfurt School.

McDonald, C. V. 'Jacques Derrida's Reading of Rousseau'. *The Eighteenth Century* (Texas), XX (1979), 82–95.

Mulligan, Kevin. 'Inscriptions and Speaking's Place: Derrida and Wittgenstein'. *The Oxford Literary Review*, VIII (1978), 62–7.

Norris, Christopher. 'Jacques Derrida's Grammatology'. *Poetry Nation Review*, VI, 2 (1978), 38–40.

Norris, Christopher. 'The Margins of Meaning: Derrida's *Spurs*'. *The Cambridge Quarterly*, IX, 3 (1980), 280–4.

Norris, Christopher. 'The Polymetaphorical Mailman' (review of Derrida's *La Carte postale de Socrate à Freud*). *The Times Literary Supplement*, 4 July 1980, 761.

Ricœur, Paul. *The Rule of Metaphor*. London: Routledge & Kegan Paul, 1978. Argues from a broadly 'hermeneutic' viewpoint not wholly sympathetic to deconstruction, but contains some interesting pages on Derrida's essay 'The White Mythology'.

Rorty, Richard. 'Derrida on Language, Being and Abnormal Philosophy'. *Journal of Philosophy*, LXXIV (1977), 673–81.

Rorty, Richard. 'Philosophy as a Kind of Writing'. *New Literary History*, X' (1978), 141–60. A lively account of Derrida's differences with 'normal' (i.e. consensual and rationalist) modes of philosophizing.

Said, Edward. 'The Problem of Textuality: Two Exemplary Positions'. *Critical Inquiry*, IV (1978), 673–714. Contrasts Derrida's textual hermeticism ('il n'y a pas de hors-texte') with Foucault's commitment to an activating rhetoric of 'worldly' discursive practices.

Silverman, Hugh J. 'Self-Decentering: Derrida Incorporated'. *Research in Phenomenology*, VIII (1978), 45–65. On Derrida's deconstruction of the transcendental ego, or self-possessed subject of traditional psychology.

Ulmer, J. L. 'Jacques Derrida and Paul de Man on/in Rousseau's Faults'. *The Eighteenth Century* (Texas), XX (1979), 164–81.

Woods D. C. 'An Introduction to Derrida'. *Radical Philosophy*, 21 (1979), 18–28. Combines lucid exposition with critique from a Marxist-activist viewpoint.

Wordsworth, Ann. 'Derrida and Criticism'. *The Oxford Literary Review*, III (1978), 47–52.

DECONSTRUCTION IN AMERICA

This section is mainly concerned with Bloom, de Man, Hartman and Miller, along with those critics who have attacked their position or entered the debate with something important to say. I have not given details of 'pre-deconstructionist' texts by the Yale critics, except (as in Hartman's case) where they offer a kind of exemplary progress through and beyond the 'old' New Criticism.

Abrams, M. H. 'How To Do Things With Texts'. *Partisan Review*, XLIV (1978), 566–88. Charges the deconstructors with practising a double and deceptive strategy: denying that language can possess any definite, communicable sense, while expecting their own texts to be carefully and properly interpreted. By no means a knock-down argument – as witness Derrida versus Searle – but a salutary riposte to deconstruction in its less circumspect forms. See also:

Abrams, M. H. 'The Limits of Pluralism: The Deconstructive Angel'. *Critical Inquiry*, III (1977), 425–38.

Altieri, Charles. 'Presence and Reference in a Literary Text: The Example of Williams' "This Is Just To Say"'. *Critical Inquiry*, V (1979), 489–510. Argues that poetry can establish its own kind of 'presence', momentarily immune to the pure *differance* of writing. Not so much a refutation of Derridean theory as a willing act of faith on the critic's part.

Bloom, Harold. *The Anxiety of Influence: A Theory of Poetry*. New York and London: Oxford University Press, 1973. (See above, Chapter 6, on Bloom.)

Bloom, Harold. *A Map of Misreading*. New York and London: Oxford University Press, 1975.

Bloom, Harold. *Poetry and Repression*. New Haven, Conn.: Yale University Press, 1976.

Bloom, Harold. *Wallace Stevens: The Poems of Our Climate*. Ithaca, NY: Cornell University Press, 1977. Contains Bloom's most explicit and hard-pressed arguments against deconstruction in its radically textual form.

Chase, Cynthia. 'Oedipal Textuality: Reading Freud's Reading of *Oedipus*'. *Diacritics*, IX (1979), 54–71.

Culler, Jonathan. *Structuralist Poetics*. London: Routledge & Kegan Paul, 1975. Basically a pre-deconstructionist treatment of structuralist theory, with distinct reservations (in the final chapter) about Derrida's then looming influence.

Culler, Jonathan. *The Pursuit of Signs*. London: Routledge & Kegan Paul, 1981. Far more sympathetic toward deconstruction, though treats it as in many ways a geared-up version of the programme announced in *Structuralist Poetics*. Essays on narrative, metaphor, genre theory, etc., showing how thought continually runs up against 'unthinkable' twists of paradox.

Culler, Jonathan. *On Deconstruction*. London: Routledge & Kegan Paul, 1982.

de Man, Paul. 'The Rhetoric of Temporality'. In Charles S. Singleton (ed.), *Interpretation: Theory and Practice*, 173–209. Baltimore, Md: Johns Hopkins University Press, 1969. Deconstructs the Romantic ideology of symbol, showing how its meanings break down into the discrete, serial structures of allegory. A brilliant essay; de Man at his most persuasive.

de Man, Paul. 'The Epistemology of Metaphor'. *Critical Inquiry*, V (1978), 13–30. On metaphor in the text of philosophy, with reference mainly to Locke and Kant. Should be read in conjunction with Derrida's 'White Mythology' (see above).

de Man, Paul. *Allegories of Reading: Figural Language in Rousseau Nietzsche, Rilke, and Proust*. New Haven, Conn.: Yale University Press, 1979. (See above, Chapter 6, for a detailed account of this sweepingly ambitious and controversial text.)

de Man, Paul. 'Autobiography as Defacement'. *Modern Language Notes*, XCIV (1979), 918–38.

Felman, Shoshana. 'Turning the Screw of Interpretation'. *Yale French Studies*, 55–6 (1977), 94–207.

Graff, Gerald. *Literature Against Itself: Literary Ideas in Modern Society*. Chicago, Ill., and London: University of Chicago Press, 1979. A polemical attack not only on deconstruction but on post-modern literature and any way of thinking which tries to drive a wedge between the text and 'reality'. Comes down to a mixture of moral indignation and flatly commonsense assertion.

Hartman, Geoffrey. *Beyond Formalism*. New Haven, Conn., and London: Yale University Press, 1970. (Discussed at length in Chapters 1 and 4.)

Hartman, Geoffrey. *The Fate of Reading and Other Essays*. Chicago, Ill., and London: University of Chicago Press, 1975.

Hartman, Geoffrey. 'The Recognition Scene of Criticism'. *Critical Inquiry*, IV (1978), 407–16.

Hartman, Geoffrey (ed.). *Deconstruction and Criticism*. London: Routledge & Kegan Paul, 1979.

Hartman, Geoffrey. *Criticism in the Wilderness*. New Haven, Conn., and London: Yale University Press, 1980. Argues for a newly adventurous 'hermeneutic' criticism aware of its own stylistic resources and open to the liberating influence of thinkers like Derrida, Heidegger and Walter Benjamin.

Jacobs, Carol. *The Dissimulating Harmony: Images of Interpretation in Nietzsche, Rilke and Benjamin*. Baltimore, Md: Johns Hopkins University Press, 1978. Follows de Man in deconstructing the metaphors and tropes that produce the illusion of straightforward textual readability. Suggestive but wayward in argument.

Jacobs, Carol. 'The (Too) Good Soldier: "A Real Story"'. *Glyph*, III (1978), 32–51. On the play of textual and historical inscription in Ford Madox Ford's *The Good Soldier*.

Jameson, Fredric. *The Political Unconscious*. London: Methuen, 1980. Argues for a more politicized approach to the deconstruction of textual gaps and inconsistencies, seen as the 'unconscious' produced by a collision of language, form and ideology. Heavy-going in places, but often persuasive in its effort to negotiate the rift between Marxist and Derridean theories of the text.

Johnson, Barbara. *Défigurations du language poétique*. Paris: Flammarion, 1979.

Krieger, Murray. 'Poetry Reconstructed'. In his *Theory of Criticism*, 207–45. Baltimore, Md, and London: Johns Hopkins University Press, 1976.

Krieger, Murray. *Poetic Presence and Illusion*. Baltimore, Md, and London: Johns Hopkins University Press, 1979. Looks to Renaissance literary theory, and poets like Sidney, for a parallel with deconstructionist debates over textual 'presence' and 'absence'. Suggests that poems may invoke an imaginary presence (like that of the desired mistress) even where the sense of unattainability is most keenly felt. Underlying Krieger's argument is a constant nostalgic appeal to the 'old' New Critical faith in the poem as a self-possessed structure of meaning.

Leitch, Vincent B. 'The Deconstructive Criticism of J. Hillis Miller' *Critical Inquiry*, VI (1980), 593–607. (See also Miller's reply, 'Theory and Practice', *Critical Inquiry*, VI (1980), 609–14.)

Lentricchia, Frank. *After the New Criticism*. London: Athlone Press, 1980. An ambitious account of American post-structuralist criticism and its main continental sources. Generally favours a 'worldly' or activist rhetoric (Foucault, Said), as opposed to what he sees as the disengaged 'pure' textuality of Derrida's closest disciples. Provocative but scrupulously argued – a valuable work of introduction.

Michaels, Walter Benn. 'Saving the Text: Reference and Belief'. *Modern Language Notes*, XCIII (1978), 771–93.

Miller, J. Hillis. *Thomas Hardy: Distance and Desire*. Cambridge, Mass.: Harvard University Press, 1970.

Miller, J. Hillis. 'The Fiction of Realism: *Sketches by Boz, Oliver Twist*, and Cruikshank's Illustrations'. In Ada Nisbet and Blake Nevius (eds), *Dickens Centennial Essays*. Berkeley, Calif.: University of California, 1971.

Miller, J. Hillis. Critical Introduction to Thomas Hardy, *The Well-Beloved*. London: Macmillan, 1976. Shrewdly latches on to the self-deconstructing elements in this strangest and least 'credible' of all Hardy's fictions.

Miller, J. Hillis. 'Ariadne's Thread: Repetition and the Narrative Line'. *Critical Inquiry*, III (1976), 57–77.

Miller, J. Hillis. 'The Limits of Pluralism, II: The Critic as Host'. *Critical Inquiry*, III (1977), 439–47.

Norris, Christopher. 'Wrestling With Deconstructors'. *Critical Quarterly*, XXII (1980), 57–62.

Norris, Christopher. 'Derrida at Yale: The "Deconstructive Moment" in Modernist Poetics'. *Philosophy and Literature*, IV (1980), 242–56.

Reed, Arden. 'The Debt of Disinterest: Kant's Critique of Music'. *Modern Language Notes*, XCV (1980), 562–84. A deconstructive reading of Kantian aesthetics, taking a cue from Derrida's remarks (in *Of Grammatology*) on Rousseau and the primacy of melody in music. Shows how a differential 'harmony' always obtrudes its disturbing overtones, just as writing invades the privileged realm of speech.

Ryan, Michael. 'The Act'. *Glyph*, II (1977), 64–87. On the rhetoric of deconstruction in Nietzsche's *Ecce Homo*.

Said, Edward. 'The Text as Practice and as Idea'. *Modern Language Notes*, LXXXVIII (1973), 1071–101.

Said, Edward. *Beginnings: Intention and Method*. Baltimore, Md, and London: Johns Hopkins University Press, 1975. An eloquent if rather long-drawn-out testimony to the impact of French post-structuralism on American critical thought. More indebted to Foucault than to Derrida, in whom Said detects and criticizes a strain of 'nihilistic radicality'. Nevertheless a crucial text for understanding the American response to deconstructionist theory.

Sussman, Henry. 'The Deconstructionist as Politician: Melville's *The Confidence-Man*'. *Glyph*, IV (1978), 33–56.

Weber, Samuel. 'Saussure and the Apparition of Language: The Critical Perspective'. *Modern Language Notes*, XCI (1976), 912–38.

White, Hayden. *Tropics of Discourse*. Baltimore, Md, and London: Johns

Hopkins University Press, 1978. Mainly concerned with historical narrative and the various tropes and patterning devices employed to make sense of history. See especially the chapters on Foucault and Derrida, the latter representing for White an 'absurdist' extreme of sceptical philosophy.

BIBLIOGRAPHY (including works cited)

Note: For this Third Edition I have collated the two previous supplementary bibliographies (1986 and 1991), along with the more recent books and articles mentioned in the 2002 Postscript. The 'Notes for Further Reading' included above is as per the first (1982) edition since it is more closely tied to the original text. I have also included a further dozen-or-so entries which may be useful for those in search of more specialised work on particular topics of interest. Among the many websites devoted to Derrida and deconstruction, readers may wish to consult Peter Krapp's splendid database (www.hydra.umn.edu/derrida/jdind.html) which has selective links to other relevant sites. The Schultz and Fried Derrida bibliography (1992: reference below) is still the most comprehensive printed source with reliable annotation for most entries. However the cut-off date – and Derrida's high productivity since that time – makes it already a limited resource for those who want the record complete. Most readers will I think find their needs and interests adequately served by the listing below.

I should especially like to to thank Jacques Derrida for his unfailing generosity in sending me copies of all his books (French-language originals) published over the past fifteen years and more. That he manages to write them faster than I – or the most dedicated exegete – can manage to read them is a regular source of amazement. Should this text ever go to a fourth edition and my bookshelves survive the strain there will no doubt be plenty more to discuss.

Abrams, M. H. (1978) 'How To Do Things With Texts'. *Partisan Review*, XLIV, 566–88.

Adams, Hazard and Searle, Leroy (eds) (1986) *Critical Theory Since 1965*. Tallahassee, Fla.: Florida State University Press.

Agacinski, Sylviane (1988) *Aparté: conceptions and deaths of Soren Kierkegaard*. Trans. Kevin Newmark. Tallahassee, Fla.: Florida State University Press.

Allison, David (ed.) (1985) *The New Nietzsche*. Cambridge, Mass.: MIT Press.

Altizer, Thomas J. *et al.* (1982) *Deconstruction and Theology*. New York: Crossroads.

Appignanesi, Lisa (ed.) (1985) *Ideas From France: the legacy of French theory*. London: ICA Publications, Documents 3.

Arac, Jonathan (ed.) (1986) *Postmodernism and Politics*. Minneapolis, Minn.: University of Minnesota Press.

—— (1987) *Critical Genealogies: historical situations for postmodern literary studies*. New York: Columbia University Press.

—— *et al.* (1983) *The Yale Critics: deconstruction in America*. Minneapolis: University of Minnesota Press.

—— and Johnson, Barbara (eds) (1990) *Consequences of Theory*. Baltimore, Md and London: Johns Hopkins University Press.

Atkins, G. Douglas (1984) *Reading Deconstruction/Deconstructive Reading*. Lexington: University of Kentucky Press.

——(1986) *Quests of Difference: reading Pope's poems*. Lexington, Kentucky: University Press of Kentucky.

——(1990) *Geoffrey Hartman: criticism as answerable style*. London: Routledge.

—— and Johnson, Michael L. (eds) (1985) *Writing and Reading Differently: deconstruction and the teaching of composition and literature*. Lawrence, Kansas: University Press of Kansas.

—— and Morrow, Laura (eds) (1989) *Contemporary Literary Theory*. London: Macmillan.

Attridge, Derek (1988) *Peculiar Language: literature as difference from the Renaissance to James Joyce*. Ithaca, NY: Cornell University Press.

——, Bennington, Geoff, and Young, Robert (eds) (1987) *Post-Structuralism and the Question of History*. Cambridge: Cambridge University Press.

Austin, J. L. (1963) *How To Do Things With Words*. London: Oxford University Press.

Baker, Peter (1995) *Deconstruction and the Ethical Turn*. Gainesville: University Press of Florida.

Barthes, Roland (1967) *Elements of Semiology*. Trans. Annette Lavers and Colin Smith. London: Jonathan Cape.

—— (1975) *S/Z*. Trans. Richard Miller. London: Jonathan Cape.

—— (1977) *Roland Barthes by Roland Barthes*. Trans. Richard Howard. London: Macmillan.

—— (1979) *A Lover's Discourse*. Trans. Richard Howard. London: Jonathan Cape.

Baudrillard, Jean (1975) *The Mirror of Production*. Trans. Mark Poster. St Louis: Telos Press.

—— (1988) *Selected Writings*. Mark Poster (ed.) Cambridge: Polity Press.

Bauman, Zygmunt (1987) *Legislators and Interpreters: on modernity, postmodernity, and intellectuals*. Cambridge: Polity Press.

—— (1993) *Postmodern Ethics*. Oxford: Blackwell.

Beardsworth, Richard (1996) *Derrida and the Political*. London: Routledge.

Beiser, Frederick C. (1987) *The Fate of Reason: German philosophy from Kant to Fichte*. Cambridge, Mass.: Harvard University Press.

Belsey, Catherine (1980) *Critical Practice*. London: Methuen.

—— and Moore, Jane (eds) (1989) *The Feminist Reader*. London: Macmillan.

Benjamin, Andrew (ed.) (1989) *Post-Structuralist Classics*. London: Routledge.

—— (1989) *Translation and the Nature of Philosophy: a new theory of words*. London: Routledge.

Bennington, Geoff (1981) 'Reading Allegory' (on de Man's *Allegories of Reading*). *The Oxford Literary Review*, IV, 83–93.

—— (1994) *Legislations: the politics of deconstruction*. London: Verso.

—— (2000) *Interrupting Derrida*. London: Routledge.

Berman, Art (1988) *From the New Criticism to Deconstruction: the reception of structuralism and post-structuralism*. Urbana-Champaign, Ill.: University of Illinois Press.

Bernasconi, Robert and Wood, David (eds) (1988) *The Provocation of Levinas: re-thinking the other*. London: Routledge.

—— and Critchley, Simon (eds) (1991) *Re-Reading Levinas*. Bloomington: Indiana University Press.

—— (1998) 'Different Styles of Eschatology: Derrida's take on Levinas's political messianism', *Research in Phenomenology*, Vol. 28, pp. 3–19.

Bernstein, Richard (1987). 'Serious Play: the ethical-political horizon of Jacques Derrida'. *Journal of Speculative Philosophy*, Vol. 1, pp. 93–117.

Blackmur, R. P. (1967) *A Primer of Ignorance*. New York: Harcourt Brace.

Bloom, Harold (1959) *Shelley's Mythmaking*. New Haven, Conn.: Yale University Press.

—— (1973) *The Anxiety of Influence: a theory of poetry*. New York and London: Oxford University Press.

—— (1975) *Kabbalah and Criticism*. New York: Seabury Press.

—— (1976) *Poetry and Repression*. New Haven, Conn.: Yale University Press.

—— (1977) *Wallace Stevens: the poems of our climate*. Ithaca, NY, and London: Cornell University Press.

—— (1982) *Agon: towards a theory of revisionism*. London and New York: Oxford University Press.

—— (1982) *The Breaking of the Vessels*. Chicago, Ill., and London: University of Chicago Press.

—— (ed.) (1985) *Modern Critical Views: Sigmund Freud*. New York: Chelsea House.

—— (1989) *Ruin the Sacred Truths: poetry and belief from the Bible to the present*. Cambridge, Mass.: Harvard University Press.

Bohrer, Karl Heinz (ed.) (1993) *Aesthetik und Rhetorik: Lektüren zu Paul de Man*. Frankfurt: Suhrkamp.

Bové, Paul A. (1986) *Intellectuals In Power: a genealogy of critical humanism*. New York: Columbia University Press.

Bowie, Malcolm (1988) *Freud, Proust, and Lacan: theory as fiction*. Cambridge: Cambridge University Press.

Boyne, Roy (1990) *Foucault and Derrida: the other side of reason*. London: Unwin Hyman.

Brannigan, John, Robbins, Ruth and Wolfreys, Julian (eds) (1996) *Applying to Derrida*. London: Macmillan.

Brodsky, Claudia J. (1987) *The Imposition of Form: studies in narrative representation and knowledge*. Princeton, NJ: Princeton University Press.

Brunette, Peter and Wills, David (1990) *Screen/Play: Derrida and film theory*. Princeton, NJ: Princeton University Press.

Bruns, Gerald L. (1989) *Heidegger's Estrangements: language, truth and poetry in the later writings*. New Haven, Conn.: Yale University Press.

Bruss, Elizabeth (1982) *Beautiful Theories: the spectacle of discourse in contemporary criticism*. Baltimore, Md: Johns Hopkins University Press.

Budick, Sanford and Iser, Wolfgang (eds) (1990) *Languages of the Unsayable: the play of negativity in literature and literary theory*. New York: Columbia University Press.

Burgass, Catherine (1991) *Challenging Theory: discipline after deconstruction*. Aldershot: Ashgate.

Butler, Christopher (1984) *Interpretation, Deconstruction and Ideology*. London: Oxford University Press.

Cain, William (1985) *The Crisis in Criticism: theory, literature and reform in English studies*. Baltimore, Md and London: Johns Hopkins University Press.

Callinicos, Alex (1990) *Against Post-Modernism: a Marxist critique*. Cambridge: Polity Press.

Cameron, Deborah (ed.) (1990) *The Feminist Critique of Language: a reader*. London: Routledge.

Campbell, Colin (9 February 1986) 'The Tyranny of the Yale Critics'. *The New York Times Magazine*, 20–8 and 43–8.

Cantor, Norman F. (1988) *Twentieth-Century Culture: modernism to deconstruction*. New York: Peter Lang.

Caputo, John D. (1987) *Radical Hermeneutics: repetition, deconstruction and the hermeneutic project*. Bloomington, Ind.: Indiana University Press.

—— (1993) *Against Ethics: contributions to a poetics of obligation with constant reference to deconstruction*. Bloomington, Ind.: Indiana University Press.

—— (1997a) *Deconstruction in a Nutshell*. New York: Fordham University Press.

—— (1997b) *The Prayers and Tears of Jacques Derrida: religion without religion*. Bloomington, Ind: Indiana University Press.

—— (1998) 'Derrida, a Kind of Philosophy: a discussion of recent literature'. *Research in Phenomenology*, Vol. 17, pp. 245–59.

Carroll, David (1982) *The Subject in Question: the languages of theory and the strategies of fiction*. Chicago, Ill.: University of Chicago Press.

—— *Paraesthetics: Foucault, Lyotard, Derrida*. London: Methuen, 1987.

—— (ed.) (1990) *The States of 'Theory': history, art and critical discourse*. New York: Columbia University Press.

Caruth, Cathy (1990) *Empirical Truths and Critical Fictions: Locke, Words-worth, Kant, Freud*. Baltimore, Md and London: Johns Hopkins University Press.

—— and Esch, Deborah (eds) (1995) *Critical Encounters: reference and responsibility in deconstructive writing*. New Brunswick, N.J.: Rutgers University Press.

Cascardi, A. J. (1984) 'Skepticism and Deconstruction'. *Philosophy and Literature*, VIII, 1–14.

—— (1987) *Literature and the Question of Philosophy*. Baltimore, Md and London: Johns Hopkins University Press.

Cavell, Stanley (1985) 'The Division of Talent'. *Critical Inquiry*, XI, 519–38.

—— (1995) *Philosophical Passages: Wittgenstein, Emerson, Austin, Derrida*. Oxford: Blackwell.

Cazeaux, Clive (ed.) (2000) *The Continental Aesthetics Reader*. London: Routledge.

Chase, Cynthia (1978) 'The Decomposition of the Elephants: Double-Reading *Daniel Deronda*'. *PMLA* XCIII, 215–27.

—— (1983) 'Getting Versed: Reading Hegel with Baudelaire'. *Studies in Romanticism*, XXII, 241–66.

—— (1986) *Decomposing Figures: rhetorical readings in the romantic tradition*. Baltimore, Md and London: Johns Hopkins University Press.

Clark, Timothy (1992) *Derrida, Heidegger, Blanchot: sources of Derrida's notion and practice of literature*. Cambridge: Cambridge University Press.

Cohen, Ralph (ed.) (1989) *The Future of Literary Theory*. London: Routledge.

Cohen, T., Cohen, B., Hillis Miller, J. and Warminski, A. (eds) (2001) *Material Events: Paul de Man and the afterlife of theory*. Minneapolis: University of Minnesota Press.

Collier, Peter and Geyer-Ryan, Helga (eds) (1990) *Literary Theory Today*. Cambridge: Polity Press.

Corlett, William (1989) *Community Without Unity: a politics of Derridian extravagance*. Durham, NC and London: Duke University Press.

Cornell, Drucilla (ed.) (1992) *The Philosophy of the Limit*. New York: Routledge.

Cornford, F. M. (1932) *Before and After Socrates*. Cambridge: Cambridge University Press.

Corngold, Stanley (1986) *The Fate of the Self: German writers and French theory*. New York: Columbia University Press.

Coward, Harold (1990) *Derrida and Indian Philosophy*. Albany, NY: State University of New York Press.

—— and Foshay, Toby (eds) (1991) *Derrida and Negative Theology*. Albany, NY: SUNY Press.

Critchley, Simon (Autumn/Winter 1988) 'A Commentary upon Derrida's Reading of Hegel in *Glas*'. *Bulletin of the Hegel Society of Great Britain*, No. 18, 6–32.

—— (1992) *The Ethics of Deconstruction: Derrida and Levinas*. Oxford: Blackwell.

—— (1999) *Ethics – Politics – Subjectivity: essays on Derrida, Levinas and contemporary French theought*. London: Verso.

—— and Dews, Peter, (eds) (1996) *Deconstructive Subjectivities*. Albany, NY: SUNY Press.

Culler, Jonathan (Winter 1972) 'Frontiers of Criticism' (review of Paul de Man's *Blindness and Insight*). *The Yale Review*, 259–71.

—— (1975) *Structuralist Poetics*. London: Routledge & Kegan Paul.

—— (1981) 'Convention and Meaning: Derrida and Austin'. *New Literary History*, XIII, 15–30.

—— (1981) *The Pursuit of Signs: semiotics, literature, deconstruction*. London: Routledge & Kegan Paul.

—— (1983) *On Deconstruction: theory and criticism after structuralism*. London: Routledge & Kegan Paul.

—— (ed.) (1988) *On Puns: the foundation of letters*. Oxford: Basil Blackwell.

—— (1989) *Framing the Sign: criticism and its institutions*. Oxford: Basil Blackwell.

Cumming, Robert D. (1994) *Phenomenology and Deconstruction*. Chicago: University of Chicago Press.

Cunningham, Valentine (1990) *In the Reading Gaol*. Oxford: Basil Blackwell.

Dasenbrock, Reed Way (ed.) (1989) *Re-Drawing the Lines: analytic philosophy, deconstruction and literary theory*. Minneapolis, Minn.: University of Minnesota Press.

Davis, R. C. (ed.) (1986) *Contemporary Literary Theory: modernism through post-modernism*. London: Longman.

—— and Schleifer, R. (eds) (1985) *Rhetoric and Form: deconstruction at Yale*. Norman, Okl.: University of Oklahoma Press.

de Bolla, Peter (1988) *Harold Bloom: towards historical rhetorics*. London: Routledge.

—— (1989) *The Discourse of the Sublime: history, aesthetics and the subject*. Oxford: Basil Blackwell.

de Graef, Ortwin (1993) *Serenity in Crisis: a preface to Paul de Man*. Lincoln, Nebr.: University of Nebraska Press.

—— (1995) *Titanic Light: Paul de Man's post-romanticism, 1960-69*. Lincoln, Nebr.: University of Nebraska Press.

de Man, Paul (1969) 'The Rhetoric of Temporality'. In Charles S. Singleton (ed.), *Interpretation: theory and practice*. Baltimore, Md: Johns Hopkins University Press.

—— (1971) *Blindness and Insight: essays in the rhetoric of contemporary criticism*. (2nd edn, expanded and revised). London: Methuen, 1983.

—— (1979) *Allegories of Reading: figural language in Rousseau, Nietzsche, Rilke, and Proust*. New Haven, Conn.: Yale University Press.

—— (1981) 'Hypogram and Inscription: Michael Riffaterre's poetics'. *Diacritics*, XI, 17–35.

—— (1981) 'Pascal's Allegory of Persuasion'. In Stephen Greenblatt (ed.), *Allegory and Representation*. Baltimore, Md: Johns Hopkins University Press, 1–25.

—— Introduction to Hans Robert Jauss, *Toward an Aesthetics of Reception*. Trans. Timothy Bahti. Minneapolis: University of Minnesota Press, 1982, vii–xxv.

—— (1982) 'Sign and Symbol in Hegel's *Aesthetics*'. *Critical Inquiry*, VIII, 761–75.

—— (1982) 'The Resistance to Theory'. *Yale French Studies*, 63, 3–20.

—— (1983) 'Dialogue and Dialogism'. *Poetics Today*, IV, 99–107.

—— (1983) 'Hegel on the Sublime'. In Mark Krupnick (ed.), *Displacement: Derrida and After*. Bloomington, Ind.: Indiana University Press, 139–53.

—— (1984) 'Phenomenality and Materiality in Kant'. In Gary Shapiro and Alan Sica (eds), *Hermeneutics: questions and prospects*. Amherst, MA: University of Massachusetts Press, 121–44.

—— (1984) *The Rhetoric of Romanticism*. New York: Columbia University Press.

—— (1986) *The Resistance to Theory*. Minneapolis, Minn.: University of Minnesota Press.

—— (1989) *Critical Writings, 1953–1978*, Lindsay Waters (ed.). Minneapolis, Minn.: University of Minnesota Press.

—— (1989) *Wartime Journalism*, W. Hamacher, N. Hertz and T. Keenan (eds). Lincoln, Nebr.: University of Nebraska Press.

—— (1997) *Aesthetic Ideology*. Minneapolis: University of Minnesota Press.

Deleuze, Gilles (1983) *Nietzsche and Philosophy* (trans. Hugh Tomlinson). London: Athlone Press.

Derrida, Jacques (1972a) *La Dissémination*. Paris: Seuil.

—— (1972b) *Marges de la philosophie*. Paris: Minuit.

—— (1973) *Speech and Phenomena, and Other Essays on Husserl's Theory of Signs*. Trans. David B. Allison. Evanston, Ill.: Northwestern University Press.

—— (1974a) *Glas*. Paris: Galilée.

—— (1974b) 'The White Mythology: Metaphor in the Text of Philosophy'. *New Literary History*, VI, 1, 7–74.

—— (1977a) *Of Grammatology*. Trans. Gayatri Chakravorty Spivak. Baltimore, Md: Johns Hopkins University Press.

—— (1977b) 'Signature Event Context'. *Glyph*, I, 172–97.

—— (1977c) 'Limited Inc. abc'. *Glyph*, II, 162–254.

—— (1978) 'Violence and Metaphysics: an essay on the thought of Emmanuel Levinas'. In *Writing and Difference*, trans. Alan Bass. London: Routledge & Kegan Paul, pp. 79–153.

—— (1978) *Writing and Difference*. Trans. Alan Bass. London: Routledge & Kegan Paul.

—— (1979) *Spurs: Nietzsche's Styles*. Trans. Barbara Harlow. Chicago, Ill.: Chicago University Press.

—— 'The Law of Genre'. *Glyph*, VII (1980), 202–29.

—— (1981) *Dissemination*. Trans. Barbara Johnson. London: Athlone Press.

—— (1981) 'Economimesis'. *Diacritics*, XI, 3–25.

—— (1981) 'Les Morts de Roland Barthes'. *Poetique*, 47, 269–92.

—— (1981) *Positions*. Trans. Alan Bass. London: Athlone Press.

—— (1981) 'Title (to be specified)'. *Substance*, 31, 5–22.

—— (1982) Interview with Christie V. MacDonald in *Diacritics*, XII, 66–76.

—— (1982) *L'Oreille de l'autre: otobiographies, transferts, traductions: textes et débats avec Jacques Derrida* (ed. Claude Lévesque and Christie V. MacDonald). Paris: VLB.

—— (1982) *Margins of Philosophy*. Trans. Alan Bass. Chicago, Ill.: University of Chicago Press.

—— (1982) 'The Time of a Thesis'. In Alan Montefiore (ed.), *Philosophy in France Today*. Cambridge: Cambridge University Press.

—— (1983a) 'Geschlecht: sexual difference, ontological difference'. *Research in Phenomenology*, Vol. 13, pp. 65–83.

—— (1983b) 'Geschlecht 2: Heidegger's hand'. Trans. John P. Leavey. In *Deconstruction and Philosophy*. John Sallis (ed.). Chicago: University of Chicago Press.

—— (1983) 'Mes Chances: Au Rendez-Vous de Quelques Stéréophonies Épicuriennes'. *Tijdschrift Voor Filosofie*, XLV, 3–40.

—— (1984) 'An Idea of Flaubert: "Plato's Letter"'. Trans. Peter Starr. *Modern Language Notes*, XCIX, 748–68.

—— (1984) 'Devant La Loi'. In A. Phillips Griffiths (ed.), *Philosophy and Literature*. Cambridge: Cambridge University Press.

—— (1984) *Feu La Cendre* (French text with Italian translation by Stefano Agosti). Firenze: Sansoni.

—— (1984) 'No Apocalypse, Not Now (Seven Missiles, Seven Missives)'. Trans. Catherine Porter and Philip Lewis. *Diacritics*, XIV, 20–31.

—— (1984) 'Of an Apocalyptic Tone Recently Adopted in Philosophy'. *Oxford Literary Review*, Vol. 6, No. 2, 3–37.

—— (1984) *Signéponge/Signsponge*. Trans. Richard Rand. New York: Columbia University Press.

—— (1987) *Ulysse gramophone: deux mots pour Joyce*. Paris: Galilée. Translation: 'Two Words for Joyce' (trans. Geoff Bennington). In Derek Attridge and Daniel Ferrer (eds). *Post-Structuralist Joyce: Essays from the French*. Cambridge: Cambridge University Press, 1984, 145–58.

—— (Winter 1985) 'Deconstruction in America' (interview with J. Creech, P. Kamuf and J. Todd). *Critical Exchange*, No. 17, 1–32.

—— (1985) *La Faculté de juger*. Paris: Minuit.

—— (1985) *The Ear of the Other: otobiography, transference, translation*. Trans. Peggy Kamuf and Avital Ronell. New York: Schocken Books.

—— (1985) 'Racism's Last Word'. Trans. Peggy Kamuf. *Critical Inquiry*, XII, 290–9. See also 'But, beyond . . . (Open Letter to Anne McClintock and Rob Nixon)'. *Critical Inquiry*, XIII (1986), 155–70.

—— (1986) *Glas*. Trans. John P. Leavey and Richard Rand. Lincoln, Nebr.: University of Nebraska Press.

—— (1986) *Memoires: For Paul de Man*. Trans. Cecile Lindsay, Jonathan Culler and Eduardo Cadava. New York: Columbia University Press.

—— (1986) *Parages*. Paris: Galilée.

—— (1986) *Schibboleth, pour Paul Celan*. Paris: Galilée, 1986. Translation: 'Shibboleth'. Trans. Joshua Wilner. In Geoffrey Hartman and Sanford Budick (eds). *Midrash And Literature*. New Haven, Conn.: Yale University Press, 307–47.

—— (1986) 'The Age of Hegel'. Trans. Susan Winnett. *Glyph*, I (new series), 3–43.

—— (1986) 'Admiration de Nelson Mandela: où les lois de la réflexion'. In

Derrida and Mustapha Tlili (eds). *Pour Nelson Mandela*. Paris: Gallimard. Translation: 'The Laws of Reflection: Nelson Mandela, in Admiration'. Trans. Mary Ann Caws and Isabelle Lorenz. In *For Nelson Mandela*. New York: Seaver Books, 1987, 13–42.

—— (1987) *Mémoires: for Paul de Man*. Trans. Cecile Lindsay, Jonathan Culler and Eduardo Cadava. New York: Columbia University Press.

—— (1987) *Psyché: inventions de l'autre*. Paris: Galilé.

—— (1987) *The Post-Card: From Socrates to Freud*. Trans. Alan Bass. Chicago, Ill.: University of Chicago Press.

—— (1987) *The Truth in Painting*. Trans. Geoff Bennington and Ian McLeod. Chicago, Ill.: University of Chicago Press.

—— (1987) 'Women in the Beehive: a seminar'. In Alice Jardine and Paul Smith (eds). *Men In Feminism*. London: Methuen, 189–203.

—— (1988a) 'Afterword: toward an ethic of discussion'. In *Limited Inc*, 2nd edn, Gerald Graff (ed.). Evanston, IL: Northwestern University Press. pp. 111–54.

—— (1988b) 'Like the Sound of the Sea Deep Within a Shell: Paul de Man's War'. Trans. Peggy Kamuf. *Critical Inquiry*, Vol. 14, No. 3, pp. 590–652.

—— (1988) 'Letter to a Japanese Friend'. Trans. David Wood and Andrew Benjamin. In David Wood and Robert Bernasconi (eds). *Derrida and Différance*. Evanston, Ill.: Northwestern University Press, 1–5.

—— (November 1988) 'The Politics of Friendship'. Trans. Gabriel Motzkin. *The Journal of Philosophy*, LXXXV, 632–45.

—— (1989) 'Biodegradables: Seven Diary Fragments'. Trans. Peggy Kamuf. *Critical Inquiry*, XV, 812–73.

—— (1989) 'Interpreting Signatures (Nietzsche/Derrida): Two Questions'. Trans. Diane P. Michelfelder and Richard E. Palmer. In Michelfelder and Palmer (eds). *Dialogue and Deconstruction: the Gadamer/Derrida encounter*. New York: State University of New York Press, 58–71.

—— (1989) 'Jacques Derrida in Conversation with Christopher Norris'. *Architectural Design*, LVIII, Nos. 1 and 2 (1989), 6–11. Reprinted in Andreas Papadakis, Catherine Cooke and Andrew Benjamin (eds). *Deconstruction: Omnibus Volume*. London: Academy Editions, 71–5.

—— (1989) *Limited Inc* (2nd edn), Gerald Graff (ed.) with Derrida's 'Afterword: toward an ethic of discussion'. Evanston, Ill.: Northwestern University Press.

—— (1989) *Of Spirit: Heidegger and the question*. Trans. Geoffrey Bennington and Rachel Bowlby. Chicago: University of Chicago Press.

—— (1990) *Du droit à la philosophie*. Paris: Galilée.

—— (1990) 'Force of Law: the "mystical foundation of authority"'. Trans. Mary Quaintance. *Cardozo Law Review*, Vol. 11, pp. 919–1045.

—— (1990) *Le Problème de la genèse dans la philosophie de Husserl*. Paris: Presses Universitaires de France. (Written 1952–3; hitherto unpublished.)

—— (1991) 'At This Very Moment in This Work Here I Am'. Trans. Ruben Berezdivin. In Robert Bernasconi and Simon Critchley (eds), *Re-Reading Levinas*. Bloomington: Indiana University Press. pp. 11–40.

—— (1992a) *Acts of Literature*, Derek Attridge (ed). London: Routledge.

—— (1992b) *The Other Heading: reflections on today's Europe*. Trans. P.-A. Brault and M.B. Haas. Bloomington, Ind.: Indiana University Press.

—— (1992c) *Given Time, I: Counterfeit Money*. Trans. Peggy Kamuf. Chicago: University of Chicago Press.

—— (1993a) *Aporias: dying – awaiting (one another at) the 'limits of truth'*. Trans. Thomas Dutoit. Stanford, CA: Stanford University Press.

—— (1993b) *Memoirs of the Blind: the self-portrait and other ruins*. Trans. Pascale-Anne Brault and Michael Naas. Chicago: University of Chicago Press.

—— (1994) *Spectres of Marx: the state of the debt, the work of mourning, and the new international*. Trans. Peggy Kamuf. London: Routledge.

—— (1995a) *On the Name*, Thomas Dutoit (ed.). Trans. Ian McLeod. Stanford, CA: Stanford University Press.

—— (1995b) *The Gift of Death*. Trans. David Wills. Chicago: University of Chicago Press.

—— (1995c) *Points: interviews, 1974-1994*, Elisabeth Weber (ed.). Trans. Peggy Kamuf and others. Stanford, CA: Stanford University Press.

—— (1996) *Archive Fever: a Freudian impression*. Trans. Eric Prenowitz. Chicago: University of Chicago Press.

—— (1997a) *The Politics of Friendship*. Trans. George Collins. London: Verso.

—— (1997b) *Adieu – à Emmanuel Levinas*. Paris: Galilée.

—— (1998) *Monolingualism of the Other, or, The Prosthesis of Origin*, trans. Patrick Mensah. Stanford, CA: Stanford University Press.

—— (2000) *Of Hospitality (Anne Dufourmantelle invites Jacques Derrida to respond)*, trans. Rachel Bowlby. Stanford, CA: Stanford University Press.

—— (2001a) *Papier Machine: le ruban de machine écrire et autres reponses.* Paris: Galilée.

—— (2001b) *L'Universit sans condition.* Paris: Galilée.

—— and Bennington, Geoff (1993) *Jacques Derrida*, trans. Bennington. Chicago: University of Chicago Press.

—— and Vattimo, Gianni (eds) (1998) *Religion.* Stanford, CA: Stanford University Press.

—— and Cixous, Hélène (1998) *Voiles.* Paris Galilée

—— and Malabou, Catherine (1999) *La Contre-Allée.* La Quinzaine Littéraire/Louis Vuitton.

—— and Elisabeth Roudinesco (2001). *De quoi demain . . . : dialogue.* Paris: Fayard-Galilée.

Descombes, Vincent (1986) *Objects of All Sorts: a philosophical grammar.* Trans. Lorna Scott-Fox and Jeremy Harding. Oxford: Basil Blackwell.

Detweiler, Robert (ed.) (1982) *Derrida and Biblical Studies.* Chico, Cal.: Scholar's Press.

Deutscher, Penelope (1997) *Yielding Gender: feminism, deconstruction, and the history of philosophy.* London: Routledge.

Dews, Peter (1987) *Logics of Disintegration: Post-Structuralist Thought and the Claims of Critical Theory.* London: Verso.

Docherty, Thomas (1990) *After Theory.* London: Routledge.

Donoghue, Denis (1976) *The Sovereign Ghost: studies in imagination.* Berkeley, Calif.: University of California Press.

Eagleton, Terry (1976) *Criticism and Ideology.* London: New Left Books.

—— (1983) *Literary Theory: an introduction.* Oxford: Blackwell.

—— (1986) 'Frère Jacques: the Politics of Deconstruction' and 'The Critic as Clown'. In *Against the Grain: selected essays.* London: Verso, 79–87 and 149–65.

—— (1989) *The Ideology of the Aesthetic.* Oxford: Basil Blackwell.

—— (1989) *The Significance of Theory.* Oxford: Basil Blackwell.

Easthope, Antony (1988) *British Post-Structuralism.* London: Routledge.

Eaves, Morris and Fischer, Michael (1986) *Romanticism and Contemporary Criticism.* Ithaca, NY and London: Cornell University Press.

Elam, Diane (1994) *Feminism and Deconstruction: ms en abime.* London: Routledge.

Eldritch, R. (1985) 'Deconstruction and its Alternatives'. *Man and World*, XVIII, 147–70.

Ellis, John M. (1989) *Against Deconstruction*. Princeton, NJ: Princeton University Press.

Empson, William (1961) *Seven Types of Ambiguity*. 2nd edn. Harmondsworth: Penguin.

Engell, James and Perkins, David (eds) (1988) *Teaching Literature: what Is needed now*. Cambridge, Mass.: Harvard University Press.

Evans, J. Claude (1991) *Strategies of Deconstruction: Derida and the myth of the voice*. Minneapolis: University of Minnesota Press.

Evans, Malcolm (1986) *Signifying Nothing: truth's true contents in Shakespeare's Text*. Brighton: Harvester Press.

Fairlamb, Horace L. (1994) *Critical Conditions: postmodernity and the question of foundations*. Cambridge: Cambridge University Press.

Farrell, Frank B. (1988) 'Iterability and Meaning: the Searle-Derrida debate'. *Metaphilosophy*, Vol. 19, pp. 53–64.

Feder, E.K., Rawlinson, M.C. and Zakin, E.Y. (eds) (1997) *Derrida and Feminism: recasting the question of woman*. New York & London: Routledge.

Fekete, John (1984) *The Structural Allegory: reconstructive encounters with the new French thought*. Manchester: Manchester University Press.

—— (ed.) (1987) *Life After Postmodernism: essays on value and culture*. Manchester: Manchester University Press.

Felman, Shoshana (ed.) (1982) *Literature and Psychoanalysis: the question of reading: otherwise*. Baltimore, Md: Johns Hopkins University Press.

—— (1983) *The Literary Speech-Act: Don Juan with J. L. Austin, or seduction in two languages*. Trans. Catherine Porter. Ithaca, NY: Cornell University Press.

—— (1985) *Writing and Madness*. Trans. Martha Evans *et al*. Ithaca, NY and London: Cornell University Press.

—— (1989) 'Paul de Man's Silence'. *Critical Inquiry*, Vol. 15, No. 4. pp. 704–44.

Felperin, Howard (1985) *Beyond Deconstruction: the uses and abuses of literary theory*. Oxford: Clarendon Press.

Fineman, Joel (1986) *Shakespeare's Perjured Eye: the invention of poetic subjectivity in the sonnets*. Berkeley and Los Angeles, Cal.: University of California Press.

Fischer, Michael (1985) *Does Deconstruction Make Any Difference? Poststructuralism and the defence of poetry in modern criticism*. Bloomington, Ind.: Indiana University Press.

—— (1989) *Stanley Cavell and Literary Skepticism*. Chicago, Ill.: University of Chicago Press.

Fish, Stanley (1989) *Doing What Comes Naturally: change, rhetoric, and the practice of theory in literary and legal studies*. New York and London: Oxford University Press.

Fish, Stanley E. (1982) 'With the Compliments of the Author: Reflections on Austin and Derrida'. *Critical Inquiry*, VIII, 693–72.

Flores, Ralph (1984) *The Rhetoric of Doubtful Authority: deconstructive readings of self-questioning narratives: St Augustine to Faulkner*. Ithaca, NY: Cornell University Press.

Flynn, Bernard C. (1984) 'Textuality and the Flesh: Derrida and Merleau-Ponty'. *Journal of the British Society for Phenomenology*, XV, 164–79.

Forrester, John (1990) *The Seductions of Psychoanalysis: Freud, Lacan and Derrida*. Cambridge: Cambridge University Press.

Foucault, Michel (1977) *Language, Counter-Memory, Practice*. Trans. Donald F. Bouchard and Sherry Simon. Oxford: Blackwell.

Frank, Manfred (1989) *What Is Neostructuralism?* Trans. Sabine Wilke and Richard Gray. Minneapolis, Minn.: University of Minnesota Press.

Frow, John (1986) 'Foucault and Derrida'. *Raritan*, V: 1 (Summer 1985), 31–42.

—— (1986) *Marxism and Literary History*. Oxford: Basil Blackwell.

Fukuyama, Francis (1992) *The End of History and the Last Man*. London: Macmillan.

Fynsk, Christopher (1986) *Heidegger: Thought and Historicity*. Ithaca, NY and London: Cornell University Press.

Garver, Newton and Seung-Chong, Lee (1994) *Derrida and Wittgenstein*. Philadelphia, PA: Temple University Press.

Gasché, Rodolphe (1986) *The Tain of the Mirror* (on Derrida's philosophical background: demanding but immensely valuable). Cambridge, Mass.: Harvard University Press.

—— (1994) *Inventions of Difference: on Jacques Derrida*. Cambridge, MA: Harvard U.P.

Gates, Henry Louis (ed.) (1986) *'Race', Writing and Difference*. Chicago, Ill.: University of Chicago Press.

Gearhart, Suzanne (Winter 1983) 'Philosophy *Before* Literature: Deconstruction, Historicity and the Work of Paul de Man'. *Diacritics*, XIII, 63–81.

Glendinning, Simon (1998) *On Being with Others: Heidegger, Wittgenstein, Derrida*. London: Routledge.

Gloversmith, Frank (ed.) (1984) *The Theory of Reading*. Brighton: Harvester Press.

Goodheart, Eugene (1985) *The Skeptic Disposition in Contemporary Criticism*. Princeton, NJ: Princeton University Press.

Goux, Jean-Joseph (1990) *Symbolic Economies: After Marx and Freud.* Trans. Jennifer Curtiss Gage. Ithaca, NY and London: Cornell University Press.

Graff, Gerald (1979) *Literature Against Itself: literary ideas in modern society.* Chicago, Ill. and London: University of Chicago Press.

—— (1987) *Professing Literature: an institutional history.* Chicago, Ill.: University of Chicago Press.

Graham, Joseph F. (ed.) (1985) *Difference in Translation.* Ithaca, NY: Cornell University Press.

Griffiths, A. Phillips (ed.) (1987) *Contemporary French Philosophy.* Cambridge: Cambridge University Press.

Griswold, Charles L. (1988) *Platonic Writings/Platonic Readings.* New York and London: Routledge.

Habermas, Jürgen (1987) *The Philosophical Discourse of Modernity: twelve lectures.* Trans. Frederick Lawrence. Cambridge: Polity Press.

Halliburton, David (1982) *Poetic Thinking: an approach to Heidegger.* Chicago, Ill.: University of Chicago Press.

Hamacher, W., Hertz, N. and Keenan, T. (eds) (1989) *Responses: on Paul de Man's Wartime Journalism.* Lincoln, Nebr.: University of Nebraska Press.

Handelman, Susan (1982) *The Slayers of Moses: the emergence of Rabbinic interpretation in modern literary theory.* Albany, NY: State University of New York Press.

Harland, Richard (1987) *Superstructuralism: the philosophy of structuralism and post-structuralism.* London: Methuen.

Harpham, Geoffrey Galt (1987) *The Ascetic Imperative in Culture and Criticism.* Chicago, Ill.: University of Chicago Press.

Harpham, Geoffrey G. (1991). 'Derrida and the Ethics of Criticism'. *Textual Practice,* Vol. 5, No. 3, 383–99.

Harris, Wendell V. (1988) *Interpretive Acts: in search of meaning.* Oxford: Oxford University Press.

Harrison, Bernard (1991) *Inconvenient Fictions: literature and the limits of theory.* New Haven: Yale University Press.

—— (1999) '"White Mythology" Revisited: Derrida and his critics on reason and rhetoric'. *Critical Inquiry,* Vol. 25, No. 3, 505–34.

Hart, Kevin (1989) *The Trespass of the Sign: deconstruction, theology and philosophy.* Cambridge: Cambridge University Press.

Hartman, Geoffrey (1970) *Beyond Formalism.* New Haven, Conn., and London: Yale University Press.

—— (1975) *The Fate of Reading and Other Essays*. Chicago, Ill., and London: University of Chicago Press.

—— (1978) 'The Recognition Scene of Criticism'. *Critical Inquiry*, IV, 407–16.

—— (1980) *Criticism in the Wilderness*. New Haven, Conn., and London: Yale University Press.

—— (5 April 1981) 'How Creative Should Literary Criticism Be?'. *New York Times Book Review*, 11, 24–5.

—— (1984) ' "Timely Utterance" Once More'. *Genre*, XVII, 37–49.

—— (1985) *Easy Pieces* (recent essays and review-articles). New York: Columbia University Press.

—— (1985) 'Wild, Fierce Yale'. In *Easy Pieces*, New York: Columbia University Press. pp. 188–98.

—— and Budick, Sanford (eds) (1986) *Midrash and Literature*. New Haven, Conn.: Yale University Press.

—— *et al.* (1979) *Deconstruction and Criticism*. London: Routledge & Kegan Paul.

Hartman, Geoffrey H. *The Unremarkable Wordsworth*. London: Routledge, 1987.

Harvey, Irene (1986) *Derrida and the Economy of Différance*. Bloomington, Ind.: Indiana University Press.

Havelock, Eric (1986) *The Muse Learns to Write: reflections on orality and literacy from antiquity to the present*. New Haven, Conn.: Yale University Press.

Hawkes, Terence (1977) *Structuralism and Semiotics*. London: Methuen.

Hawthorn, Jeremy (1987) *Unlocking the Text: fundamental issues in literary theory*. London: Edward Arnold.

Herman, L., Humbeeck, K., and Lernout, G. (eds) (1989) *Discontinuities: Essays on Paul de Man*. Amsterdam: Rodopi.

Hertz, Neil (1985) *The End of the Line: essays on psychoanalysis and the sublime*. New York: Columbia University Press.

Hirsch, David (1991) *The Deconstruction of Literature: criticism after Auschwitz*. Providence, RI: Brown University Press.

Hobson, Marian (1981) 'Scroll-Work' (on Derrida's *La Verité en Peinture*). *Oxford Literary Review*, IV, 94–102.

—— (1998) *Jacques Derrida: opening lines*. London: Routledge.

Holdheim, Werner (1989) 'Jacques Derrida's Apologia'. *Critical Inquiry*, Vol. 15, No. 4, 784–96.

Holland, N.J. (ed.) (1997) *Feminist Interpretations of Jacques Derrida*. Philadelphia, PA: Pennsylvania University Press.

Howells, Christina (1998) *Derrida: from phenomenology to ethics*. Cambridge: Polity Press.

Hughes, Daniel (1981) 'Geoffrey Hartman, Geoffrey Hartman'. *Modern Language Notes*, XCVI, 1134–48.

Husserl, Edmund (1964) *The Phenomenology of Internal Time-Consciousness*. Trans. James S. Churchill. Bloomington, Ind.: Indiana University Press.

—— (1970) *The Crisis of the European Sciences and Transcendental Phenomenology*. Trans. David Carr. Evanston, Ill.: Northwestern University Press.

Jacobs, Carol (1978) *The Dissimulating Harmony: images of interpretation in Nietzsche, Rilke and Benjamin*. Baltimore, Md: Johns Hopkins University Press.

—— *Uncontainable Romanticism: Shelley, Brontë, Kleist*. Baltimore, Md and London: Johns Hopkins University Press, 1989.

Jacobus, Mary (1986) *Reading Woman: essays in feminist criticism*. London: Methuen.

—— (1989) *Romanticism, Writing and Sexual Difference: essays on The Prelude*. Oxford: Clarendon Press.

Jameson, Fredric (1971) *Marxism and Form*. Princeton, NJ: Princeton University Press.

—— (1972) *The Prison-House of Language*. Princeton, NJ: Princeton University Press.

—— (1988) *The Ideologies of Theory* (Vol. 1, *Situations of Theory* and Vol. 2, *Syntax of History*). London: Routledge.

—— (1990) *Postmodernism, or the Cultural Logic of Late Capitalism*. Durham, NC: Duke University Press.

Johnson, Barbara (1981) *The Critical Difference: essays in the contemporary rhetoric of reading*. Baltimore, Md: Johns Hopkins University Press.

—— (ed.) (1981) *The Pedagogical Imperative* (*Yale French Studies*, 63). New Haven, Conn.: Yale University Press.

—— (1987) *A World of Difference*. Baltimore, Md and London: Johns Hopkins University Press.

—— (1990) 'The Surprise of Otherness: a note on the wartime writings of Paul de Man'. In Peter Collier and Helga Geyer-Ryan (eds), *Literary Theory Today*. Ithaca, NY: Cornell University Press. pp. 13–22.

—— (1994) *The Wake of Deconstruction*. Oxford: Blackwell.

Johnson, Christopher (1993) *System and Writing in the Philosophy of Jacques Derrida*. Cambridge: Cambridge University Press.

—— (1997) *Derrida*. London: Phoenix.

Judowitz, Dalia (1988) *Subjectivity and Representation in Descartes: the origins of modernity.* Cambridge: Cambridge University Press.

Kamuf, Peggy (ed.) (1991) *A Derrida Reader: between the blinds.* New York: Columbia University Press and London: Harvester-Wheatsheaf.

—— (1988) *Signature Pieces: on the institution of authorship.* Ithaca, NY and London: Cornell University Press.

Kaplan, Alice Jaeger (1986) *Reproductions of Banality: Fascism, literature and French intellectual life.* Minneapolis, Minn.: University of Minnesota Press.

Kauffman, Linda (ed.) (1989) *Feminism and Institutions: dialogues on feminist theory.* Oxford: Basil Blackwell.

—— (ed.) (1989) *Gender and Theory: dialogues on feminist criticism.* Oxford: Basil Blackwell.

Kennedy, Alan (1990) *Reading Resistance Value: deconstructive practice and the politics of literary critical encounters.* London: Macmillan.

Kermode, Frank (1983) *Essays on Fiction, 1971–82.* London: Routledge & Kegan Paul.

Kierkegaard, Soren (1954) *Fear and Trembling.* Trans. Walter Lowrie. New York: Anchor Books.

Kimball, Roger (1990) 'The Case of Paul de Man', in *Tenured Radicals: how politics has corrupted our higher education.* New York: Harper & Row. 96–115.

Kirwan, James (1990) *Literature, Rhetoric, Metaphysics: literary theory and literary aesthetics.* London: Routledge.

Knellwolf, Christa and Norris, Christopher (eds) (2001) *The Cambridge History of Literary Criticism,* Vol. 9: *twentieth-century historical, philosophical and psychological perspectives.* Cambridge: Cambridge University Press.

Koelb, Clayton (1988) *Inventions of Reading: rhetoric and the literary imagination.* Ithaca, NY and London: Cornell University Press.

—— and Lokke, Virgil (eds) (1987) *The Current in Criticism: essays on the present and future of literary theory.* West Lafayette, Ind.: Purdue University Press.

Kofman, Sarah (1984) *Lectures de Derrida.* Paris: Galilée.

—— (1985) *The Enigma of woman: woman in Freud's writing.* Trans. Catherine Porter. Ithaca, NY and London: Cornell University Press.

Kramer, Matthew H. (1991) *Legal Theory, Political Theory, and Deconstruction: against Rhadamanthus.* Bloomington, Ind.: Indiana University Press.

Kreiswirth, Martin and Cheetham, Mark (eds) (1990) *Theory Between the*

Disciplines: authority/vision/politics. Ann Arbor, Mich.: University of Michigan Press.

Krell, David Farrell and Wood, David (eds) (1988) *Exceedingly Nietzsche: aspects of contemporary Nietzsche interpretation*. London: Routledge.

Krieger, Murray (1979) *Poetic Presence and Illusion*. Baltimore, Md, and London: Johns Hopkins University Press.

—— (ed.) (1987) *The Aims of Interpretation: subject/text/history*. New York: Columbia University Press.

—— (1988) *Words about Words about Words: theory, criticism and the literary text*. Baltimore, Md and London: Johns Hopkins University Press.

Kristeva, Julia (1989) *Language, the Unknown: an initiation into linguistics*. Trans. Anne M. Menke. London: Harvester-Wheatsheaf.

Krupnick, Mark (ed.) (1983) *Displacement: Derrida and after*. Bloomington, Ind.: Indiana University Press.

LaCapra, Dominick (1985) *History and Criticism*. Ithaca, NY and London: Cornell University Press.

—— (1989) *Typography: mimesis, philosophy, politics*. In Christopher Fynsk (ed.). Cambridge, Mass.: Harvard University Press.

Lacoue-Labarthe, Philippe and Nancy, Jean-Luc (eds) (1981) *Les Fins de l'homme*. Paris: Galilée.

—— and Nancy, Jean-Luc (1988) *The Literary Absolute: the theory of literature in German romanticism*. Trans. Philip Barnard and Cheryl Lester. Ithaca, NY: State University of New York Press.

Lang, Berel (1990) *The Anatomy of Philosophical Style: literary philosophy and the philosophy of literature*. Oxford: Basil Blackwell.

Latimer, Dan (ed.) (1989) *Contemporary Critical Theory*. New York: Harcourt, Brace Jovanovich.

Lawlor, L. (1991) 'A Little Daylight: a reading of Derrida's "White Mythology"'. *Man and World*, Vol. 13, 285–300.

—— (1992) *Imagination and Chance: the difference between the thought of Ricoeur and Derrida*. Albany, NY: SUNY Press.

—— (ed.) (1994) *Derrida's Interpretation of Husserl*. Memphis: Memphis University Press.

Leavey, John P. (1982) 'Jacques Derrida's *Glas*: A Translated Selection and Some Comments on an Absent Colossus'. *Clio*, XI, 327–37.

—— (ed.) (1986) *Glassary* (commentary on Derrida's *Glas*). Lincoln, Nebr.: University of Nebraska Press.

Leavis, F. R. (1937) 'Literary Criticism and Philosophy' (reply to René Wellek). *Scrutiny*, VI, 59–70.

Lecercle, Jean-Jacques (1985) *Philosophy Through the Looking-Glass: language, nonsense, desire*. La Salle, Ind.: Open Court Publishers.

Le Doeuff, Michèle (1989) *The Philosophical Imaginary* (trans. Colin Gordon). London: Athlone Press.

Lehman, David (1991) *Signs of the Times: deconstruction and the fall of Paul de Man*. London: Deutsch.

Leitch, Vincent (1987) *American Literary Criticism from the Thirties to the Eighties*. New York: Columbia University Press.

—— (1983) *Deconstructive Criticism: an advanced introduction*. New York: Columbia University Press.

Lentricchia, Frank (1980) *After the New Criticism*. London: Athlone Press.

—— (1983) *Criticism and Social Change*. Chicago, Ill.: University of Chicago Press.

—— and McLaughlin, Thomas (eds) (1990) *Critical Terms for Literary Study*. Chicago, Ill.: University of Chicago Press.

Levinas, Emmanuel (1969) *Totality and Infinity*. Trans. A. Lingis. Pittsburgh: Duquesne University Press.

—— (1981) *Otherwise than Being, or Beyond Essence*. Trans. A. Lingis. The Hague: Martinus Nijhoff.

Lévi-Strauss, Claude (1961) *Tristes Tropiques*. Trans. John Russell. London: Hutchinson.

—— (1966) *The Savage Mind*. London: Weidenfeld & Nicolson.

Lipovetsky, Gilles (1992). *Le crepuscule du devoir*. Paris: Gallimard.

Llewelyn, John (1985) *Derrida on the Threshold of Sense* (offers some acute philosophical commentary). London: Macmillan.

—— (Autumn/Winter 1988) 'Glasnostalgia'. *Bulletin of the Hegel Society of Great Britain*, No. 18, 33–42.

Lodge, David (1977) *The Modes of Modern Writing: Metaphor, Metonymy, and the Typology of Modern Literature*. London: Edward Arnold.

—— (ed.) (1988) *Modern Criticism and Theory: A Reader*. London: Longman.

Loesberg, Jonathan (1991) *Aestheticism and Deconstruction*. Princeton, NJ: Princeton University Press.

Lotringer, Sylvère and Cohen, Sande (eds) (2001) *French Theory in America*. London: Routledge.

Lukacher, Ned (1987) *Primal Scenes: Literature, Psychoanalysis, Philosophy*. Ithaca, NY and London: Cornell University Press.

MacCabe, Colin (1985) *Theoretical Essays: Film, Linguistics, Literature*. Manchester: Manchester University Press.

MacCannell, Juliet Flower (1984) 'Portrait: de Man'. *Genre*, XVII, 51–74.

Macey, David (1988) *Lacan In Contexts*. London: Verso.

Macherey, Pierre (1978) *A Theory of Literary Production*. Trans. Geoffrey Wall. London: Routledge & Kegan Paul.

Machin, Richard (1986) *Paul de Man*. London: Croom Helm.

—— and Norris, Christopher (eds) *Post-Structuralist Readings of English Poetry*. Cambridge: Cambridge University Press, forthcoming.

Madison, G.B. (ed.) (1993) *Working Through Derrida*. Evanston, IL: Northwestern University Press.

Magliola, Robert (1984) *Derrida on the Mend*. West Lafayette, Ind.: Purdue University Press.

Malachowski, Alan (ed.) (1990) *Reading Rorty: critical responses to Philosophy and the Mirror of Nature and beyond*. Oxford: Basil Blackwell.

Mapp, Nigel (Spring 1990) On Paul de Man's *The Resistance to Theory* (review-article). *Textual Practice*, IV: I, 122–37.

—— (1990) 'Deconstruction'. In Martin Coyle, Malcolm Kelsall and John Peck (eds) *Encyclopedia of Literature and Criticism*. London: Routledge, 777–90.

Margolis, Joseph (1989) *Texts Without Referents: Reconciling Science and Narrative*. Oxford: Basil Blackwell.

Martin, Bill (1992) *Matrix and Line: Derrida and the possibilities of postmodern social theory*. Albany, NY: SUNY Press.

Marx, Karl (1968) 'The Eighteenth Brumaire of Louis Bonaparte'. In *Marx and Engels: selected works*, 96–179. London: Lawrence & Wishart.

McCarthy, Thomas (1991) *Ideals and Illusions: on reconstruction and deconstruction in contemporary critical theory*. Cambridge, MA: MIT Press.

McDonald, Henry (1990) 'Crossroads of Scepticism: Wittgenstein, Derrida, and ostensive definition'. *Philosophical Forum*, Vol. 21, No. 3, pp. 261–76.

McGann, Jerome J. (1988) *Social Values and Poetic Acts*. Cambridge, Mass.: Harvard University Press.

McKenna, W.R. and Evans, J.C. (eds.) (1995) *Derrida and Phenomenology*. Boston: Kluwer.

McQuillan, Martin (2001) *Paul de Man*. London: Routledge

Meese, Elizabeth and Parker, Alice (eds) (1989) *The Difference Within: feminism and critical theory*. Amsterdam: John Benjamins Publishing Company.

Megill, Alan (1985) *Prophets of Extremity: Nietzsche, Heidegger, Foucault, Derrida*. Berkeley and Los Angeles: University of California Press.

Mehlman, Jeffrey (1979) *Revolution and Repetition*. Berkeley & Los Angeles, Calif.: University of California Press.

—— (1995) 'Perspectives: on Paul de Man and *Le Soir*', in *Genealogies of the Text: literature, psychoanalysis and politics in modern France*. Cambridge: Cambridge University Press. pp. 113–30.

Melville, Stephen (1986) *Philosophy Beside Itself: on deconstruction and modernism*. Minneapolis: University of Minnesota Press.

Merleau-Ponty, Maurice (1962) *The Phenomenology of Perception*. London: Routledge & Kegan Paul.

—— (1964) *Signs*. Trans. McCleary. Evanston, Ill.: Northwestern University Press.

Merod, Jim (1986) *The Political Responsibility of the Critic*. Ithaca, NY and London: Cornell University Press.

Merquior, J. G. (1986) *From Prague to Paris: a critique of structuralist and post-structuralist thought*. London: Verso.

Merrell, Floyd (1985) *Deconstruction Reframed*. West Lafayette, Ind.: Purdue University Press.

Meyer, Michel (ed.) (2001) *Questioning Derrida, with his replies on philosophy*. Aldershot: Ashgate.

Michaels, Walter Benn and Knapp, Steven (1982) 'Against Theory'. *Critical Inquiry*, VIII, 723–42.

Middleton, Peter (1983) 'The Revolutionary Poetics of William Blake: silence, syntax and spectres'. *Oxford Literary Review*, VI, 35–51.

Mileur, Jean-Pierre (1990) *The Critical Romance: the critic as reader, writer, hero*. Madison, Wisc.: University of Wisconsin Press.

Miller, J. Hillis (1966) 'The Geneva School'. *The Critical Quarterly*, VII, 305–21.

—— (1970) *Thomas Hardy: distance and desire*. Cambridge, Mass.: Harvard University Press.

—— (1977) 'The Limits of Pluralism, II: The Critic as Host'. *Critical Inquiry*, III, 439–47.

—— (1981) 'Remembering and Disremembering in Nietzsche's "On Truths and Lies in a Non-Moral Sense"'. *Boundary 2*, IX, 41–54.

—— (1982) *Fiction and Repetition: seven english novels*. Oxford: Blackwell.

—— (1984) 'The Search for Grounds in Literary Study'. *Genre*, XVII, 19–36.

—— (1985) *The Linguistic Moment: Wordsworth to Stevens*. Princeton, NJ: Princeton University Press.

—— (1987) *The Ethics of Reading*. New York: Columbia University Press.

—— (1991) *Hawthorne and History*. Oxford: Basil Blackwell.

—— (1991) *Parables, Tropes, Performatives: essays on twentieth-century literature*. London: Harvester-Wheatsheaf.

—— (1991) *Victorian Subjects*. London: Harvester-Wheatsheaf.

Mitchell, Sollace (1983) 'Post-Structuralism, Empiricism and Interpretation'. In Sollace Mitchell and Michael Rosen (eds). *The Need for Interpretation*. London: Athlone Press, 54–89.

Mitchell, W. J. T. (ed.) (1985) *Against Theory: literary studies and the new pragmatism*. Chicago, Ill.: University of Chicago Press.

Mohanty, J. N. (1989) *Transcendental Phenomenology*. Oxford: Basil Blackwell.

Mohanty, S. P. (1990) *Literary Theory and the Claims of History*. Oxford: Basil Blackwell.

Moi, Toril (1985) *Sexual/Textual Politics: feminist literary theory*. London: Methuen.

Morris, Michael (2000) 'Metaphor and Philosophy: an encounter with Derrida'. *Philosophy*, Vol. 75, 225–44.

Mouffe, Chantal (ed.) (1996) *Deconstruction and Pragmatism*. London: Routledge.

Moynihan, Robert (1986) *A Recent Imagining: interviews with Harold Bloom, Geoffrey Hartman, J. Hillis Miller, Paul de Man*. Hamden, Conn.: Shoe String Press.

Mueller-Volmer, Kurt (ed.) (1986) *The Hermeneutics Reader: texts of the German tradition from the enlightenment to the present*. Oxford: Basil Blackwell.

Muller, John P. and Richardson, William J. (eds) (1987) *The Purloined Poe: Lacan, Derrida and psychoanalytic reading*. Baltimore, Md and London: Johns Hopkins University Press.

Nägele, Rainer (1987) *Reading After Freud: Essays on Goethe, Hölderlin, Habermas, Nietzsche, Brecht, Celan and Freud*. New York: Columbia University Press.

—— (1989) *Benjamin's Ground: new readings of Walter Benjamin*. Detroit, Mich.: Wayne State University Press.

Natoli, Joseph (ed.) (1989) *Literary Theory's Future(s)*. Urbana-Champaign, Ill.: University of Illinois Press.

—— (1987) *Tracing Literary Theory*. Urbana-Champaign, Ill.: University of Illinois Press.

Nealon, J.T. (1993) *Double Reading: postmodernism after deconstruction*. Ithaca, NY: Cornell University Press.

Neel, Jasper (1988) *Plato, Derrida and Writing*. Carbondale, Ill.: Southern Illinois University Press.

Nelson, Cary (ed.) (1988) *Theory in the Classroom*. Urbana-Champaign, Ill.: University of Illinois Press.

—— and Grossberg, Lawrence (eds) (1988) *Marxism and the Interpretation of Culture*. Urbana-Champaign, Ill.: University of Illinois Press.

Newton, K. M. (ed.) (1987) *Twentieth-Century Literary Theory: A Reader*. London: Macmillan.

——(1990) *Interpreting the Text: a critical introduction to the theory and practice of literary interpretation*. London: Harvester-Wheatsheaf.

Nietzsche, Friedrich (1954) *The Portable Nietzsche*. Trans. and ed. Walter Kaufmann. New York: Viking.

—— (1977) *A Nietzsche Reader*. Selected and trans. R. J. Hollingdale. Harmondsworth: Penguin.

—— (1986) *Human, All Too Human: a book for free spirits*. Trans. R. J. Hollingdale. Cambridge: Cambridge University Press.

—— (1990) *Unmodern Observations* (*Unzeitgemässe Betrachtungen*, trans. and ed. William Arrowsmith). New Haven, Conn.: Yale University Press.

Norris, Christopher (1983) *The Deconstructive Turn: essays in the rhetoric of philosophy*. London: Methuen.

—— (Summer 1985) 'Reason, Rhetoric, Theory: Empson and de Man'. *Raritan*, V. 1, 89–106.

—— (1985) *The Contest of Faculties: deconstruction, philosophy and theory*. London: Methuen.

—— (1987) *Derrida*. London: Fontana.

—— (1988) *Paul de Man: deconstruction and the critique of aesthetic ideology*. New York and London: Routledge.

—— (1988) *Deconstruction and the Interests of Theory*. London: Pinter and Norman, Okl.: University of Oklahoma Press.

—— (February 1988) 'Paul de Man's Past'. *The London Review of Books*, X: 3, 7–11.

—— (1988a) *Paul de Man: deconstruction and the critique of aesthetic ideology*. New York: Routledge.

—— (1988b) 'Law, Deconstruction and the Resistance to Theory'. In *Deconstruction and the Interests of Theory*. London: Pinter Publishers. 126–55.

—— (1989) 'Derrida's "Vérité"'. In Elinor Shaffer (ed.). *Comparative Criticism*, XI. Cambridge: Cambridge University Press, 235–51.

—— (1989a) 'Deconstruction, Postmodernism and Philosophy: Habermas on Derrida'. *Praxis International*, VIII: 4 (January), 426–46.

—— (1989b) 'Deconstruction as *Not* just a "Kind of Writing": Derrida and the claim of reason'. In R. W. Dasenbrock (ed.) *Re-Drawing the Lines: analytic philosophy, deconstruction, and literary theory*. Minneapolis, Minn.: University of Minnesota Press, 189–203.

—— (1990) *Spinoza and the Origins of Modern Critical Theory*. Oxford: Basil Blackwell.

—— (1990) *What's Wrong with Postmodernism: critical theory and the ends of philosophy*. Baltimore: Johns Hopkins University Press.

—— (1994) *Truth and the Ethics of Criticism*. Manchester: Manchester University Press.

—— (1996) *Reclaiming Truth: contribution to a critique of cultural relativism*. London: Lawrence & Wishart.

—— (1997a) *New Idols of the Cave: on the limits of anti-realism*. Manchester: Manchester University Press.

—— (1997b) *Against Relativism: philosophy of science, deconstruction and critical theory*. Oxford: Blackwell.

—— (2000a) *Minding the Gap: philosophy of science and epistemology in the two traditions*. Amherst, MA: University of Massachusetts Press.

—— (2000b) *Deconstruction and the Unfinished Project of Modernity*. London: Athlone Press.

—— and Benjamin, Andrew (1988) *What Is Deconstruction?* London: Academy Editions.

Novitz, David (Winter 1985) 'Metaphor, Derrida, and Davidson'. *Journal of Aesthetics and Art Criticism*, XLIV: 2, 101–14.

O'Hara, Daniel T. (ed.) (1985) *Why Nietzsche Now?* Bloomington, Ind.: Indiana University Press.

Olsen, Stein Haugom (1987) *The End of Literary Theory*. Cambridge: Cambridge University Press.

Ong, Walter J. (1962) *The Barbarian Within*. New York: Macmillan.

Parker, Andrew (1981) 'Taking Sides (on History): Derrida re-Marx'. *Diacritics*, XI, 57–73 (review of Lentricchia, *After the New Criticism*).

Parker, Ian and Shotter, John (eds) (1990) *Deconstructing Social Psychology*. London: Routledge.

Parker, Patricia (1987) *Literary Fat Ladies: rhetoric, gender, property*. New York and London: Routledge.

—— and Hartman, Geoffrey (eds) (1985) *Shakespeare and the Question of Theory*. London and New York: Methuen.

Patrick, Morag (1997) *Derrida, Responsibility and Ethics*. Aldershot: Ashgate.

Pavel, Thomas G. (1989) *The Feud of Language: a history of structuralist thought*. Oxford: Basil Blackwell.

Pêcheux, Michel (1982) *Language, Semantics and Ideology*. London: Macmillan.

Perpich, Diane (1998). 'A Singular Justice: ethics and politics between Derrida and Levinas'. *Philosophy Today*, Vol. 42 (supplement), 59–70.

Petrey, Sandy (1990) *Speech Acts and Literary Theory*. New York and London: Routledge.

Petterson, Torsten (1988) *Literary Interpretation: Current Models and a New Departure*. Abo (Finland): Abo Academic Press.

Pirsig, Robert M. (1974) *Zen and the Art of Motorcycle Maintenance*. London: The Bodley Head.

Pitstock, Catherine (1998) *After Writing: on the liturgical consummation of philosophy*. Oxford: Blackwell.

Plato (1960) *The Gorgias*. Intro. and trans. Walter Hamilton. Harmondsworth: Penguin.

—— (1973) *The Phaedrus and Letters VII and VIII*. Intro. and trans. Walter Hamilton. Harmondsworth: Penguin.

Postone, Moishe (1998) 'Deconstruction as Social Critique: Derrida on Marx and the New World Order'. *History and Theory*, Vol. 37, No. 3. 370–87.

Pradhan, S. (Spring 1986) 'Minimalist Semantics: Davidson and Derrida on Meaning, Use and Convention'. *Diacritics*, XVI: 1, 66–77.

Prendergast, Christopher (1990) 'Making the Difference: Paul de Man, Fascism and deconstruction'. In Bruce Robbins (ed.), *Intellectuals, Aesthetics, Politics, Academics*. Minneapolis: University of Minnesota Press.

Priest, Graham (1994) 'Derrida and Self-Reference'. *Australasian Journal of Philosophy*, Vol. 72, No. 1, 103–111.

—— (1995) *Beyond the Limits of Thought*. Cambridge: Cambridge University Press.

Putnam, Hilary (Autumn 1985) 'A Comparison of Something with Something Else'. *New Literary History*, XVII: 1, 61–79.

Raffoul, François (1998) 'The Subject of the Welcome: on Jacques Derrida's "Adieu à Emmanuel Levinas"'. *Symposium*, Vol. 2, No. 2, 211–22.

Rainsford, Dominic and Woods, Tim (eds) (1999) *Critical Ethics: text, theory and responsibility*. London: Macmillan.

Rajan, Tilottama *The Supplement of Reality: Figures of Understanding in Romantic Theory and Practice*. Ithaca, NY: Cornell University Press.

Rajnath (ed.) (1989) *Deconstruction: a critique*. London: Macmillan.

Rand, Richard (ed.) (2001) *Futures: of Jacques Derrida*. Stanford, CA: Stanford University Press.

Rapaport, Herman (1984) 'Geoffrey Hartman and the Spell of Sounds'. *Genre*, XVII, 159–77.

—— (2001) *The Theory Mess: deconstruction in eclipse*. New York: Columbia University Press.

Raval, Suresh (1981) *Metacriticism*. Athens, Georgia: University of Georgia Press.

Ray, William (1984) *Literary Meaning: From Phenomenology to Deconstruction*. Oxford: Blackwell.

Rée, Jonathan (1987) *Philosophical Tales: an essay on philosophy and literature*. London: Methuen.

Reed, Arden (ed.) (1984) *Romanticism and Language*. London: Methuen.

Reising, Russell (1986) *The Unusable Past: theory and the study of American literature*. New York and London: Methuen.

Reiss, Timothy J. (1988) *The Uncertainty of Analysis: problems in truth, meaning and culture*. Ithaca, NY and London: Cornell University Press.

Rice, Philip and Waugh, Patricia (eds) (1989) *Modern Literary Theory: A Reader*. London: Edward Arnold.

Richards, I. A. (1924) *Principles of Literary Criticism*. London: Paul Trench Trubner.

—— (1936) *The Philosophy of Rhetoric*. London and New York: Oxford University Press.

Ronell, Avital (1986) *Dictations: on haunted writing*. Bloomington, Ind.: Indiana University Press.

Rorty, Richard (1978) 'Philosophy as a Kind of Writing'. *New Literary History*, X, 141–60.

—— (1982) *Consequences of Pragmatism*. Brighton: Harvester.

—— (1984) 'Deconstruction and Circumvention'. *Critical Inquiry*, XI, 1–23.

—— (1985) 'Texts and Lumps'. *New Literary History*, XVII, 1–15.

—— (1986) 'The Higher Nominalism in a Nutshell: A Reply to Henry Staten'. *Critical Inquiry*, XII, 461–6.

—— (Spring 1989) 'Is Derrida a Transcendental Philosopher?' *Yale Journal of Criticism*, II: 2, 207–17.

—— (1989a) *Contingency, Irony, and Solidarity*. Cambridge: Cambridge University Press.

—— (1989b) 'Two Meanings of "Logocentrism": a Reply to Norris'. In R. W. Dasenbrock (ed.) *Re-Drawing the Lines: analytic philosophy, deconstruction, and literary theory*. Minneapolis, Minn.: University of Minnesota Press, 204–16.

—— (1991) *Essays on Heidegger and Others*. Cambridge: Cambridge University Press.

Rose, Gillian (1984) *Dialectic of Nihilism: post-structuralism and law*. Oxford: Blackwell.

Rosen, Stanley (1987) *Hermeneutics as Politics*. New York and Oxford: Oxford University Press.

—— (1988) *The Quarrel Between Philosophy and Poetry: Studies in Ancient Thought*. New York and London: Routledge.

Royle, Nicholas (1995) *After Derrida*. London: Routledge.

—— (ed.) (2000) *Deconstructions: a user's guide*. London: Macmillan.

Russell, Bertrand (1954) *A History of Western Philosophy*. London: Allen & Unwin.

Ryan, Michael (1982) *Marxism and Deconstruction: A Critical Articulation*. Baltimore, Md: Johns Hopkins University Press.

—— (1989) *Politcs and Culture: working hypotheses for a post-revolutionary society*. Baltimore, Md and London: Johns Hopkins University Press.

Rylance, Rick (ed.) (1987) *Debating Texts: a reader in twentieth-century literary theory and method*. Milton Keynes: Open University Press.

Said, Edward (1978) *Orientalism*. New York: Pantheon.

—— (1979) 'The Text, the World, the Critic'. In Josué V. Harari (ed.), *Textual Strategies: perspectives in post-structuralist criticism*, 161–88. London: Methuen.

—— (1984) *The World, the Text and the Critic*. London: Faber & Faber.

Sallis, John (ed.) (1988) *Deconstruction and Philosophy: The Texts of Jacques Derrida*. Chicago, Ill.: University of Chicago Press.

Salusinszky, Imre (1987) *Criticism In Society: Interviews with Jacques Derrida, Northrop Frye, Harold Bloom, Barbara Johnson, Frank Lentricchia, J. Hillis Miller, Geoffrey Hartman, Frank Kermode and Edward Said*. London: Methuen.

Saussure, Ferdinand de (1974) *Course in General Linguistics*. Trans. Wade Baskin. London: Fontana.

Schauber, Ellen and Spolsky, Ellen (1986) *The Bounds of Interpretation: linguistic theory and literary text*. Stanford, Cal.: Stanford University Press.

Schleifer, Ronald (1984) 'The Anxiety of Allegory: de Man, Greimas, and the Problem of Referentiality'. *Genre*, XVII, 215–37.

Scholes, Robert C. (1990) *Protocols of Reading*. New Haven, Conn.: Yale University Press.

—— (1985) *Textual Power: Literary Theory and the Teaching of English*. New Haven, Conn.: Yale University Press.

Schrift, Alan D. (1990) *Nietzsche and the Question of Interpretation: between hermeneutics and deconstruction*. London: Routledge.

Schultz, William R. and Fried, Lewis L.B. (eds) (1992) *Jacques Derrida: an annotated primary and secondary bibliography*. New York: Garland Publishing.

Searle, John R. (1972) *Speech Acts: an essay in the philosophy of language*. Cambridge: Cambridge University Press.

—— (1977) 'Reiterating the Differences' (reply to Derrida). *Glyph*, I, 198–208.

Sedgwick, Peter (2001) *Descartes to Derrida: an introduction to European philosophy*. Oxford: Blackwell.

Selden, Raman (1984) *Criticism and Objectivity*. London: Allen & Unwin.

—— *A Guide to Modern Literary Theory*. Brighton: Harvester Press, 1985.

—— (ed.) (1995) *The Cambridge History of Literary Criticism, Vol. 8: from formalism to poststructuralism*. Cambridge: Cambridge University Press.

Seung, T. K. (1982) *Structuralism and Hermeneutics*. New York: Columbia University Press.

Shusterman, Richard (January 1986) 'Analytic Aesthetics, Deconstruction, and Literary Theory'. *Monist*, LXIX: 1, 22–38.

—— (Autumn 1986) 'Deconstruction and Analysis: confrontation or convergence'. *British Journal of Aesthetics*, XXVI: 4, 311–27.

Siebers, Tobin (1988) *The Ethics of Criticism*. Ithaca, NY and London: Cornell University Press.

Silverman, Hugh J. (1987) *Inscriptions: between phenomenology and structuralism*. New York and London: Routledge, 1987.

—— (ed.) (1988) *Philosophy and Non-Philosophy since Merleau-Ponty*. London: Routledge.

—— (ed.) (1989) *Derrida and Deconstruction*. London: Routledge.

—— (ed.) (1990) *Postmodernism – Philosophy and the Arts*. London: Routledge.

—— and Aylesworth, Gary (eds) (1990) *The Textual Sublime: deconstruction and its differences*. Albany, NY: SUNY Press.

—— and Ihde, Don (eds) (1985) *Hermeneutics and Deconstruction*. Albany: State University of New York Press.

—— and Welton, Donn (eds) (1988) *Postmodernism and Continental Philosophy*. Albany, NY: State University of New York Press.

Simpson, David (ed.) (1988) *The Origins of Modern Critical Thought: German aesthetics and literary criticism from Lessing to Hegel*. Cambridge: Cambridge University Press.

Siskin, Clifford (1988) *The Historicity of Romantic Discourse*. New York and Oxford: Oxford University Press.

Skinner, Q. (ed.) (1985) *The Return of Grand Theory in the Human Sciences*. Cambridge: Cambridge University Press.

Sloterdijk, Peter (1988) *Critique of Cynical Reason*. Trans. Michael Eldred. London: Verso.

Smith, Barbara Herrnstein (1988) *Contingencies of value: alternative perspectives for critical theory*. Cambridge, Mass.: Harvard University Press.

Smith, John H. (1987) *The Spirit and its Letter: traces of rhetoric in Hegel's philosophy of Bildung*. Ithaca, NY and London: Cornell University Press.

—— and Kerrigan, William (eds) (1984) *Taking Chances: Derrida, psychoanalysis and literature*. Baltimore: Johns Hopkins University Press.

Smith, Paul (1988) *Discerning the Subject*. Minneapolis, Minn.: University of Minnesota Press.

Solomon, J. Fisher (1988) *Discourse and Reference in the Nuclear Age*. Norman, Okl.: University of Oklahoma Press.

Solomon, Robert C. (1988) *Continental Philosophy Since 1750: the rise and fall of the self*. Oxford: Oxford University Press.

Spanos, William V. *et al*. (eds) (1982) *The Question of Textuality: strategies of reading in contemporary criticism*. Bloomington, Ind.: Indiana University Press.

Spivak, Gayatri C. (1987) *In Other Worlds: essays in cultural politics*. New York and London: Methuen.

—— (1990) *The Post-Colonial Critic: Interviews, Strategies, Dialogues* (ed. Sarah Harasym). London: Routledge.

—— (1980) 'Revolutions that as yet have no Model: Derrida's *Limited Inc.*'. *Diacritics*, X, 29–49.

—— (1981) 'Reading the World: Literary Studies in the 1980s'. *College English*, LXIII, 671–9.

—— (1981) 'Sex and History in *The Prelude* (1805): books nine to thirteen'. *Texas Studies in Language and Literature*, XXIII, 324–60.

Sprinker, Michael (1987) *Imaginary Relations: Aesthetics and Ideology in the Theory of Historical Materialism*. London: Verso.

—— (ed.) (1999) *Ghostly Demarcations: a symposium on Jacques Derrida's Spectres of Marx*. London: Verso.

Starobinski, Jean (1988) *Jean-Jacques Rousseau: Transparency and Obstruction*. Trans. Arthur Goldhammer. Chicago, Ill.: University of Chicago Press.

Staten, Henry (1984) *Wittgenstein and Derrida*. Lincoln, Neb. and London: University of Nebraska Press.

—— (1986) 'Rorty's Circumvention of Derrida', *Critical Inquiry*, XII, 453–61.

—— (Winter 1988) 'Wittgenstein and the Intricate Evasions of "Is" '. *New Literary History*, XVIII: 2, 281–300.

—— (1990) *Nietzsche's Voice*. Ithaca, NY and London: Cornell University Press.

Steiner, George (1989) *Real Presences*. Chicago, Ill.: University of Chicago Press.

Sussman, Henry S. (1989) *High Resolution: critical theory and the problem of literacy*. New York: Oxford University Press.

—— (1982) *The Hegelian Aftermath: Readings in Hegel, Kierkegaard, Freud, Proust, and James*. Baltimore, Md: Johns Hopkins University Press.

Sychrava, Juliet (1989) *Schiller to Derrida: Idealism in Aesthetics*. Cambridge: Cambridge University Press.

Tate, Allen (1953) *The Forlorn Demon*. Chicago, Ill.: Regnery.

Taylor, Mark C. (1984) *Erring: A Postmodern A/theology*. Chicago, Ill.: University of Chicago Press.

—— (ed.) (1986) *Deconstruction in Context: literature and philosophy*. Chicago, Ill.: University of Chicago Press.

—— (1987) *Altarity*. Chicago: University of Chicago Press.

Thody, Philip (1977) *Roland Barthes: a conservative estimate*. London: Macmillan.

Todorov, Tzvetan (ed.) (1989) *French Literary Theory Today: a reader*. Trans. R. Carter. Cambridge: Cambridge University Press.

—— (1988) *Literature and its Theorists: a personal view of twentieth-century criticism*. Trans. Catherine Porter. Ithaca, NY and London: Cornell University Press.

Tomlinson, Hugh (1980) 'Derrida's Differance (sic)'. *Radical Philosophy*, 25, 30–3.

Ulmer, Gregory L. (1984) *Applied Grammatology: Post(e) Pedagogy from Jacques Derrida to Joseph Beuys*. Baltimore, Md: Johns Hopkins University Press.

—— (1990) *Teletheory: grammatology in the age of video*. London: Routledge.

Valdés, Mario J. and Miller, Owen (eds) (1985) *The Identity of the Literary Text*. Toronto: University of Toronto Press.

Vattimo, Gianni (1988) *The End of Modernity: nihilism and hermeneutics in postmodern culture*. Trans. Jon R. Snyder. Oxford: Basil Blackwell.

—— (1990) *The Adventure of Difference: philosophy after Nietzsche and Heidegger*. Trans. Cyprian Blamires. Oxford: Basil Blackwell.

Vickers, Brian (1989) *In Defence of Rhetoric*. Oxford: Oxford University Press.

Ward, Graham (1995) *Barth, Derrida, and the Language of Theology*. Cambridge: Cambridge University Press.

Warminski, Andrzej (1987) *Readings in Interpretation: Hölderlin, Hegel, Heidegger*. Minneapolis, Minn.: University of Minnesota Press.

Warner, Martin (1989) 'On Not Deconstructing the Difference between Literature and Philosophy'. *Philosophy and Literature*, Vol. 13, 16–27.

Warner, William Beattie (1986) *Chance and the Text of Experience: Freud, Nietzsche and Shakespeare's 'Hamlet'*. Ithaca, NY and London: Cornell University Press.

Waters, Lindsay and Godzich, Wlad (eds) (1989) *Reading de Man Reading*. Minneapolis, Minn.: University of Minnesota Press.

Weber, Samuel (1982) *The Legend of Freud*. Minneapolis: University of Minnesota Press.

—— (1987) *Institution and Interpretation*. Minneapolis, Minn.: University of Minnesota Press.

Webster, Roger (1990) *Studying Literary Theory: an introduction*. London: Edward Arnold.

Weedon, Chris (1987) *Feminist Practice and Post-Structuralist Theory*. Oxford: Basil Blackwell.

Wellek, René (1986) *A History of Modern Criticism*, Vols 5 and 6 (*English Criticism, 1900–1950* and *American Criticism, 1900–1950*). New Haven, Conn.: Yale University Press.

Wheeler, Samuel C. (January 1986) 'The Extension of Deconstruction'. *Monist*, LXIX: 1, 3–21.

—— (Winter 1988) 'Wittgenstein as Conservative Deconstructor'. *New Literary History*, XVIII: 2, 239–58.

—— (2000) *Deconstruction as Analytic Philosophy*. Stanford, CA: Stanford University Press.

White, Hayden (1987) *The Content of the Form: narrative discourse and historical representation*. Baltimore, Md and London: Johns Hopkins University Press.

Wihl, Gary (1994) *The Contingency of Theory: pragmatism, expressivism, and deconstruction*. New Haven: Yale University Press.

Wimsatt, William K. (1954) *The Verbal Icon: studies in the meaning of poetry*. Lexington, Ky: University of Kentucky Press.

—— (1970) 'Battering the Object: the ontological approach'. In Brad-
    bury and Palmer (eds), *Contemporary Criticism*. London: Edward
    Arnold.

Wittgenstein, Ludwig (1953) *Philosophical Investigations*. Trans. G. E. M.
    Anscombe. Oxford: Blackwell.

Wolfreys, Julian (1998) *Deconstruction: Derrida*. New York: St Martin's
    Press.

Wolin, Richard (ed.) (1993) *The Heidegger Controversy: a critical reader*.
    Cambridge, MA: MIT Press.

Wood, David (1989) *The Deconstruction of Time*. Atlantic Highlands, NJ:
    Humanities Press International.

—— (ed.) (1990) *Philosophers' Poets*. London: Routledge.

—— (ed.) (1990) *Writing the Future*. London: Routledge.

—— (ed.) (1992) *Derrida: a critical reader*. Oxford: Blackwell.

—— and Bernasconi, Robert (eds) (1988) *Derrida and Différance*. Evan-
    ston, Ill.: Northwestern University Press.

Wordsworth, Ann (1982) 'Household Words: alterity, the unconscious and
    the text'. *Oxford Literary Review*, V, 80–95.

Worton, Michael and Still, Judith (eds) (1990) *Intertextuality: theories and
    practices*. Manchester: Manchester University Press.

Wright, Edmond (1982) 'Derrida, Searle, Contexts, Games, Riddles'. *New
    Literary History*, XIII, 463–77.

Wright, Elizabeth (1984) *Psychoanalytic Criticism: theory in practice*. London:
    Methuen.

Wyschogrod, Edith (1983) 'Time and Non-Being in Derrida and Quine'.
    Journal of the British Society for Phenomenology, XIV, 112–26.

Young, Robert (ed.) (1981) *Untying the Text: a post-structuralist reader*.
    London: Routledge & Kegan Paul.

—— (1982) 'Post-Structuralism: the end of theory'. *Oxford Literary Review*,
    V, 3–20.

—— (1990) *White Mythologies: writing, history and the west*. London:
    Routledge.

INDEX

2090071LV000011B/36/A

16 December 2010

LaVergne, TN USA